Evangelicals and Conservatives in the Early South

George Whitefield (1714–1770), by James Moore after Andrew Miller after M. Jenkin
—National Portrait Gallery, Smithsonian Institution, Washington, D.C.

EVANGELICALS AND CONSERVATIVES
in the Early South, 1740–1861

by **Robert M. Calhoon**

University of South Carolina Press

Copyright © University of South Carolina 1988

Published in Columbia, South Carolina, by the
University of South Carolina Press

First Edition
Manufactured in the United States of America

LIBRARY OF CONGRESS

Library of Congress Cataloging-in-Publication Data

Calhoon, Robert M. (Robert McCluer)
    Evangelicals and conservatives in the early South, 1740-1861 / by
Robert M. Calhoon. — 1st ed.
        p.   cm.
    Bibliography: p.
    Includes index.
    ISBN 0-87249-577-9
    1. Evangelicalism—Southern States—History—18th century.
    2. Conservatism—Southern States—History—18th century.
    3. Southern States—Church History—18th century. 4. Southern
States—Church history—19th century. 5. Evangelicalism—Southern
States—History—19th century. 6. Conservatism—Southern States-
-History—19th century. 7. Southern States—History—Colonial
period, ca. 1600-1775. 8. Southern States—History—1775-1865.
9. Southern States—Intellectual life.   I. Title.
BR1642.U5C34   1988
277.5'07—dc19   88-20641
                                                          CIP

for
Claudia Marie

Contents

John C. Calhoun (1782–1850), by William James Hubard
—In the collection of The Corcoran Gallery of Art, Museum Purchase, Gallery Fund, 1889

Preface

Early in 1970 Richard Current suggested that I read the account of the American Revolution in Guilford County, North Carolina, recorded in Eli Caruthers's *Life and Character of the Reverend David Caldwell* (1842). There, in an appendix, I found two surviving Caldwell sermons. One of them, "The Character and Doom of the Sluggard" (1775), examined the impulse to revolt against British authority, and invoked theological justification for the American cause, with a penetration and resourcefulness surpassing anything I had seen in the famous New England political sermons of the Revolutionary era. My curiosity aroused, I began to collect material on religion and the American Revolution, first in North Carolina, and then in Virginia, South Carolina, and Georgia as well.

Whereas New England had a unitary social core tugged at by external metropolitan and frontier forces—and perhaps vitiated by subtle changes from within the New England town itself—the region that would become the American South consisted of a well-settled low country and a newly settled backcountry then in the early stages of an imperfect amalgamation and hungry for a sense of identity. Some of the most compelling language expressing that hunger was religious discourse: Anglicans yearning for dignity, Presbyterians for order, Moravians for harmony, Methodists for assurance, Lutherans and German Reformed for traditional learning, Baptists for purity, within a highly individualistic religious community, and black people in various worshiping contexts for liberation from bondage.

Piecing together the late eighteenth-century sermons, correspondence, disciplinary records, denominational proceedings, hymn books, liturgies, and prayers that expressed these yearnings promised to be a feasible, engrossing task. The honeymoon did not last long. The absence of transitional dates—1763, 1776, 1783, 1800, and 1815 had relatively little religious significance—induced me to range back to the 1740s and forward into the nineteenth century, eventually to

Preface

the eve of the Civil War, and into new terrain, to gauge the rhythm of the religious change I had encountered gathering strength in the 1770s and 1780s. When I started research in 1973, John B. Boles's, *The Great Revival*, George William Pilcher's biography of Samuel Davies, and a few seminal articles by Donald G. Mathews, Bertram Wyatt-Brown, and Rhys Isaac rounded out the list of recent scholarship. By the early 1980s the field was becoming crowded with scholars who had also sensed the opportunities in the study of early southern religious life.

Accordingly, I put aside for the time being a case study of a particular evangelical community—undertaken in collaboration with Professor Mathews—to concentrate on southern evangelicalism as a belief system across the life span of this religious phenomenon from marginality to respectability. Mathews not only generously supported my change in focus; through his writings and our conversations helped me understand a belief system as an integrated understanding of existence and the cosmos based on assumptions, structured by traditions and theology, given authenticity and vitality by ritual and practice, and capable of sustaining within itself paradoxes inherent in the human condition. The life cycle of a religious movement encompasses the overflow of religious convictions from the cauldron of personal and collective experience and its spilling into, and reacting with, a surrounding social environment.

As I focused on these matters, and as I reflected on my earlier work on loyalists and on moderate patriots, I was struck by the utility of viewing faith and spirituality from the perspective of authority and politics, and vice versa. That approach dictated expanding my only recently narrowed project into a comparative intellectual history of southern evangelicalism and conservatism. This volume is the result, and the organization of the book expresses in the broadest terms what I have learned from the experience of bringing religious testimony and political inquiry together in the same study.

The book has four interrelated purposes. The first and most important is to depict evangelicalism as a spiritually shared, socially expansive, and publicly intrusive religious experience; the second, and nearly as important, purpose is to probe the acknowledged values of a society—the American South—into which evangelicals intruded, as those values are revealed in a significant body of sources—normative discourse about public life or, in a word, conservatism. The third aim is to place southern evangelicals in the context of western civilization

Preface

by reminding readers that evangelicals were children of the Protestant Reformation and that the Reformation fused theology and political thought—spiritualizing politics and politicizing faith. The final purpose is to show how Protestant evangelicalism challenged public philosophy in the American South and, in turn, became imbued with the political values of southerners; this ebb and flow of evangelical zeal and political reaction created a three-stage interaction of religion and politics in which evangelicals first antagonized colonial conservatives, then challenged conservatives in the new republic, and finally brought ambiguous comfort to the defenders of order in the antebellum South.

The structure of the book reflects both the separate integrity and the interconnectedness of religion and politics. The prologue examines the connection between the theology and politics of the Reformation, defines evangelicalism and conservatism, and previews their parallel development in the American South from 1740 to 1861. Each of the three chronological parts of the book contains a chapter on evangelicalism treating that religious impulse on its own terms but also paying attention to the spiritual empowering, sanctioning, and controlling of evangelical converts, that is, to the politics of evangelicalism. Likewise, each part includes a chapter on conservatism that is sensitive to the moral and religious implications of normative political thought. Finally, each part concludes with an excursus pinpointing where evangelicals and conservatives intersected and how they interacted. The epilogue sketches the persistence of some of those interactions since the Civil War and especially during the twentieth century.

Approximately a tenth of the text excerpts earlier writings used here with publishers' permissions: "The Floridas, the Western Frontier, and Vermont: Thoughts on the Hinterland Loyalists" in Samuel Proctor, ed., *Eighteenth-Century Florida: Life on the Frontier* (Gainesville: University Presses of Florida, 1976); "Civil, Revolutionary, or Partisan: The Loyalists and the Nature of the War for Independence," *Military History of the American Revolution* (Washington: U. S. Government Printing Office for the Air Force Academy, 1976); "The Character and Coherence of the Loyalist Press," Bernard Bailyn and John B. Hench, eds., *The Press & the American Revolution* (Worcester, Mass.: American Antiquarian Society, 1980), written in collaboration with Janice Potter; "The Reintegration of the Loyalists and the Disaffected," Jack P. Greene, ed., *The American Revolution: Its Character and Limits* (New York: New York University Press, 1987), pp. 51–74; "Lutheranism in Early

Preface

Southern Culture," H. George Anderson and Robert M. Calhoon, eds., "*A Truly Efficient School of Theology*": *The Lutheran Theological Southern Seminary in Historical Context, 1830–1980* (Columbia, S. C.: Lutheran Theological Southern Seminary, 1981); "An Evangelical and Agrarian Culture," Lindley S. Butler and Alan D. Watson, eds., *The North Carolina Experience: An Interpretive and Documentary History* (Chapel Hill, N. C.: University of North Carolina Press, 1984): review of books by Fred J. Hood, Anne C. Loveland, and Donald G. Mathews, *William and Mary Quarterly*, (April 1982).

I gratefully acknowledge invitations to present preliminary findings before informed and critical audiences from: the Algie Newlin-Rembert W. Patrick Symposium on Southern History at Guilford College in 1980; the Southeastern region of the American Academy of Religion in Atlanta, Georgia and the Historical Society of North Carolina at Campbell University, both in 1981; the Craigsville Beach consultation of the Association for the Study of American Evangelicals and the Organization of American Historians in Los Angeles, California, both in 1984—in particular Martha Cooley, Carole W. Troxler, Joel Carpenter, and Ronald Hoffman deserve thanks for arranging those meetings.

Research for this book was made possible by a Research Grant from the National Endowment for the Humanities, a Ford Fellowship from the American Council of Learned Societies, and successive grants and leaves from The University of North Carolina at Greensboro where Ann Saab, Robert L. Miller, Stanley L. Jones, Elisabeth Zinser, William E. Moran, and John W. Kennedy were especially supportive. Bobbie Carter eased my work in many ways, and Elizabeth Hunt typed the manuscript.

For teaching me a great deal about this subject and enabling me in many ways to pursue it, I am especially grateful to Richard Bardolph, Richard N. Current, the late Warren Ashby, and the late James S. Ferguson.

Elizabeth Calhoon, Nathan O. Hatch, William A. Link, Mark A. Noll, Thomas T. Taylor, and Robert M. Weir read and commented on the manuscript, and H. George Anderson, Raymond M. Bost, Barbara Clowse, Richard O. Curry, Gary Freeze, Lawrence B. Goodheart, Charles Headington, Scott H. Hendrix, Henry S. Levinson, Paul Mazgaj, John M. Mulder, Karl A. Schleunes, and Andrew F. Weisner read and criticized particular passages.

Preface

Loren Schweninger called several useful pieces of evidence to my attention and helped interpret and decipher others; conversations with Converse D. Clowse about colonial historiography showed me connections between my research and recent scholarship. Among those who shared material or made useful suggestions were Murray Arndt, Timothy M. Barnes, Walter Beale, Camilla Cornelius, Don Higginbotham, C. William Hill, Samuel S. Hill, Gene Hyde, John Douglas Minyard, Rob Sikorski, Durward T. Stokes, Guy Ritter, Stephen Ruzicka, David Turner, Lowry Ware, James P. Whittenburg, and Clyde N. Wilson. Cindy Hanford, Rodney Boback, and JoAnn Williford helped with the research.

All of the archives and libraries I visited provided gracious assistance, and I am particularly grateful to Alice Cotton, North Carolina Collection, and Richard Shrader, Southern Historical Collection, University of Carolina at Chapel Hill Library; Virginia Shadron, Georgia State Archives; Mary Lane and Jerrold Brooks, Presbyterian Historical Foundation, Montreat; John Creasey, Dr. Williams's Library, London; Julie Myrick, Gaylor Callahan, and Sigrid Walker, Jackson Library, University of North Carolina at Greensboro; Paul Hoffman, Barbara Cain, and Robert Cain, North Carolina Archives, Raleigh; Johanna Mims, North Carolina Lutheran Synod Archives, Salisbury; Virginia Aull, South Carolina Lutheran Synod Archives, Columbia; and John Woodard, Baptist Collection, Wake Forest University Library.

Doris Calhoon listened appreciatively to the whole story as it unfolded and tried, I hope successfully, to keep the argument from running ahead of the evidence. Our daughter was two months old when she accompanied us on a trip to Williamsburg so that I could attend a conference on religion and the American Revolution, which confirmed my choice of this research topic. There she bounced on Jack Greene's knee and slept through lunch at Christiana Campbell's Tavern. By the time the book was nearing completion thirteen years later, she knew it and its author well enough to help select the title. To paraphrase a line of Frederick Tolles's, she deserves, and has, an entire page of the book to herself.

Greensboro, North Carolina   R.M.C.
Feast of St. Ambrose 1987

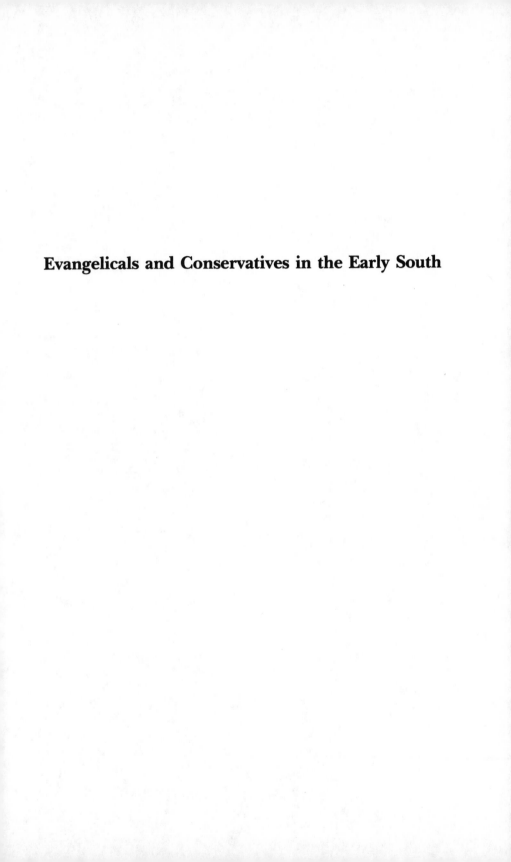

Evangelicals and Conservatives in the Early South

Prologue:

Experience and Order in the Reformation

Evangelical Christianity is the proclamation of salvation through faith in Christ. It emphasizes the atonement for human sins through Christ's crucifixion, relies on Scriptural authority, and affirms the victory of God's grace over His law. As such, evangelical Christianity is a religious belief shared by converts and observable by those inside and outside the faith. *Evangelicalism* is a different term, an academic concept, identifying the bond between proclaimers and believers and the social energy which conversion releases into a surrounding human environment.[1]

While evangelical Christianity is as old as the Acts of the Apostles, it became a distinct phenomenon during the Protestant Reformation. The reformers of the sixteenth century struggled with issues of freedom, community, and truth and in doing so injected a new kind of individualism into religious thought and the consciousness of western civilization. To introduce evangelicals and to begin to understand evangelicalism requires at least a brief look at the Reformation, particularly at Martin Luther, John Calvin, and their followers' sense of existing within the cosmos as fallen and redeemed human creatures. Evangelicals in the American South, the primary subjects of this book, would inherit and perpetuate that Protestant search for personal solitude and shared consolation. Freedom and community were, moreover, political as well as religious questions, and evangelicals operated within a highly charged political context. The secondary cast of characters in this book, political conservatives in the South, would also inherit ideas about power that crystallized during the Reformation.

Early in his career, Luther faced the question of how Christians practice fellowship and remain, at the same time, particular souls. In the spring of 1518—nine months after Luther first attacked indulgences—Pope Leo X directed the Thomist scholar, Sylvester Prierias, to rebut Luther's views. In an imagined dialogue between

1

Prologue

Luther and himself, Prierias emphasized the issues he felt were at stake: the authority of the Pope over all of Christendom, the inability of a conscientious pope to err, the consistency between Scripture and papal guidance of the faithful, the inseparability of the practices and teachings of the Church, and the heretical error of judging the former by the latter. "The stupid dolt wrote such wretched stuff that I had to laugh," Luther later recalled; "since then I've never been frightened."

If not intimidated, Luther must have been concerned. He was not yet ready to confront the issue of papal authority, and would not do so until 1521 when he concluded that the Pope had perverted the pastoral role of the Church. In his 1518 response to Prierias, Luther tried to thread his way between blasphemous presumption, in claiming alone to know God's will, and political impotence, in drawing the stinger from his attack on indulgences. His solution was to make the Resurrection—the ongoing reality of Christ's victory over death—into a source of authority over both believers and the Church. "Christ lives and he not only lives but reigns, not just in heaven but also in Rome, no matter how much she rages," Luther declared; "if I am cursed for the truth, I will bless the Lord. The censure of the Church will not separate me from the Church if the truth of the Church joins me."[2] In that statement, Luther took an important political step. Drawing on his medieval ecclesiastical orientation, he admitted that the Church could empower him so long as it remained obedient to the truth; acknowledging his doctoral oath to teach the Scriptures faithfully, he assumed personal responsibility for his fidelity to the truth.

His appreciation of ecclesiastical power and his sense of standing alone before God and men sensitized Luther to the solitary condition of the soul and the elusiveness of communication between human beings. Luther could face these realities because he believed that God used human isolation and pain as means of grace—a way of injecting healing love into people's lives. "The summons of death comes to us all, and no one can die for another," he explained; "we can shout into another's ears, but everyone must himself be prepared for the time of death." That isolation, Luther contended, was part of the human condition that Christ died to redeem. "Faith must always remain pure and unmovable in our hearts, never wavering," he told his listeners on the first Sunday in Lent, 1522, explaining to them how redemption entered human experience; "love bends and turns so that our neighbor can grasp it."[3]

Experience and Order

Determining the relationship between human experience and the order of the universe was a major task of the Protestant reformers. "The difference between us and the papists," Calvin declared, "is that they do not think the Church can be the 'pillar of the truth'[4] unless she presides over the word of God. We, on the other hand, assert that it is because she reverently subjects herself to the word of God that the truth is preserved by her and passed on to others by her hands."[5] The quintessential Calvinist experience, therefore, was proclamation of the word by the doctrinally orthodox. Where Luther's fidelity to conscience and Scripture marked a hard-won conclusion, Calvin's sense of discipleship was a point of departure. Lutheran confessions—historic creeds hammered out as Lutheran leaders sought security in a troubled world—centered on Baptism and the Eucharist as means of grace. Calvin's *Institutes* more ambitiously undertook to reconcile many of the divergent beliefs given fresh credence by the Reformation. Calvin blurred the question of whether the Bible or trinitarian creeds like the Nicene Creed was the more basic bedrock of faith; the Bible gave individuals the resources to understand salvation for themselves while historic creeds buttressed the authority of church bodies to preserve Christian orthodoxy. Calvin also positioned himself in between the teaching of Ulrich Zwingli that the bread and wine in the Lord's Supper were symbols and Luther's that they were the real presence of Christ. And his teaching on predestination conveyed both the personal consolation and the grim inevitability of knowing that salvation rested in the hands of the Almighty. The Calvinist, or Reformed, tradition in post-Reformation Europe and America hinged on these delicate accommodations and compromises.

Calvin regarded these compromises as a framework of freestanding theological bulwarks against evil and error. Shielded by these bulwarks, human action could be guided by divine truth. "True knowledge," one scholar paraphrased Calvin, came from "the interaction of the knower, the known, and the Spirit of God."[6] These three elements in revelation worked together, as parts of a harmonious creation, to enlarge human freedom and to vouch for the dependability of God's promises. As Calvin put it, "the Lord has joined together the certainty of His Word and His Spirit by a mutual bond, in order that the solid religion of the Word may dwell in our souls . . . that we in our turn may embrace the Spirit in no fear of hallucination when we recognize Him in His image, that is in the Word." There was a creative tension in that passage between power and love, between Scriptural authority and the gentle transmission of demanding truths. That tension would divide Protestants over the next two centuries into rival camps of "Calvinists," emphasizing the power of the triune creator, and "Arminians," influenced by Jacobus Arminius, sixteenth century Dutch theologian, who stressed God's compassionate grace. For his part, Calvin embraced both tendencies:

> God did not set the Word in the midst to make a sudden show, for it to be abolished immediately by the advent of His Spirit, but he sent down the same Spirit by whose power he had bestowed the Word, in order that He should complete His work by His effective confirmation of the Word.[7]

This paradoxical, evangelical belief in the present activity and timeless verity of a Creator-redeemer energized Protestant Christianity for the next three centuries. The same persistent vitality in Lutheran and Reformed theology and liturgy spilled into family, community, education, law, commerce, and especially, into politics.[8] Reformation political thought—like theology—struggled to comprehend the nature of authority and to create a secure sphere for the practice and preservation of liberty. While Luther and Calvin each instructed their followers to " 'be subject unto the higher powers, for there is no power but of God'," quoting Romans 13:1, neither man could bring himself to stop with that categorical view of obedience.[9] By the time they had explained why Christians should obey constituted authority and only passively resist tyranny, the great reformers had larded their teachings on submission with qualifications and ambiguities that allowed followers to restrict the claims of political rulers and hold princes and kings accountable to God and their fellow men.

What Luther conceded to rulers when he affirmed that "the temporal power is ordained of God to punish the wicked and protect the good ... without restriction, ... whether it affects Pope, bishops, priests, nuns or anyone else," he partly took back when he insisted that the prince "must devote himself" to his subjects, "protect and maintain them in peace and plenty, ... take unto himself the needs of his subjects, dealing with them as though they were his own needs."[10] Calvin warned that obedience to earthly rulers "is never to lead us away from obedience to Him, to whose will the desire of all kings ought to be subject." Starting in the 1539 edition of his *Institutes*, Cal-

Experience and Order

vin endorsed the principle of "avengers," called by God to "deliver the people, oppressed in unjust ways, from miserable calamity."[11]

Converting these intimations—that misrule was an offense to God and that personal conscience might take precedence over the dictates of the prince—into a full-blown right of resistance and revolution challenged Protestant resourcefulness. In 1530 Luther's princely followers devised two competing justifications for resistance. Philip of Hesse proposed a constitutional theory explaining why a ruler lacked the power to tamper with conscience. John of Saxony offered a simpler legal doctrine declaring that conscience was simply an area into which a ruler could not intrude. Abruptly, in October 1530, Luther, Philip Melanchthon, and other Lutheran theologians endorsed John of Saxony's private law theory.[12]

Luther could not tamper lightly with St. Paul's teaching in Romans against resisting authority when that epistle was the bedrock of his theology of grace. The princes, on whose support Luther depended, needed a clear justification of their own legitimacy. The Hessian constitutional theory, balancing the princes' power against their duty to their subjects and against the power of the Emperor, looked precarious. Saxon juristic theory, in contrast, did not impair their authority so long as they did not trample on rights of conscience. Luther's table talk in the 1530s tried to put more teeth into passive resistance by observing that a magistrate who exceeds the bounds of his office "reduces himself to the status of a felonious private citizen"[13] and ceases to merit obedience. Melanchthon went further and found private law justification for resisting oppression by force of arms. Eventually, the Lutheran scholar, Andreas Osiander, returned to a constitutional theory of resistance when he argued that Charles V had violated standards of good faith implicitly required by his election as Emperor. Martin Bucer next set forth a full-scale Lutheran argument that lesser magistrates, the Lutheran princes, shared power with the supreme ruler, the Emperor. Thus, while Saxon legal doctrine became official Lutheran teaching, the Lutheran constitutionalists (Philip of Hesse, Osiander, and Bucer) provided their Protestant allies, French Calvinists, or Huguenots, with a more powerful arsenal of arguments in favor of resisting Catholic tyranny.[14]

The first generation of Huguenots employed the constitutionalism borrowed from Lutheran writings in defense of freedom of conscience in Catholic France. Until the early 1570s they saw as complementary Calvin's notion of avenging deliverers and Bucer's assign-

Prologue

ment of the avenging role to inferior princes. But after the killing of thousands of Huguenot leaders in the St. Bartholomew's Day massacre in 1572, Huguenots boldly changed the direction of their search for political understanding. Recognizing that Counter-Reformation Catholics were deeply split between a dominant wing favoring royal absolutism and Papal authority and a minority believing that Church Councils rather than the Papacy should determine the future of the faith, Huguenots sought common ground with Catholic conciliarists. This wing of Catholicism used an extraordinary range of scholarship—Roman law, medieval scholasticism and political theory, and French humanist philosophy—as the basis for allocating authority within Catholic Europe among the Papacy, Church Councils, and secular rulers.[15] Enriching Huguenot arguments with moderate Catholic erudition, Quenton Skinner explains, later Huguenot writers "rejected the characteristically Protestant tendency to suppose that God places all men in a condition of political subjection as a remedy for their sins. Instead they . . . argue[d] that the original and fundamental condition of the people must be one of natural liberty."[16] By reaching out to Catholic constitutionalists after 1572, Huguenots radicalized Calvinist political teaching about the supremacy of conscience over dictates of political tyrants.

A further task was to take an equally close look at the human qualities of political subjects—the people ruled by potentially despotic monarchs. Puritans and many Anglicans in seventeenth-century England took that step, and John Locke in the early 1680s brought English Protestant constitutionalism to its highest level of insight and elegance. His theory of government by implicit contract—in which the ruler provided protection and the subject obedience to the law—synthesized more than six decades of parliamentary assertions about consent and Puritan teaching about the depravity of absolutist monarchs. Locke argued that gross violations of the contract by the ruler required the people to rise in revolt; this contention closely resembled the mature Huguenot justification for resisting tyranny. Unique and original in Locke's politics were, first, his explanation of how the mind equipped people to resist tyranny and, second, how only a government of laws could cleanse the community of destructive irrationality.[17]

Locke's theory of the mind, which held that all learning is sensory and that people can organize sense impressions into perceptions

Experience and Order

and complex ideas, served his political theory well. The experience of work and the enjoyment of the fruits of one's own labor taught human beings about creation, human society, and the meaning of liberty. "God gave the world to men in common," he wrote, "for the use of the industrious and rational, . . . not to the fancy or covetousness of the quarrelsome and contentious."[18] The knowledge that life and property could not be wrenched away arbitrarily, except on the finding of a court of law, allowed individuals the luxury of rational reflection on their situation. Arbitrary rule, conversely, threatened to plunge the subject into irrational fear and loathing of authority. To respect the rule of law, Locke declared, was to obey the law of nature, and to impose arbitrary rule mocked natural law. "In transgressing the law of nature," Locke graphically declared, "the offender declares himself to live by another rule than that of reason and common equity," to be "one of those wild savage beasts with whom men can have no society nor security."[19] The compact, he believed, united people in the common task of excluding brutal men from the company of civilized human beings. In exchange for the security of liberty and property, the Lockean compact cajoled people to forego the gratifications of vengeance and aggression.

This sketch of Reformation theology and politics suggests several patterns of religious and civic activity. The first is a divergence of the two over time. Protestant political thinkers by Locke's time were, to be sure, orthodox Christians but were also more circumspect about their faith than their counterparts had been a century earlier. While the wars and political upheavals of the sixteenth century threatened the immediate survival of the Protestant flock, those of the seventeenth century served more deliberately to define the modern state and determine how it should deal with claims of conscience. During the Enlightenment of the eighteenth century, rationalism would further separate political philosophy from religion.

The same theological and political events pointing to divergence, secondly, also show that belief and political thought could oscillate, now touching, then dividing, and later converging again. Toleration became a flash point in England in the early 1680s because of the prospect of James, Duke of York, ascending the throne. The St. Bartholomew's Day massacre compelled French Calvinists to move boldly into Catholic constitutional thought in search of political realism equal to the dangers they faced. Luther's and Calvin's cautious

Prologue

traditionalism about those in political authority prompted their followers to explore the limits of obedience allowed by St. Paul's injunction in Romans 13:1.

A third possible implication of this material is that theology and politics in the Reformation were intertwined. Protestant theology was inherently political because it enabled individuals to visualize their own proximity to the forces of darkness and light and to think about appropriate human action; the politics of the Reformation juxtaposed liberty and authority, based in large part on the Biblical concept of a sovereign, divine power and freely choosing human subjects.

The diverging, oscillating, and intrinsic intertwining patterns are hypotheses that are not mutually exclusive or all-explaining, though in the pages that follow, the intertwining model most often serves to make sense out of the evidence. Patterns cry out for recognition in historical sources as people speak of the structure they perceive in the reality of their lives and of their need for a perspective on their experience. This book will examine the persistent search for structure and perspective among religious evangelicals and political conservatives in the middle Atlantic southern colonies and states from the First Great Awakening to the eve of the Civil War. Conservatism was a form of political thought evangelicals frequently encountered in the early South.

Conservatism is normative discourse about politics and society which insists that historical experience and cultural tradition should impinge on human choice and social achievement. Respect for the authority of the past is not unique to conservatives; liberals—children of the Enlightenment who believe that institutions ought to be responsive to human needs—considered themselves participants in a long struggle for freedom, and radicals have appealed to a golden age in the past for the outlines of a new order. "Conservatism is an attitude of mind that tends to promote resistance to change," Leonard W. Labaree opined in his classic lectures on *Conservatism in Early American History*, delivered in 1947.[20] But the reverse is also true; conservatism can encourage and welcome change as a way of cushioning its impact.[21] The internal arguments among conservatives have transformed conservative opinions into ideological conservatism, that is, into a textured appreciation of the past and apprehension of the present and future. The competing normative voices of different conservatives in the same society produce a kind of creative dissonance.

Evangelicals and conservatives helped to shape early southern

Experience and Order

society during three readily recognizable periods of history. First, during the late colonial era (roughly 1740–1775), evangelicals appeared on the fringes of polite society as disturbers of accepted norms of religious decorum. Their talk of liberation sounded to many Anglicans, Crown officials, and members of the planter elite vaguely subversive—and in one South Carolina episode explicitly seditious. For their own part, Presbyterian, Baptist, and just as the colonial era ended, Methodist revivalists and their flocks, regarded themselves as people liberated from the standards of the world and a joyful vanguard of the Kingdom of God.

The Revolution and the early republic (1776–1815) brought to power a new elite of planters and lawyers who did not seek an egalitarian society but did believe that power belonged to the whole body of the people and that constitutions ought to prescribe how government used that power in the public interest. After disestablishing the Anglican Church in the southern states, the new state governments looked to all Protestant churches to inculcate discipline and civic virtue among the people. These developments provided all Protestant churches, especially evangelical ones, with an unprecedented opportunity to seek adherents and to infuse into the new ethos of republicanism a strong dose of piety.

The success of evangelical churches as flourishing institutions in virtually every community during the antebellum period (1815–1861) brought with it respectability and a stake in the preservation of slavery. American evangelicals became immersed in the seemingly feasible task of leading all of society to salvation, and southern white evangelicals shared in this strenuous vision. Perplexed, troubled, and embarrassed by slavery, they decided that God must have some special plan by which slavery would be miraculously transformed, under the guidance of the Holy Spirit, into a humane labor system. Black evangelicals, both slave and free, had no such illusions, but they appropriated the elements of the Christian message dealing with human dignity and liberation that met their spiritual needs, and they celebrated this discovery.

Superficially then, evangelicals and conservatives in the South first encountered each other as adversaries; they became autonomous collaborators during the revolutionary and republican decades; and they fell into an awkward embrace during the antebellum era. That is the consensus historians have thus far tentatively reached. It is essentially correct, although evidence also indicates that the late colonial

Prologue

antagonism was not as adversarial or antebellum accommodation as cozy as they have often been depicted. The most significant dynamic, however, did not arise from dealings between evangelicals and conservatives but within each community of belief and action. Evangelicals were torn between Calvinist assumptions and Arminian practices and between spontaneity and structure; conservatives sensed the precariousness of political practices and social forms and raged against the certainty that the old would pass away. Religious-political contact—whether adversarial or collaborative or accommodationist—became exciting or painful when it intensified convictions or exacerbated tensions within evangelicalism and within conservatism.

The story should therefore proceed at two levels. The first will be the manifest progression of evangelicals and conservatives from conflict to independent action to collaboration as seen through the eyes of those persons in tune with their own culture who believed they understood the relationship of spirituality and power. Around the edges of that movement of events and beliefs—and sometimes at the center of action—will appear the church people and politicians who were not so sure they had a fix on each other.

Part I.

THE LATE COLONIAL PERIOD

1.

Colonial Evangelicalism

Evangelical principles soon took possession of his vigorous mind and susceptible heart, and in his life their influence was conspicuous. . . . Having made religion his chief pursuit, he . . . spent much of his time in meditation, prayer, and reading the scripture, . . . enjoying delightful intercourse with God in private. But he was not contented with a solitary devotion. His experience . . . prompted an ardent desire that others . . . should participate in the same blessing.

anonymous description of
Richard Furman,
Richard Furman Papers,
Furman University Library

The heart of evangelical Christianity was the experience of conversion—the realization by individuals that Christ had died for their sins and that they were thereby connected spiritually to all other recipients of this grace. That discovery often occurred in a sharply focused and highly charged moment of awareness for each convert, but the beginnings of conversion could stretch far back into memory and reverberate throughout a lifetime. Their sense of connectedness with others transformed the way evangelical converts perceived reality; they felt enriched most intimately by those who delivered to them the message of salvation, then by those who shared with them the common experience of conversion, next by the larger fellowship of believers, and more remotely, but still within the circle of concern, fellow human beings who had not yet experienced conversion.[1]

The two essential ingredients in evangelical belief—awareness of redemption and fellowship with other saints—together prompted strong autobiographical and narrative impulses. Evangelicals had a story to tell and an understanding of the human context within which to place their stories.

The Late Colonial Period

Among the most telling of evangelical narratives were those of Presbyterian ministers who, in the course of seeking converts among white yeoman farmers in Virginia in the 1740s and 1750s, recorded the responses of slaves to the Christian message. "For about a year and a half past, I have had more success among the poor Negroes," Samuel Davies wrote in 1757; "I have baptized in all 150 adults and at the last sacramental occasion I had the honor (for so I esteem it) of sitting down at the table of the Lord with about 60 of them." Davies's deliberate prose conveyed the powerful impulses at work in building a fellowship among slaves and racial outcasts. "Multitudes of them," he explained, "are eager to learn to read . . . , some from a pious thirst after Christian knowledge, some from curiosity, and some from ambition."

This division of the slave community—or at least that large segment of it which seemed open to Christian instruction—into the pious, the curious, and the ambitious suggests the complexity of the religious impulse about which Davies was writing. It was an insight that was at once disturbing and exciting: "Whatever be the present principle" or motivation, "I hope many happy effects will follow from this acquisition" of knowledge "as it will render them more capable of being their own instructors and of receiving instruction from others." Davies described a forty-year-old man, "a very stupid lubberly fellow in appearance and but indifferently acquainted with our language," who seemed a hopeless student but proved to be amazingly adept. "I . . . despaired of his ever being taught to read and resolved to instruct him in the principles of Christianity in the best manner I could. . . . But he, unexcited [by which Davies meant unaided] by me, somehow learnt the letters and began to spell, and even before I so much as expected it, was almost prepared to read." So Davies gave him books and special tutoring and soon he could "read English almost as intelligibly as he could speak it." This man, however, was probably not very literate for Davies described his spoken confession of belief and experience "a very broken account," but impressive as a triumph of the will; "his life," Davies exulted, was a magnificent example of piety, serenity, and generosity.

Running through Davies's account of the building of a Christian fellowship of slaves was an undercurrent surprise at the unpredictability of events. Seeking souls and converts, he was nonetheless taken aback by the intensity of the psychological and intellectual liberation his charges experienced in Christian life. "The hardest task I have to perform," he explained, "is . . . to deal with them in a proper manner.

Colonial Evangelicalism

I am afraid of discouraging them... by imposing high forms of admission to baptism and am cautious of swelling the number of proselytes with only nominal Christians." His dilemma was not so much a legalistic one as it was a problem in the application of theology to ministerial practice: "I find it the hardest thing in the world"—the repetition of this phrase is suggestive of struggle—"at once to convince their judgments and make their hearts properly sensible of the reasonableness, the glory, and the necessity of a mediatory religion, or, in other words, the Christian scheme of salvation thro' Christ."

It was not that the slaves were uncomprehending or unreceptive; rather they brought to Davies's services presuppositions that he had never before encountered. They had "high notions of the necessity and efficacy of Baptism" so that as soon as they realized what it meant to be in "a state of heathenism," they desired baptism as an immediate, refreshing, and purifying act of cleansing and renewal without grasping "the necessity of proper preparative qualifications for it." This restless state of mind intrigued and perplexed Davies; "many of them only seem to have a desire to be," he groped for the right words, "they know not what." Pondering that insight, he found a startling implication. Some slaves considered baptism a fashion—a light-hearted communal rite linking them to their fellows. More ominously to Davies, baptism appealed to others as a means to "be put upon an equality with their masters." Many confessed such an improper motivation so that, Davies admitted, with conflicting emotions, "I am obliged to exclude them from that ordinance." His pragmatic solution was to avoid close attention to belief and instead "make their temper and conduct, rather than their speculative notions, the standard of my judgment concerning them." Assessed in this manner, most slave converts qualified as "proper members of the Christian church, 'tho they be ignorant of many of its important doctrines."

What Davies had done was extraordinary. Making "conduct and temper" substitutes for confessional orthodoxy introduced into evangelical ministry an unpredictable new element; Davies sensed that he had entered new terrain. A faint but unmistakable note of perplexity appeared in his attempt to pin down what was happening. "There is... a number of them," he concluded, "who, I have not the least doubt, are genuine children of Abraham by Faith; some of them seem to have made a greater progress in experimental religion than many sincere Christians of a fairer colour." "Experimental religion" proudly labeled evangelicalism as a distinctive religious practice in which the individual played a conscious role in the drama of his or her own

The Late Colonial Period

salvation. Read in the context of Samuel Davies's ministry to slaves and yeoman farmer whites in Hanover County, Virginia, experimental religion suggests a belief system in which personal experience, within a voluntary fellowship of other believers, became the life of the church. This participatory, self-conscious quality sprang from the human need for a personal identity and a desire to be empowered and revitalized by the "mediatory" intervention of Jesus in the eternal destiny of individual souls. Just as strong as these individualistic needs and rewards was the sense of entry into a privileged fellowship of baptized communicants.[2]

Black spirituality was enthralling and disturbing to Davies because it challenged him to accelerate his efforts to redeem and transform those "of a fairer colour." Until Davies and other Pennsylvania Presbyterians came to Hanover County, Virginia, the only Presbyterians in the southern colonies were among pockets of Scottish and Scots Irish settlement in the Valley of Virginia and on its eastern shore, the Cape Fear valley in North Carolina, and among French, Swiss, and German Calvinists in South Carolina and Georgia. Sometime around 1740 a Hanover County man named Samuel Morris, impressed by the writings of Luther and the English revivalist, George Whitefield, began to preach to ever increasing crowds of his neighbors. About the same time, the New Brunswick Presbytery ordained a man named "One-Eyed" William Robinson, the son of a Quaker merchant blinded and scarred by smallpox, to visit Scots Irish settlements in western Virginia and North Carolina. Robinson's success as a preacher in the Valley of Virginia prompted him to cross the Blue Ridge to the east and preach in Lunenberg and Amelia counties. There he heard of Samuel Morris and agreed in 1743 to bring the message of the Great Awakening to Hanover County—the first intrusion of a Presbyterian into Anglican tidewater jurisdiction. He stayed only four days but, in that time, he "alarmed" large numbers of previously unconcerned people with "apprehensions of their dangerous condition, ... of their former entire ignorance of religion," and he left them "anxiously inquiring what they should do to be saved."[3] Other middle colony Presbyterians, including Davies in 1747, came to Hanover to exploit this new opening. Unlicensed to preach in Virginia and viewed with suspicion, these clergymen felt intense isolation.

Davies's correspondence with British evangelicals, like that of other Presbyterian clergymen in Virginia, returned again and again

Colonial Evangelicalism

to his sense of isolation: a contrast between their attainment of communion with other souls and the lack of a sense of community with stable elements in the society in which they found themselves. "The condition of this part of the country is very melancholy," one minister explained, "there is little inquiry after good books among our great folks; plays, races, cock-fighting, etc. are more acceptable."[4] That was more than a complaint about anti-intellectualism. Evangelical clergy in Virginia felt their spiritual life suffocated because "there is little seriousness amongst us here in this country." Seriousness was an essential precondition to the consideration of self and the cosmos that evangelicalism entailed. Davies frequently thanked the Society for Promoting Religious Knowledge among the Poor for sending him books for his ministry—hymnals and psalms by Isaac Watts, Bibles, and copies of the classic treatise of popular British evangelicalism, Philip Doddridge, *The Rise and Progress of Religion in the Soul.*

Davies's letters concerning the conversion of blacks and the Society's gifts of devotional books to evangelical clergymen were parts of a trans-Atlantic communications network that significantly magnified the influence and scope of Calvinist revivalism in the British Empire during the mid-eighteenth century. Organized by Philip Doddridge and his friends, this network publicized the work of Jonathan Edwards and George Whitefield, collected and disseminated conversion narratives as a way of documenting the reality of revivalism as a cultural form, and linked scattered ministers and congregations on the periphery of British and colonial societies into a well-organized association.[5]

Davies's appreciation of these books, especially Doddridge, highlighted the potency of the printed word on the periphery of the civilized world of British culture. The most popular and effective of all the evangelical self-help books of the eighteenth century, *Rise and Progress*, followed the spiritual and emotional life of the convert from irreligious unhappiness to step by step engagement with the scheme of salvation and the process of discipleship. Its direct, conversational tone instilled in the reader confidence in an unseen yet familiar voice. "Will any one of us presume to say that religion has a universal reign among us?" Doddridge asked at the outset:

> Will any one suppose that it prevails in every life, that it reigns in every heart? Alas! the avowed infidelity, the profanation of the name and day of God, the drunkenness, the lewdness, the injustice, the falsehood, the

The Late Colonial Period

pride, the prodigality, the base selfishness and stupid insensibility to the spiritual and eternal interests of themselves and others, which so . . . loudly proclaim to the contrary.

The cadences and rhetorical self-confidence of such a passage suggest why it filled a human void in dissenting churches and households in colonial Virginia, and a typical chapter, "A Serious Persuasive to . . . a Method of Spending Our Days . . . " typified the guidance and help that Davies craved for his parishioners. "I know," Doddridge here comforted his readers, "that the mind is very fickle and inconstant, and that it is a hard thing to preserve . . . government and authority over our thoughts. . . . But so much of the honour of God, and so much of our own true happiness, depends upon it that I beg you give me a patient and attentive hearing while I am pleading with you . . . and then judge whether a care and conduct like that which I have advised be not in itself reasonable. . . . "[6]

Davies's sense of isolation was accentuated by his belief that his adversaries were the apathy and the superficiality of the lives of his white parishioners. His account of a series of revival services in which he participated in Lunenberg County in June 1756 emphasized his yearning for meaning and authenticity. "In 13 days, I preached 11 or 12 sermons with encouraging signs of success. . . . At the sacrament in that wilderness there were about 2000 hearers and 200 communicants, and a general seriousness and attention appeared among them; a considerable number of thoughtless creatures are solicitously enquiring after religion": seriousness, attention, solicitous inquiry, these were the indications of cultural transformation and hard-won repudiation of existing social norms which Davies craved.

Something of the emotional cost of this struggle appeared when he assisted his neighbor, the Rev. John Todd, at a joint service. "It was a time of unusual anxiety to me," he recalled; "I hardly ever felt so much of a pastoral heart, I mean an affection and concern for my flock, and yet I had not a proportionate liberty to vent it. However, I hope it was a refreshing time to some hungry souls. I had the pleasure of seeing the table of the Lord adorned with about 44 black faces. . . . In the land of their slavery, they have been brought into the glorious liberty of the sons of God. But alas! notwithstanding these promising appearances, an incorrigible stupidity generally prevails thro' this guilty land."[7]

For Davies, therefore, joy and exultation were partial, finite grati-

Colonial Evangelicalism

fications. In contrast, the conversion experience—which was completely in the hands of God—much more nearly approached the sublime, and Davies celebrated its power and intensity. When men "first see their sins" and "their hearts" are "broken with penetential sorrows," a miracle occurs within their character, Davies contended; "their lives" stand as convincing testimony that conversion truly transforms a convert. "Are not the savages transformed into lambs and doves? . . . Are they not habitually humble and meek, dutiful, faithful, diligent, and the reverse of what they once were?" The powerful linkages between the "broken heart" and the entire personality of the convert epitomized the evangelical perception of reality—one that stressed the interconnectedness of all reality and the essential role of salvation in this web of relationship. The objection that "Christianizing the Negroes" would "make them proud and saucy and . . . imagine themselves on a equality with white people," Davies argued, flowed from ignorance of Christianity and its inculcation of "meekness, faithfulness, and every grace and virtue." The connection between the spirit of the Lord and the character traits of the convert was, for Davies, isomorphic. "Is the true Christian spirit haughty and insolent?" he demanded to know; the answer was self-evident. "As they are not sufficiently polished to dissemble with good grace, they express the sentiments of their souls so much in the language of simple nature . . . that it is impossible to suspect their professions, especially when attended with a true Christian life and exemplary conduct." Their lack of sophistication validated their credibility to any rational observer.[8]

If the fruits of the spirit radiated throughout the behavior and consciousness of individuals—one pattern of evangelical connectedness—so also the baneful effects of secular culture pervasively stifled spiritual life. Acutely aware that the gentry acted as cultural arbiters, a Richmond County, dissenting minister lamented the hedonism and restlessness of most planters. "No wonder that their slaves are neglected," he concluded; Sundays found slaves either working in the fields or fishing; curses filled their vocabulary; worst of all, they seemed "ignorant as brutes" about the dangerous consequences of this pattern of living. Only "two or three" slaves of his acquaintance "seem" to have become Christians and to have reformed their lives, and a group of "ten" came to his weekly prayer meetings to receive religious instruction. A few of these had even learned to read the Bible. In contrast with his own struggle, and minister pointed to

The Late Colonial Period

"Mr. Davies's people" where "religion seems to flourish; it is like the very suburbs of heaven."[9] James Reid, an obscure Presbyterian school-master in Virginia, reacted to the stylized gregariousness of the planters with an elaborate satire entitled, *The Religion of the Bible and the Religion of K[ing] W[illiam] County Compared* (1769). "A King Wil-liamite," Reid explained, "is... neither atheist, sceptic, nor unbe-liever, but he is a real dogmatist. He believes or denies a thing not from any reason or knowledge he has of it, but only because he will do so. He thinks so, and therefore he believes; he believes so, and therefore he thinks.... The whole reason he gives for doing so is contained in this laconic phrase, 'G–d d—n me if I don't'."[10]

Evangelicals' sense of the intensity of slave conversion and uneas-iness about what it meant to a white Christian to witness such an experience appeared in a letter from Elizabeth Colson, wife of the director of the Bethesda Orphanage in Savannah, to the patroness of that institution, the Countess of Huntington, in 1773: "I want nothing but the life and power of God in my soul," she exclaimed in a state-ment typical of the outspoken piety of letters to the Countess. "I feel for the poor Negroes, tho most people gives them very bad carictor and that it is in vain to preach to them. One night my heart was drawn to preach to them. They heard me, [were] very attentive, & one woman was drowned in tears."[11] Evangelicals like Elizabeth Colson believed that the emotions were points of entry into the interior of human consciousness, and that habit, indifference, feelings of superiority or inferiority blocked these openings until the word of God and the workings of the Spirit pierced this protective layer of inhibitions. John Murratt, a young irrepressible, free, black musician born in New York, tried on a dare to disrupt a religious service in Charlestown in 1769 by blowing his horn during George Whitefield's sermon. "I was pushing the people to make room to get the horn off my shoulder and blow it, just as Mr. Whitefield was naming his text," Murratt later recalled; "looking around and, as I thought, directly upon me, and pointing his finger, he uttered these words, 'PREPARE TO MEET THY GOD, O ISRAEL'... I was struck to the ground, and lay speechless and sense-less...." When he regained consciousness, "every word I heard from the minister was like a parcel of swords thrust into me."[12]

George Whitefield, the evangelist Murratt thus encountered, had first visited Charlestown, South Carolina, in late August and early September, 1738, on his way from Savannah back to London to seek Anglican ordination. During this visit he called on the Anglican Com-

Colonial Evangelicalism

missary in Charlestown, the Rev. Alexander Garden, and the two men conversed amiably. By the time he returned to Charlestown on January 1, 1740, he had not only become an ordained minister of the Church of England, he returned as a controversial religious reformer—highly critical of the theology of most Anglican clerics and almost all of the Church's hierarchy and scornful of any discipline or reproach cast in his way. He was a figure in transit, constantly moving, speaking, writing, making his presence felt; his message too, an amalgam of Calvinist rigor, Wesleyan warmth and appeal, and urgent revivalism, followed an uncertain trajectory.[13]

In England he affronted his fellow Anglicans by preaching when and wherever the Spirit moved him and hearers assembled, without regard for whose parish he invaded; he inveighed against the Arminian theology of many Anglican clerics and refashioned the idea of salvation through grace of unregenerate sinners into a wholesale reform of church and society. His notorious sermon, *What Think Ye of Christ?* published in Philadelphia in 1739, drew the line between evangelicalism and conventional Anglicanism: "It is the divinity of our Lord that gives a sanction to his death . . . , and whatsoever Minister of the Church of England makes use of her forms and eats of her bread and yet holds not this doctrine (as I fear too many such have crept in amongst us) belongs to the *Synagogues of Satan.*" Or, as he put the same suspicion even more bluntly, respected Anglican homiletician, Archbishop Tillotson, "knew no more of Christianity than Mahomet." A reputation for such sentiments and attitudes preceding him, Whitefield returned to Charlestown a sensational figure and soon tangled publicly with the feisty Anglican commissary, Alexander Garden.[14]

He presented himself at Garden's church in Charlestown, St. Philips, on Sunday, January 6, 1740, but was barred from the pulpit by a curate, probably acting on his superior's orders. Garden was conveniently out of the city. Because a large number of people wanted to hear him—Whitefield characteristically estimated that "most of the town" were "eager"—he preached that afternoon in the Calvinist church of Josiah Smith. Whitefield's reading of his audience accurately gauged the ease with which Charlestown society savored the spectacular quality of Whitefield's style while missing the essentials of his message: "The audience was large but polite. I question whether the court-end of London could exceed them in affected finery, gaiety of dress, and deportment"—traits "ill-becoming persons who have had such divine judgments lately sent amongst them. I reminded

The Late Colonial Period

them of this in my sermon; but I seemed to them as one that mocked." The following day, however, when he preached in the Huguenot church of Timothy Millechamp, a similarly fashionable congregation exhibited genuine depth of feeling; "instead of . . . going out (as they did yesterday) in a light unthinking manner, a visible concern was in most of their faces." The following day, while preparing to leave for Savannah, he surveyed the whole religious state of the British Empire and concluded that "the heads of the Church of England seemed resolved to shut out the Kingdom of God. . . . Why [is] there so little religion in" South Carolina? he asked himself; because the Christian ministers present there were "dry bones" and because Commissary Garden was "strict in the outer discipline of the Church"—a scathing indictment of Arminian formalism and spiritual deadness.[15]

When Whitefield returned to Charleston in March, 1740, Garden was ready for a showdown. He received the young evangelist in his rectory and demanded proof of his charges against the Anglican clergy. Whitefield replied that the very fact Anglicans did not preach justification by faith alone proved his case. They debated the issue inconclusively, and then Garden forbade Whitefield from preaching in any Anglican church in the province. Whitefield said he would treat that order with the same respect he would a papal bull.[16]

At work in these disputes were several kinds of conflict of which the most immediate was a clash of personality. Whitefield was a supremely confident figure, buoyed up by an international reputation and strengthened in certitude by the sound of his own voice. He prided himself on his ability to transcend personal rancor, and his tone to Anglicans like Garden was insufferably smug. "By your conversation, sermon, and letter," he wrote to Garden in March 1740, "I perceive that you are angry over much. . . . I would stay [quiet] until the cool of the day," he confided to Garden as his own way of coping with feelings of hostility; "your letter more and more convinces me that my charge against the clergy is just and reasonable." As though he could hear Garden's angry rebuttal coming, he sidestepped it: "It would be endless to enter into such private debate as you propose."[17]

Beneath this grating of colliding egos lay fundamental religious and intellectual differences. Whitefield's insistence on "the utter inability of man to save himself and absolute necessity of his dependence on the rich mercies and free grace of God in Christ Jesus for his restoration" drove Garden to reaffirm that "I firmly believe and have always taught that *good works* do as necessarily spring from and

Colonial Evangelicalism

accompany a true and *lively* faith ... as light and heat do the sun."
Judging from the scornful intensity of Garden's *Six Letters to George
Whitefield,* the conduct the Commissary found most reprehensible in
the young evangelist was Whitefield's freewheeling criticism of the
irresponsibility and callousness of slave owners. The thrust of this
argument, like Davies's sermon to the planters, was the duty of the
master to see to the religious instruction of his own slaves. But joined
to this strategy of reconciling slaves to their bondage by converting
them to Christianity was Whitefield's Cassandra-like warning that
slave ownership was an integral part of a pagan, irreligious culture
which cried out to God for chastisement:

> your dogs are caress'd and fondled at your tables, but your slaves, who
> are frequently stiled dogs or beasts, have not equal privilege.... Con-
> sidering what usage they commonly meet with, I have wondered that we
> [don't] have more instances of self-murder among the Negroes.... My
> blood has frequently run cold within me to consider how many ...
> slaves have neither food to eat or proper raiment ... , notwithstanding
> most of the Comforts you enjoy were solely owing to their ... labours.[18]

Whitefield's condemnation of slavery was a judgment on the sinfulness, pride, and arrogance of the unconverted. He could therefore
move easily from lashing masters with accusations of inhumanity to
beseeching them with appeals for religious instruction of their slaves.
"There is a vast difference between civilizing and Christianizing a
Negroe. A black man ... may be civilized by outward restraints and
afterwards break thru those restraints again. But I challenge the whole
world to produce a single instance of a Negroe's being made a thorough Christian and thereby a worse servant. It cannot be."[19] Whitefield's glowing description of the fervent and dutiful Christian slave
mocks his castigation of slaveowning, but only because it compares so
poorly with evangelical attacks on slavery from the later eighteenth
and nineteenth centuries. As James D. Essig points out in his study of
eighteenth-century evangelical antislavery, Whitefield's "abrasive criticism of the slaveowning class ... and his prophesy of divine judgment
on the offending provinces ... led him away from accommodation to
a rejection of slavery."[20] His sense of the collective sinfulness of
slaveowning—not a self-evident proposition in mid-eighteenth century America—can be seen as calling into question his pragmatic argument that Christianized slaveowning was less than reprehensible.

The Late Colonial Period

Garden saw at once this tendency in Whitefield's rhetoric. The very idea of linking divine wrath to a particular social arrangement in this world, he fumed, smacked of blasphemy. "What is it you had in mind to inform them [i.e., slaveowners in the southern colonies]? . . . You THINK God has a quarrel with them. . . . Had God sent you charged with this special *Message*, you might well say, that you must inform them of it; but as 'tis only a matter of your own *thoughts*, the necessity of it does not so well appear."[21]

The issue here was more than a forensic point. Although obtuse about Whitefield's Calvinism, Garden recognized clearly the prophetic role Whitefield had assigned himself and the disorder in the minds and security of men that such prophetic utterances could cause. It may be a "very just thought" that God is angry with those who are cruel to their fellow men, Garden continued, but what evidence did Whitefield offer for this indictment? None at all: "you only *think* it to be so, and *fear* it, and *believe* it." It was this presumptuous moral progression from thought to emotion to conviction that was to Garden the fruit of a disordered mind; to Whitefield it was simply using all human faculties in obedience to conscience and as an act of faithful discipleship. Garden bluntly told Whitefield that in many parts of the South he could be indicted for mouthing incendiary notions "which may endanger the peace and safety of the community." Indeed in contrast with Whitefield's fanciful rhetoric, Garden insisted that the "lives" of slaves "in general are more happy and comfortable in all temporal respects (the point of liberty only excepted) than . . . three-fourths of the hired farming servants" in Great Britain. Certain that he had placed Whitefield on the defensive, Garden pressed the attack. Because this rosy picture of slave contentment was, in Garden's view, based on actual observation of "the generality of slaves, . . . what *apology* can suffice either for the manner or matter of your letter?" Was it "hearsay or report?"[22]

Whitefield's sense that sin was collective as well as individual revealed to Garden how potentially radical and irresponsible the itinerant was, and his pleas for evangelization of the slaves further exposed to Garden a dangerous presumption. Garden readily conceded Whitefield's claim that Christians, even Christian slaves, were meek, tractable, peaceable folk; objections to religious education of slaves, he admitted, were "wild and extravagant." But, Garden noted, Whitefield inserted into his plea phrases which were deeply troubling: "*Christianizing*" blacks; "mak[ing] them *thorough Christians*"; and "*the gospel*

Colonial Evangelicalism

preached" to slaves "*with power.*" These words implied that human beings could appropriate to themselves the "power" to convert, to indict
the sinful, to forgive, to proclaim salvation—all functions which only
God, the Holy Spirit, exercised. "Men may teach *true Christianity*, but
no man can MAKE a true *Christian*."[23] That was precisely what Whitefield believed men could do, what revivalism was all about.

Two of Whitefield's South Carolina converts, the prominent
Beaufort area planters, Hugh and Jonathan Bryan, took very seriously
the teaching that, as new creatures in Christ, they should proclaim the
need to repent and the dangers of impiety to all South Carolina society. The Bryans moved boldly to announce the apocalyptic message of
impending judgment. A conventionally dutiful Anglican, Hugh Bryan
came to evangelical conversion first through the influence of his wife,
Catherine. She, in turn, had been a pious student of the writings of
Archbishop John Tillotson until she encountered Whitefield's sermons on *The New Birth* and *Justification*. These writings confirmed for
her—with what seemed uncanny precision—the reality of her earlier
conversion. Taking Catherine to Georgia to meet the author of those
writings, Hugh listened to Whitefield preach and felt profound uneas-
iness when hearing Whitefield brought him no "real change of heart"
but left him "in the very gall of bitterness and bonds of iniquity," he
later put it. This awakening to the terrors of isolation from grace in
Bryan was, of course, the classic precondition for evangelical conversion, and he passed quickly through the necessary stages that followed: realization that "to flee from [God's] justice was impossible"; a
request to Whitefield for the sacrament of the Lord's Supper; a day
spent in prayer and study; and finally, "illuminations and assurance of
God's favor to [his] soul."[24]

Events soon thrust Bryan into religious controversy for which neither his social eminence nor his new found spirituality prepared him.
In recent natural and political calamities in South Carolina, he saw a
clear indication of God's impending wrath. Bryan's letter, elaborating
on those fears, categorically indicted the colony's Anglican clergymen
for their hostility to revivalism and indifference to theology; they
"have," he charged, "no bowels of love, no pity for poor perishing
souls that are wandering in worse than Egyptian darkness."

Uncertain of the theological subtleties of this pronouncement,
Hugh and Jonathan Bryan waited anxiously until they could consult
with Whitefield before making their views public. In December 1741
Whitefield returned to South Carolina, read Hugh's draft letter to the

The Late Colonial Period

public, and made some revisions in it. On January 1, 1742, it appeared in the *South Carolina Gazette*, and ten days later Whitefield, Hugh Bryan, and the printer of the *Gazette* were all jailed briefly, and then released on bail, for this breach of public decorum.[25]

Whitefield soon left the province, and Bryan turned his attention to the leadership of an interracial community of converts—his slaves, now treated as spiritual and even personal brothers and sisters, as well as white neighbors. By the end of 1741, his deep involvement in this community, especially its black members, convinced Bryan that divine wrath was about to descend on South Carolina. Accordingly, he sent a journal in which he had recorded his apocalyptic ruminations to William Bull, Speaker of the Assembly. Even before this extraordinary document reached Bull, rumors of Bryan's spiritual conviviality with blacks led to demands in the Assembly for Bryan's prosecution. Though Bryan's journal mysteriously disappeared, at least one person who read it reported that it contained the prediction of the destruction of "Charles Town and the [surrounding] country as far as Ponpon Bridge [forty miles from the city but well clear of Bryan's own plantation near Beaufort] . . . by fire and sword . . . by the negroes before the first day of the next month." A few days before he was indicted by the Grand Jury in early March 1742, for spreading rumors of "SECRET DESIGNS contrary to the peace and tranquillity of government," Bryan suddenly emerged from a vigil in the woods of his plantation and announced it had all been a mistake. He had not meant to alarm or terrify his contemporaries and begged their forgiveness.[26]

> You should participate in the pleasure we enjoyed yesterday [Eliza Pinckney wrote to her friend, Mary Bartlett], by hearing that Mr. B[ryan] is come to his senses and acknowledges with extreme concern he was guided by a spirit of delusion which carried him the length he has lately gone under a notion of inspiration. Poor man! With what anguish he must reflect on making the spirrit of God the author of his weaknesses and of disturbing the whole community [which knew] him to be no prophet but dreaded . . . his prophesies coming to the ears of his African Hosts.[27]

The very idea that the slaves he taught had served as his "hosts" suggested that Bryan had abandoned the world of social convention to commune with those of the dark unknown. "I hope he will be a warning to all pious minds," she wrote, "not to reject reason and revelation and set up in their stead their own wild notions." Specifically,

Colonial Evangelicalism

he had expressed the "wild notion" that certain "sacred Oracles" provided support for his apocalyptic vision—as "did all the broachers of herisey in the primitive church." Worst of all, there was no need for his falling into delusion because the "bountiful author of our being" had first "revealed," and then "set up in every man's mind," the intellectual ability to distinguish delusion from true inspiration. The key, for Mrs. Pinckney, was the abundance of God's gifts to man and the rationally discernible nature of existence. "Tho' their may be things in the Xtian sistem above reason such as the incarnation of our Saviour, etc., yet surely they dishonour our religion who affirm their is anything in it contrary to reason." Such a patient willingness to work with the resources of reason and not to venture into the dangerous unknown beyond what was rationally discernible was what Eliza had in mind when she told her brother "that fortitude" was a "virtue so necessary in all stations of life and to all people.... Heat of temper and a certain fierceness" were widely confused with "courage,... but how truly different... is the truely amiable virtue fortitude, or strength of mind, which is hardened against evil upon rational principles, that is so guarded with reason and consideration that no outward event is able to raise any violent disturbance in it."[28]

Violent disturbance was exactly what Hugh Bryan had at first felt certain God was sending upon Charlestown and what he should announce to the world. A serious fire in the southeast part of the city in November 1740, coming only a year after an abortive slave rebellion on the Stono River and just five months after the defeat of General James Oglethorpe's expedition against the Spanish at St. Augustine, had convinced Bryan that "surely, God's judgments are upon us." "We have been hardened under the sunshine, the bounteous dispensations of his Providence," he asserted, "and tho'... scourging us by drought, by... diseases on man and beast, by insurrections of our slaves, and... by baffling... our enterprise against our enemy, so as to make us a by-word and a hissing among the heathen that are round about us" yet after all this warning "we have not laid it to heart to turn to HIM. As are the people, so are the priests: everyone seeking after gain."[29]

Bryan was a dangerous man because he claimed religious, specifically Scriptural, authority for a radical critique of South Carolina society and culture. Eliza Pinckney groped toward this judgment when she compared Bryan's motivation with the authors of early Christian heresies. What she could not bring herself to examine directly was

The Late Colonial Period

Bryan's use of Old Testament prophesy—doubtless with Whitefield's tutoring. From Lamentations he drew language about the "vain and foolish things" that hypnotized sinners into stupefication and from Jeremiah "woe" on "pastors that scatter and destroy the sheep of my pasture" and the warning to "give ear and be not proud for the Lord hath spoken."[30] These passages were thinly veiled assaults on the hubris of the Carolina aristocracy.

Bryan's prophetic vision arose from a passage in Ezekiel:

> Wherefore, thus saith the Lord God; Woe to the bloody city, to the pot whose scum *is* therein and whose scum is not gone out of it. . . . For her blood is in the midst of her; she set it upon the top of a rock; she poured it not upon the ground to cover it with dust; that it might cause fury to come up to take vengeance; I have set her blood upon the top of a rock, that it should not be covered. Therefore thus saith the Lord God, woe to the bloody city! I will even make the pile for fire great. Heap on wood, kindle the fire, consume the flesh, and let the bones be burned.[31]

"Blood," "fire," "vengeance," "flesh," "bones" were searing images that Bryan drove home with horrifying candor: "His drought hath spoken; his diseases inflicted on us and our cattle have spoken," Bryan declared, referring to recent natural calamities. Then, closer to the dreadful truth,

> the insurrections of our slaves have spoken; our *Augustine* expedition hath spoken; the faithful of CHRIST's ministers have lately, in a remarkable manner, been speaking; and the yet greater dreadful fire of *Charles-Town* hath spoken terror; and if we regard not this to lay it to heart, humble ourselves, and repent truly of our sins, the just GOD will yet pour out upon us more terrible vials of his wrath.

All of these portents, all of the known, angry character of God, and the manifest inability of South Carolina leaders to extricate themselves from worldly circumstances and spiritual indifference pointed to a single, haunting Biblical event from Daniel, "hand writing of God on the wall which the great *Belshazzer* understood not." Daniel translated the mysterious words that told the king that God had judged him unworthy and would distribute his kingdom to the Medes and the Persians.[32]

Colonial Evangelicalism

Like Whitefield, Bryan held the Anglican clergy chiefly responsible for moral laxity and spiritual stupor. To Whitefield's charge that the "priests," no less than the "people," were greedily pursuing their own gain, Bryan added callous disregard for the work of the devil to his indictment of the Anglican clergy: "Thieves and robbers" were roaming the world to entrap unwary sinners; "how many poor, careless souls have we in every parish," he asked,

> that stand in need of being informed of their danger and of the absolute necessity of being born again of GOD, and having Christ's personal righteousness imputed to them, before they can have any well-grounded hope of being finally saved? ... Shall our clergy at this day persecute Christ's faithful ministers for not conforming exactly to ... the decrees and canons of the Church ... and have no bowels of love, no pity for the poor perishing souls that are wandering in worse than *Aegyptian* darkness?"

Here Bryan touched a tender nerve. "Egyptian darkness" implied persons in bondage and darkness, and Egyptian further suggested black skin and African origins. And, he turned the social hierarchy upside down by proposing as a remedy that

> our KING wou'd humble himself, lest his Principalities should come down, even the Crown of his glory; for GOD regardeth not princes except their thrones are established in righteousness. O! that all in authority... would humble themselves and duly consider that the great GOD, by whom they enjoy any power, will strictly require at their hands a due and conscientious improvement of the talents committed to their trust.[33]

As William H. Kenney has observed, "Bryan ... had crossed the very fine line that separated religious debate from sedition," or as one English evangelical put it, "the Negroes lately converted at Mr. Jonathan Bryan's ... thirst after inward and outward knowledge" which should inspire Christians everywhere "to be instrumental in Ethiopia's bowing her head to Jesus."[34]

More surprised than chagrined by his failure to instill the fear of the Lord into his contemporaries among the South Carolina elite, Bryan turned his attention from 1743 until his death a decade later to building an evangelical, biracial community of family, neighbors, and slaves on his plantation at Huspah Neck. At the center of that commu-

The Late Colonial Period

nity was the Stoney Creek Independent Congregational Church, which later affiliated with the Presbyterians.

There were pockets of Baptists in the South in the early eighteenth century—called "Regular" Baptists—who adhered rigorously to a Calvinist belief in depravity, election by grace, and predestination in addition to adult baptism. As it did among the Presbyterians, the Great Awakening caused a surge of Baptist migration and evangelization into Virginia and the Carolinas. In 1755, a "Separate" Baptist from Connecticut named Shubal Stearns led fifteen followers to a new settlement at Sandy Creek in present-day Randolph County, North Carolina. Within three years, the membership of Stearns's church had grown to 606, and by 1772 his followers had founded forty-two Separate Baptist churches in the southern colonies.

In Caroline County, Virginia, an unidentified Anglican clergyman, probably the Reverend Archibald Dick of St. Mary's Parish, strode into a Baptist meeting in one of those churches in April 1771 during the singing of an opening hymn. Moving among the gathered worshipers, he flicked the tip of his whip across the open pages of the hymnals while ominously "running the end of the horsewhip in his mouth," an intriguing oral display of insecurity. As the singing ended, the intruder "violently jerked" the Baptist minister, John Waller, "off the stage, caught him by the back part of his neck, beat his head against the ground," dragged the half conscious Waller outside where "a gentleman" administered "not less than twenty lashes with his horsewhip" and "the parson give him abominable ill language." Their point made, the parson, his curate, and the gentleman departed. Waller picked himself up, returned to the meeting, "singing praises to God . . . and preached with a great deal of liberty."[35]

The episode illustrated the ill-defined boundaries between sacred and profane that Anglicans and Baptists understood to exist. Order, decorum, gentility, and subordination as expressed in Anglican liturgy, church architecture, and moral admonition preserved the sacred in vessels fit for the deity and savior of mankind. Rhys Isaac emphasizes the symbolic power of Anglican church buildings in which "tall windows were elegantly arched and designed to let light freely into these temples of rational religion" and "fine rubbed brickwork dignified the plain lines of the great door and windows" that greeted approaching mounted or carriage borne parishioners.[36] The visual object the Baptists seized upon in their depiction—the horsewhip!—symbolized gentry superiority and Anglican hauteur that intensified

Colonial Evangelicalism

the voice of the Lord through the din of blows and curses. "B[rother] Waller... was asked by one of us if his nature did not interfere at the time of the violent persecution when whiping, &c. He answered that the Lord stood by him of a truth and poured his love into his soul without measure, and brethren and sisters about him singing praises to Jehovah, so that he could scarcely feel the stripes for the love of God."[37] The Mill Creek Baptist Church "solemn Covenant," Berkeley County, Virginia, adopted on May 25, 1761, accentuated the communalism implicit in Christian abasement:

> We who desire to walk together in the fear of the Lord and through the assistance of his holy spirit, express our deep and sincere humility for all our transgressions and we do also solumnly in the presence of God and of each other, in the sence of our own unworthiness, give up ourselves to the Lord in a church state, according to the gospel order and practice of the Apostle's constitution, ... humbly submitting ourselves to the discipline of the gospel.

Each of the eight articles of the church constitution that followed this promise stipulated the tangible meaning of a spiritual community— "holy conversation ... to render our communion delightful to God"; "promise to watch over each other's conversation, ... to warn, reprove, rebuke, and admonish one another"; and "to bear with each other's weaknesses and infirmities."[38]

Samuel Frink, Anglican minister in Savannah, watched closely for signs that the evangelical frenzy might subside. "I find the people more constant in their attendance upon Christian Ordinances than at first," he wrote in 1769; "owing partly, I imagine to Mr. Whitefield's longer absence than usual from Georgia. However we are never free from one or more of that stamp in this province. But politicks has of late so much engaged the attention of that sort of people that they have neglected Methodism, 'that one thing needful', as they call it."[39] Frink's phraseology vibrates with distaste, with a sensation of having uncovered the secret of religious dissent and enthusiasm without learning to account for its appeal. "If any of you are willing to be reconciled to God," Whitefield declared in his definition of the "one thing needful," "God ... is willing to be reconciled to you.... O then, though ye have no peace as yet, come away to Jesus Christ.... He has made peace betwixt God and offending man."[40] This sense of urgency, this sense that there is something that people can and must do—in

The Late Colonial Period

spite of their fears and the strangeness of the deed—was an existential moment of sublime terror. It occurred just before a person felt convicted of depravity and—almost—simultaneously rescued by Christ's sacrifice and was the uniquely realistic thread linking the consciousness of the saints. Almost every element of this turning to the Lord appears in the scathing account of backcountry Baptist revivals in South Carolina in the 1760s written by the Anglican itinerant, Charles Woodmason:

> Another vile matter that does and must give offence to all sober minds is what they call their *experiences*. It seems that before a person can be dipp'd [baptized by immersion], he must give an account of his secret calls, conviction, conversion, repentance &c &c; . . . to heighten the farse, to see two or three fellows with fix'd countenances and grave looks, hearing all this nonsense for hours together, and making particular enquiries, when, how, where, in what manner these miraculous events happen'd—to see, I say a sett of mongrels under pretext of religion sit and hear for hours together such a string of vile, cook'd up, silly and senseless lyes . . . and to encourage such gross inventions must grieve, must give great offence to ev'ry one that has the honour of Christianity at heart.[41]

Woodmason's vehemence did not impair his accuracy. "Secret calls, conviction, conversion, and repentence" were the necessary steps in what evangelicals called "experimental religion." The searching of the Holy Spirit for lost souls, the feeling of being a helpless prisoner before the bar of justice who is convicted of sin, the realization and acceptance of salvation, and the sinking-in of a sense of unworthiness all occurred more or less simultaneously, but Woodmason was right about the desired sequence of these discoveries as phases of tumultuous self-discovery.

Richard Furman, the South Carolina Baptist clergyman, experienced just this kind of conversion in the early 1770s. Born in New York in 1755, he grew up in Virginia in an area "not favored with religious institutions" among folk "addicted to rustic sport and social gaiety" in the words of a family friend. Settling in the South Carolina backcountry in 1770 he fell under the influence of a noted Baptist preacher, Joseph Reese, whose witness to Furman is a model of evangelical persuasion and spirituality:

> Under the ministry of Mr. Reese his convictions became deep. The justice, spirituality, universal extent & application of the divine law

Colonial Evangelicalism

were displayed to his view, with his inability as a sinner to fulfill its requisitions or make satisfaction for its violation. The inevitable ruin involved in this condition filled him with apprehension of instant destruction, & he regarded the lightning as the messenger of vengeance. Penetrated with these feelings he was prepared for a discovery of the free grace & mercy of God in the gospel, & was led by the spirit of truth to embrace the righteousness & salvation of the redeemer.[42]

The language of this account is crucial to understanding evangelical sensibility. The preacher *displayed* salvation to him so thoroughly that it *filled* his consciousness; the peril in which he then found his soul *penetrated* deeply into his personality so that of his own volition he could *embrace* salvation. The sexual imagery [43] here accurately conveyed the passionate nature of Christ's pursuit of lost souls in evangelical theology.

This kind of structure was a necessary counterweight to the intense individualism evangelicals experienced in the new birth. Structure not only gave the individual a perspective on the myriad of feelings that washed across his or her consciousness, it also allowed the individual to plunge into the sublime knowing that each kind of ecstasy was but one level of an orderly, intelligible spiritual universe. "Can I feel my soul in sacred raptures, burning with love of God and of Christ, and [have]all my best passions alive?" asked Josiah Smith, Whitefield's chief defender in Charlestown, rhetorically; "can I feel the secret pleasure in the word, ordinances, and communion of God? Can I taste all the powers of the world to come? Can I groan under the burthen of my corruptions or exult in the liberty of spirit?" Smith, like all evangelicals, could ask these questions because he had experienced secret raptures and groaning mortification and he had been taught that they were integral parts of larger whole.[44]

The shifting, uncertain world in which Davies, Whitefield, Bryan, and Furman sought to bring order and security to the souls of men and women underwent during the middle decades of the eighteenth century an ominous series of political disturbances. As population and prosperity surged upward, and as the southern colonies became the most valuable portions of the Empire, Crown officials and a handful of local leaders noted the dangerous fissures in the framework of British administration.

2.

Augustan Conservatism

Sea-girt Britannia! mistress of the isles!
  Where Faith, and Liberty, united reign;
Around whose fertile shores glad Nature smiles,
  And Ceres crowns with gifts the industrious swain!

Thy generous daring sons have nobly toil'd,
  To guard thy cliffs from arbitrary sway;
In well fought fields the baffled tyrant foil'd,
  Where glorious Freedom led the arduous way!

Now through the land Dissention stalks confest;
  With foul Distrust, and Hatred in her train;
The dire infection runs from breast to breast,
  And statesmen plan—and patriots plead in vain!

All-gracious Heaven, avert the impending storm,
  Bid every jealous, jarring faction cease;
Let sweet Content resume her lovely form,
  And o'er the land diffuse perpetual peace:

And, when again our colours are unfurl'd,
  May Britons nobly join one common cause!
With rapid conquests strike the wondering world,
  In firm support of Liberty and Law.

William Eddis,
Maryland Gazette, July 23, 1772

An angry yet elegant debate in the columns of the *South Carolina Gazette* in 1769 argued whether the people of the province should resist the Townshend duties. Four men were principally involved: Wil-

Augustan Conservatism

liam Henry Drayton and William Wragg denounced the tactic of a trade boycott enforced by an extralegal General Committee of activists; Christopher Gadsden and John MacKenzie defended nonimportation and castigated Drayton and Wragg for their betrayal of provincial liberty.

Although in some respects the controversy duplicated disputes over British policy and colonial rights throughout America in the 1760s, the clash of these four personalities—and their ideas and styles—was peculiar to South Carolina. Drayton was a literalist, oblivious to nuance and subtlety, who considered the attempt to coerce people into supporting nonimportation as a violation of individual conscience and regarded the creation of the General Committee as dangerously destabilizing. MacKenzie retorted that the Townshend duties were the product of unbridled power and that the recruitment of opponents of that measure was a legitimate appeal to their "interest," which "is the great director of human affairs. As an individual I have a right to deal with whom I please. . . . Any part of society has the same right." Gadsden sought to rally and mobilize the available resources of virtue and public service among his contemporaries so that "even the most callous, selfish, narrow minded man in the province, . . . however reluctantly and against the grain . . . [will] make the public good . . . the scale of his actions." Wragg coolly took the measure of his adversaries and their use of language. "Shall a railing accusation," he sarcastically asked Gadsden, "serve as a pretense to a return to a state of nature?"[1]

The sharp thrusts and the intimacy of these exchanges reflected a quintessentially South Carolinian conversation about power and authority, liberty and virtue. The combatants ornamented their essays with quotes from English and Roman literature that they knew would be recognized: Shakespeare, Locke, Blackstone, Pope, Bolingbroke, and King James Bible; Juvinal, Horace, Ovid, and Virgil. Drayton could claim that his reply to Gadsden served "more to guide than spur the muse's steed; restrain his fury, than provoke his speed," quoting Pope's *Essay on Criticism*, and Gadsden tossed back in Latin a line from Horace, "What will this boaster produce in keeping with such mouthing?"[2] Not only did the antagonists share a similar education, set of literary models, and fondness for verbal combat, their essays rested on a common body of assumptions about the nature of politics. They all equated freedom with moral and intellectual independence, assigned to the legislature responsibility for checking arbitrary

The Late Colonial Period

power, and agreed that men of property had a moral duty to join in defense of the public good. The sense of trusteeship and respect for the conscientious individual were the coordinates of public philosophy in colonial South Carolina; the nonimportation debate, as Robert M. Weir has discovered, showed how divergent these values had become as controversy made Gadsden and MacKenzie into tribunes of the people and confirmed Drayton and Wragg as "paragons of personal independence."[3]

The Townshend duties controversy in South Carolina exposed a deep cleavage in eighteenth-century British conservatism. The dominant viewpoint was that of the Whig magnates who governed Britain during the "Augustan" age following 1713. Led by Robert Walpole and later by the Duke of Newcastle, Parliamentary and ministerial officeholders and their supporters celebrated British stability and commercial prosperity like that of first-century Rome, and they prized values of subordination, economic interest, and in most cases, Anglican orthodoxy. Burgeoning patronage, national debt, imperial trade, and bureaucracy undergirded the new self-confidence. Members of the bureaucracy, especially the Board of Trade and the Treasury, articulated this metropolitan philosophy, and the Townshend duties perfectly expressed the establishment outlook—the obligation of the colonists to pay for some of the benefits of the Empire and the need for a special secret fund to be used to reinvigorate royal administration.

In condemning resistance to the Townshend duties, however, Wragg drew in part on a different set of political principles, known to historians as the "country ideology." In Britain, this set of ideas challenged Augustan orthodoxy, and in South Carolina and elsewhere in the colonies, usually became a vehicle for resistance against imperial centralization. Alienated from the "court" party of ministerial, Parliamentary, and financial insiders at the center of the British political system, a loose network of political and social outsiders, called the "country" party, denounced moneyed politics, official hauteur, and the fusion of Parliamentary and ministerial power; they yearned for a return to a simpler, agrarian past; the group's most skilled theorist, Lord Bolingbroke, wanted Britain to have a "patriot king" who would rise above parties and interests. By teaching that commercial and financial interests corrupt men and that service of the public good ennobles them, the country ideology divided the political world into

Augustan Conservatism

spheres of darkness where power mattered and of light where virtue abounded.[4]

From the 1720s and 1730s until the early 1770s, the orthodox core of British conservatism and its encircling country party critics formed a stable, if stressful, framework of political thought. In the colonies, however, the availability of these alternative philosophies more readily destabilized politics. Opposition thought manifestly emboldened critics of royal and proprietary administration. Inspired by the history of the Roman Republic, the country ideology became after 1775—as we shall see—a major influence on the polity of the American Republic and the celebration of republicanism as a political and social way of life. Less dramatic, opposition pessimism about the fragility of society during the late colonial period seeped into the outlook of the defenders of British authority. "Foul distrust . . . runs from breast to breast," lamented William Eddis in Maryland, doubting whether "Britons" without divine intervention could ever again "join one common cause . . . in firm support of liberty and laws."[5]

Thus MacKenzie and Gadsden employed the country ideology to identify the aggressive ambition behind the Townshend duties while Wragg and Drayton exposed the same flaws in libertarian crusaders. Profoundly conservative, both applications of oppositionist ideology in South Carolina repudiated dangerous, novel assaults on the public good. Likewise, the disciplining of the colonies through the Townshend duties was conservative—an expression of the vigorous statecraft of Renaissance princes, recent enlightened despots, and contemporary British bureaucracy. Just as evangelicalism was the socially shared experience of private beliefs, so conservatism was not a single normative creed but rather the clashing, sharpening, and refining of several prescriptive voices within the same society.

Until John C. Calhoun, in the antebellum period, constructed a defense of South Carolina's interests and a vindication of his own political integrity from a variety of historical and philosophical sources, no one in South Carolina engaged in normative discourse so skillfully as William Wragg. With deceptive ease, Wragg fit the old stereotype of colonial conservative as a proto-loyalist: fearful of change, privileged, rigid, haughty, and opinionated. A wealthy planter born into a prosperous Charlestown merchant family, he had close ties to England and lived in London from age four years until he was thirty-seven. After settling in South Carolina, he served on the Royal

The Late Colonial Period

Council. He alone had voted in the Commons House against sending delegates to the Stamp Act Congress; he could find no second to his motion in 1766 to build a statue of George III; he refused to sign a nonimportation subscription in 1768, the South Carolina Revolutionary Association in 1775, and in 1777 to abjure allegiance to the King. Banished from the province, he died in shipwreck en route to England.[6]

On closer examination, however, Wragg did not at all fit the stereotype of an unbending conservative. His positions in the pre-Revolutionary controversy and in earlier political contentions—he properly delighted in reminding his contemporaries—ran directly counter to his self-interest. Far from being alienated from the values and ideology of the pre-Revolutionary movement in South Carolina, Wragg internalized the prevailing social creed of the personal and communal virtue that fueled opposition to royal authority in South Carolina.

Wragg's brief but tumultuous tenure on the South Carolina Royal Council—to which he was appointed in 1753, two years after his return to the province, and from which he was summarily dismissed four years later—had a profound effect on the rest of his political career in the province and suggested strongly that he was much more than a prerogative-minded ally of the Crown. Wragg infused into every action a style of personal aggressiveness and intellectual mastery of the situation that unintentionally cut him off from other men and drew both Wragg and his adversaries into postures of defensiveness.

> I thought myself very justifiable in delivering my opinion upon every question which was proposed with resolution and virtue; nor was I in the least anxious whether my almost constant attention and freedom of speech were acceptable or not; for I could not be brought to believe that it was answering the honor and trust reposed in me by his Majesty, if I had through a blamable deference, subscribed to any opinion I was not really of and like one of an herd, implicitly . . . followed a leader with a bell.[7]

Wragg sought to impress Governor James Glen with his learning, intellectual curiosity, and independence as though these qualities in a councillor were of special value to the Crown.

Augustan Conservatism

Those qualities, in fact, made Wragg an undependable supporter of royal administration. In March 1756 Wragg clashed with Glen over a minor procedural matter and demonstrated his outrage by resigning two commission posts Glen had given him. Glen's successor, William Henry Lyttelton, in November 1756 dismissed Wragg from the Council, observing with judgmental but penetrating insight that Wragg "is a zealous stickler for the rights and privileges, real or imaginary, of that body of which he is a member because he derives his own importance from it."[8] Only Lyttelton's close connections with the Duke of Newcastle enabled him to make the dismissal stick. "The suspension was the most important event in Wragg's life," George C. Rogers has written; "it touched upon two threads in his career. The suspension involved a constitutional question; it was also a personal matter." The dismissal meant that the governor was really hostile to the proper balance of Crown, Council, and Commons in the South Carolina constitution; it struck directly at Wragg's concept of his civic responsibility, one in Rogers's words, "marked out by study and fortified by conscience."[9]

In Wragg's eyes, his opposition to the coming of the Revolution was a natural extension of this style of opposition politics. Almost all of his public writings dilated on the function of individual conscience in a political culture. Conscience was the propellant force by which virtue insinuated itself into the life of the community; collective action by men who subordinated conscience to their mutual interest was the source of tyranny over the individual. The only kind of collective action that could legitimately impinge on another man's liberty was the balanced and constitutionally prescribed functioning of the Crown, Lords, and Commons. Wragg felt compelled to make test cases out of his own dissents, to rub in the faces of his contemporaries their duty to respect his conscience. "He must be a very weak or a very wicked man and know very little of me," he said in 1775, "who thinks me capable of surrendering my judgment, my honor, and my conscience upon any considerations whatever."[10]

"Weak" and "wicked" were terms synonymous for Wragg with political folly and degeneration, and he was determined to be both strong and virtuous in the exercise of public duty. His original appointment to the Council, he pointedly told Lyttelton, testified to the active power of virtue in politics: "as you well know," he had been appointed to the Council on the recommendation of Governor James Glen, who knew Wragg's principles with "perfect intimacy," had noth-

The Late Colonial Period

ing personal to gain by securing the appointment, and could vouch for Wragg's "knowledge of the constitution," "experience in the laws of the mother country," "equity," and "thorough acquaintance with the several connections and general interest of the province." Wragg, therefore, felt explicitly obligated to the Crown to serve as an "advisor" to the governor "in many cases, *and in others to be a check upon him.*" "These several trusts," Wragg concluded, called into play all of his talents and defined his role.[11]

Wragg's self-image as an agent of virtue in a mixed government, giving his assent to the actions of others only when morally justified in doing so and withholding it at any whiff of impropriety, belied the allegation that he was a "willful, self-centered, cantankerous old man"—George Rogers's apt summary of Wragg's reputation. "I hope my aspiring after *uprightness* will not be in vain," he wrote to his constituents after his reelection in 1768; "he that sets no value on such qualities, or has them not, is certainly in the right not to boast of them."[12] During the Stamp Act crisis he had refused to be "intimidated by any supercilious brow or forbidding countenance," and, in the difficult years that followed, he had "ever been studious to preserve the peace of society." He only stated his opposition to nonimportation when it "casually became the subject of private conversation."[13] Once his views had caused an uproar, he felt free to make a typically acid comment on the jeopardy in which nonimportation had placed South Carolina: it created a demand for the illegal importation of woolen hats from one province to another and therefore might tempt the ministry to seek an expansion of the number of items taxed under the Townshend duties, "were they of the disposition imputed to them."[14]

Conscientious virtue not only helped Wragg locate himself politically; it also required him to externalize the demands of his conscience in terms other men could understand and from which he himself could derive astringent consolation. "Though briars and thorns be with me," he quoted Ezekiel, "be not afraid of their words nor dismayed at their looks." His writings abounded with literary attempts to explain the sense of isolation and pain and his hunger for consolation and inner certainty. He contrasted the "seeming security of swimming with the stream" with the "violence" it would do to his own judgment. "The freedom of the constitution and the genuine, undepraved text of the law," he declared, upheld concretely his "claim to an indisputable right of withholding my assent to propositions I disapprove of and which are in their nature altogether discretionary"

Augustan Conservatism

and provided graphic evidence of the sources of his conviction. His mother's Huguenot ancestors, "who severely suffered by the persecutions of Louis XIV for exercising a liberty of conscience" taught him that "rancour" and persecution were "the worst of tyrannies."[15] Wragg claimed that he found no pleasure in his contentious role, but rather preferred the known terrors of being a pariah in his own community to the unknown ones of subjection to evil demands or futile recriminations against his detractors. Instead, Wragg assumed the stance of a reasonable man who sought to persuade others of his integrity in terms that were, most importantly, satisfying to himself.

For this reason, his refusal of the post of Chief Justice of South Carolina was an event charged with emotional and ideological significance. In 1769 he had indicated his unwillingness to seek reelection and his preference for political retirement. Gadsden accused him of angling for a Crown appointment. The offer of the Chief Justiceship a week later provided him with a magnificent opportunity to demonstrate that conscience alone, and not interest, ambition, or forensic opportunism, lay at the base of his conduct. "A fairer opportunity, I imagined, would never offer [itself] to raise my reputation to the summit of my wishes." In the face of repeated urgings from the ministry to accept the position, he declined it, hoping that the Colonial Secretary would understand that his "actions flowed from a principle of supporting government and not from a view of preferment."[16]

Wragg's sensitivity to the way others viewed his character and motivation, and his careful fostering of an image of moral and political independence, reflected his lifelong fascination with the psychology of persuasion. "When I assert that no man's assent can be forced or compelled," he declared in his refusal to sign the final South Carolina Association in August 1775, "you know, sir, that I found my assertion upon the authority of two of the most acute and solid reasoners that ever existed: Mr. Locke, in his *Essay upon the Human Understanding*, and Dr. Clarke, in various parts of his works. . . . " From Locke, he drew his evidence that personal consent to an action was ultimately an intellectual act and that a man's liberty to give or withhold his assent depended, in the final analysis, on his freedom to employ all of his senses and perceptual powers without interference or intimidation.[17] The Anglican rationalist, Samuel Clarke, brought this process most clearly into shape in Wragg's thinking. In Wragg's refusal to sign the Revolutionary Association, he referred to "various parts" of Clarke's works before quoting from one of the radically Arian, Anglican cleric's sermons: "to attempt to influence the will by force is like applying sounds to the eyes or colors to the ears; the absurdity in both cases is exactly the same; for as nothing affects the eyes but light, nor the ears but sound, so nothing affects the will and understanding, but reason and judgment."[18] Wragg was apparently familiar with the ten-volume edition of Clarke's sermons published in 1744, books replete with such titles as "The Liberty of Moral Agents," "A Virtuous Heart the Best Help to Understand True Religion," "The Practice of Wickedness Generally Attended with Great Evil," "The Character of Oppressive Power in Religion," "The Nature of Religious Truths," and "Against Persecution in Religion"—all of which condemned attempts to terrify, overpower, delude, or intimidate audiences of religious discourse.[19]

Wragg's joining of Locke and Clarke was the closest he ever came to defining his conservatism philosophically—and as formal philosophy his views were almost incoherent. Clarke was a Platonist who elevated rationality to the level of an ideal essence while Locke had repudiated idealism and made sensory learning and reflection on accumulated sets of sense impressions the highest and best capacity of the human mind. But as a political practitioner and commentator, situated on the periphery of the Augustan world, Wragg drew creatively from metropolitan sources to construct a defensible doctrine of individual freedom and social obligation. "I should look upon myself with the greatest abhorrence," he declared in a characteristic reminder of his scourging self-criticism, "if I was capable upon any considerations of subscribing to any opinion contrary to the dictates of judgment." First, he refused to take the oath of allegiance to the revolutionary movement because it was too general and open-ended, committing the signer to endorse future and unspecified actions the Continental Congress might take. Moreover, the oath presupposed the guilt of anyone who in the future opposed political actions that no one could yet predict or delimit. Second, Wragg protested that oaths binding on an individual could only be prescribed by Parliament or the common law; oaths based on any other authority sanctioned arbitrary and extralegal power and threatened "the common liberty" of all. Finally, the new oath could not be morally binding for it violated prior oaths to uphold and support George III; "a prior obligation, truly valid," he declared, "cannot be annulled by a subsequent oath." A capricious oath taken now to support a revolutionary movement that had not yet fully come into being, Wragg complained,

Augustan Conservatism

would rob him of his most precious possession: his reputation; "what reliance could be had upon a man of so unsettled and flexible a conscience?"

At every point the coercive machinery of the revolutionary move- ment denied Wragg's right to participate in measures for which he would be responsible, fettered his freedom to inject statements of conscience into the political process, and cast doubt upon future loy- alty to his society without specifying what offenses constituted disloy- alty and what evidence supported that hypothetical suspicion. In this state of total war between conscience and force, it was unthinkable to Wragg that he could relinquish the one weapon that could still pre- serve his integrity. "I have withdrawn from all public concerns . . . ; my intentions and conduct have no tendency towards opposition and if I differ with you, I differ without disguise or reserve, neither insidi- ously nor malevolently," he declared, his righteous posture now pru- dently limited and circumscribed; "but I cannot renounce but with life the noble prerogative of speaking freely in a free country." Wragg wanted to be certain that circumstances beyond his control would not cheat him of his own independence as a moral agent. "Fiat Justitia, ruat Coelum," his statement ended: "Justice be done though the heav- ens fall."[20]

The "noble prerogative of speaking freely," which Wragg valued so highly, established his own conscience and integrity as well as the corpus of Augustan political orthodoxy as the internal guidance sys- tem of his thought and pronouncements. Conservatism in the late colonial South varied widely in subtlety, discrimination, and pur- poses; it was a kind of family dialogue in which individuals drew on both British Court and Country orientations for arguments and as- sumptions. Two native-born Crown officials in the southern colonies, James Wright and William Bull—men personally wounded and finally politically destroyed by the American Revolution—defined in the midst of that experience norms of colonial subordination on which the Empire depended. Though part of the imperial establishment, they brought to the service of the Crown something of Wragg's indi- vidualism and stubborn integrity.

Wright was an unusually able Crown official who enjoyed unu- sual opportunities to exercise power effectively. As governor of Geor- gia from 1760 to 1775 he presided over the creation of a burgeoning plantation economy in a young royal colony; he was the only royal governor with troops under his personal command, and he used them

The Late Colonial Period

adroitly to enforce the Stamp Act in 1765; during the War for Independence, Georgia was the only colony in which Britain reestablished civil government, and Wright reassumed the governorship in 1779. The son of the Chief Justice of South Carolina, Wright appreciated the fragility of royal authority and the ease with which centrifugal forces of opposition could disrupt imperial administration.[21]

Enforcing laws he sometimes considered unwise, exercising power he knew to be extremely limited, confronting and denouncing opposition he sensed to be potent and growing, Wright watched his reputation among the Georgia elite erode. His resilience and resourcefulness stiffened and hardened. What preserved his professionalism and preserves a fine example of Augustan political thought was an ability to think conceptually. Broken into component parts, his letter to the Colonial Secretary, Lord Hillsborough, of August 15, 1769, contained seven basic arguments:

[1] I should hope that the People on this Continent, seeing the United Concurrence and Resolution . . . and also the Generous Disposition of His Majesty and the Parliament towards them, would be induced Cheerfully to submit to that Supreme and Sovereign Authority.

[2] The Opposition which has been given to the . . . Legislative Authority of Great Britain has not proceeded from any Spirit or Principle . . . of disaffection to His Majesty's Person. . . .

[3] But, my Lord, the Americans are deeply Convinced that they are not Represented in the British Parliament and . . . are so Enthusiastically Possessed with an Opinion that they cannot Constitutionally be Taxed by a Parliament in which they are not Represented or . . . taxed by Laws to which they have not consented. . . .

[4] The Spirit of Discontent . . . will nevertheless Continue and be as Violent as ever, for the Grievance complained of [i.e., the Townshend duties], whether real or imaginary will still remain unredressed. . . .

[5] Believe me, my Lord, the time and the only time has been Missed . . . for setting the Power or Right of Parliament to tax America. . . . [The Townshend duties and like measures] are now Considered not as the Real and true sense of either Parliament or People [of Britain], but as the effect of Ministerial Influence.

[6] My Opinion has ever been . . . that According to the Present Constitution the Parliament has an absolute Right to bind the Colonies and that America is and can be bound by any and every Act of the British Parliament in all Cases whatever. . . .

Augustan Conservatism

[7] But, My Lord, when People first Emigrated to America it was not thought ... that America would soon, if ever, become that Vast, Populous, and Opulent Empire ... that it now is. May it not therefore my Lord in Point of True Policy, as well as from Motives and Principles of Equity and Justice, may it not now become Expedient to make Some Alteration in the Present Constitution Relative to America?[22]

Taken together, these forthright, quotable opinions were a remarkable analysis of the dilemma of rational governance of the Empire in the face of colonial assertiveness. Wright shared an insight with only one other future loyalist, William Smith of New York,[23] when he spoke of the need for an "alteration in the ... constitution" according to dictates of "equity and justice."

The inner structure of Wright's analysis adhered closely to the fragile underpinnings of Augustan conservatism. He faced hard issues by juxtaposing them against others still harder. The frail "hope" that the colonists could be "induced" to "submit" stood in awkward association with the manifest "generous disposition" of the British government toward America. Wright knew that his scenario rested on tenuous assumptions about colonial attachment to the parent state. The data to examine in the light of those assumptions resisted firm definition; the distinction between "opposition" as "disaffection" and "deep" conviction that America was being unconstitutionally governed might seem a trivial matter of semantics to British officialdom but to a knowledgeable royal governor like Wright the distinction was crucial to statesmanship. Two highly problematic methods for testing colonial governability occurred to Wright: inducing cheerful obedience was one and the other involved changing colonial perceptions, but "the only time has been missed" for that to work with any reasonable expectation of success. Conclusions arising from this inquiry and their long-range implications were likewise at odds with each other. The Declaratory Act language about Parliament's power to bind the colonists was legally and historically right but "true policy" involved political ethics, or at least ethical sensitivity, which transcended issues of right and authority.

During Wright's governorship from 1760 to 1775, Georgia was a textbook case of Augustan conservatism in practice. British capital, royal administration, military security, and Indian trade regulation all energized society and at the same time held in check proclivities to

The Late Colonial Period

disorder with a framework of rational, externally mandated constraints. By fostering what Wright called the "wealth & strength of the southern American colonies" as "the chief means of their becoming opulent and considerable," royal administration earned the loyalty and affection of Georgians. And if the bad example of radicals in other colonies caused trouble, "a small check from home or disapprobation of their proceedings" would "set all right here." Impressed with Wright's ability and candor and the realism of his analysis, historians accept for his explanation of the Revolution in Georgia as imitation of South Carolina and other colonies to the north. A few historians have also sensed the ironic truth that imperially mandated order and vitality worked only in the short run. A recent study shows that Wright's brilliant achievement of a complex cession of Cherokee land to the Crown in 1773, its sale to white settlers, and the use of proceeds to pay debts owed by the Cherokees to creditors and merchants in Georgia and London, buttressed and undermined stability at the same time. The transaction did not, and could not, take into account every interest group with a stake in frontier expansion. Violent clashes between Creek Indians—ignored by Wright's land policy—and "cracker" frontiersmen, as well as assaults by anti-British "Liberty Boys" against the wealthy British land speculator, Thomas Brown, sapped Wright's credibility throughout 1774 and 1775. Unable to establish peace on the frontier or to protect Crown officials and supporters from intimidation and violence, Wright beseeched the Georgia Assembly to realize that "only . . . the due course of law and support of government . . . can insure the enjoyment of your lives, your liberties, and your estates." He believed that liberty was a "substance" fabricated from the available resources of imperial practice rather than an illusory "shadow" of popular emotion and desire.[24]

Wright was royal governor for fifteen years prior to the Revolution, and Lieutenant Governor William Bull of South Carolina served as acting governor in between the terms of appointed governors five times between 1760 and 1775.

At the core of Bull's discreet, benign manner was his respect for unvarnished truth. "In the present temper of the times," he wrote to Colonial Secretary Lord Dartmouth as the Georgia Assembly prepared to elect delegates to the second Continental Congress, "when all power constitutionally to be called on in support of government is drawn into the popular scale, . . . the very attempt to defeat the measure of sending delegates by a governor so circumstanced would have

Augustan Conservatism

given rise to fruitless altercation and exposed me to useless insult." In the lexicon of Augustan conservatism, this was biting language: the dominance of "popular" power and the pitiful isolation of "a governor so circumstanced" signaled the collapse of the uneasy structure of governmental favors offsetting public acquiescence. Uncharacteristically, Bull made his gentle sarcasm explicit: "authority and reason, unsupported by real power are too weak to stem the torrent of popular prejudices swelled to the highest inundation by claims of privileges . . . increasing near ten years past."[25]

Bull came to these conclusions by way of a decade or more of effort to comprehend—imaginatively as well as objectively—the sources of instability and the slackening of self-interest as a constraint on colonial political exuberance. In 1769 he had responded to calls for colonial production of finished goods previously purchased from Britain by pointing out "to them the inviting plan of improving our agriculture in such articles as silk, wine, hemp, tobacco, and flour which will be of real and mutual benefit to both the Mother Country and this colony." *Real and mutual benefit* came as close to expressing a fundamental value, an enduring human achievement, as Bull ever allowed himself to contemplate, He hoped that his tactful, shrewd handling of the Assembly and his willingness to represent the colony's interests to Crown officials would "sow the seeds of such future benefits to Great Britain and this province as will ripen into perfection as soon as the genial warmth of restored confidence and affection shall break forth upon us."[26]

The processes at work in restoring "genial warmth" marked Bull as an insightful, engaged social figure. "With design," he explained to Lord Hillsborough, "I . . . avoided mentioning the reciprocality of advantage" that imperial trade brought to South Carolina and Great Britain. "In the present unhappy temper of the times," he explained, such talk "would rather slacken than enforce their attention."[27] The image of a short attention span and churlish sensitivity to talk of adult responsibilities in Bull's language suggested that colonial political leaders were like adolescent children; that analogy in itself was significant, for the standard language of the London bureaucracy portrayed the colonists as children of the parent state—brats deserving of swift punishment for their insolence.[28] But for Bull colonial discontent was a volatile mixture of peer pressure and worldly environmental influences. "The political principles now prevailing in Boston," he told Hillsborough in 1768, "kindles a kind of enthusiasm very likely to

The Late Colonial Period

predominate in popular assemblies" like the South Carolina Commons House of Assembly where "loud cries silence the weaker voice of moderation."[29]

Bull's reticence over engaging in controversy, his sense of the futility of provoking already resentful assemblymen, and his respect for volatility of debates over liberty all combined in a characteristic report to Hillsborough: "I thought it prudent to be silent with regard to the concurrence of the Assembly with the Virginia resolutions" protesting the quartering at provincial expense of British troops. "The sovereign authority of the British Parliament does not stand in need of the feeble voice of an American Governor to support its right," and "reviving disputes now on such subjects would only serve to produce fruitless altercation and render the minds of people thereby more irritated."[30]

Bull's concern for the truth in public affairs and his fascination with the actual motivation of his provincial adversaries converged in a telling retort to a rebuke by Lord Hillsborough in 1769: "I have always conceived it to be my duty, and that his Majesty's ministers expect, that I shall not, in order to make my representation of our affairs appear more agreeable, make them less consistent with the whole truth of their state, which is more especially necessary at this critical and important juncture, big with present discontent and future hopes."[31] Bull's spacious conception of political reality as a mixture of discontent and hope exhibited the most thoughtful and generous characteristics of Augustan conservatism. Dr. Samuel Johnson had the same cast of mind, and his biographer, Walter Jackson Bate, found at the core of Johnson's intellect a tension between the "hunger of imagination ... and the stability of truth." Facing discontent unflinchingly certainly taxed Bull's imagination; envisioning future hope required the patience to wait for truth to prevail.[32]

Bull's hunger for imaginative understanding also resembled Dr. Johnson's hard-won appreciation of "the vanity of human wishes." Bate describes Johnson's mastery of self in terms that dovetail closely with Bull's efforts to maintain personal and political equanimity: "Despite the transitoriness of things, despite the chronic lack of satisfaction our ambitions bring, the first need of the heart is to turn outward and avoid paralysis and self-concentration."[33] Bull kept his frustrations and official dignity under strict discipline and recognized the need of legislators to explore the public meaning of their fears and excitement. "In the warmth of argument, which is an artful method of ex-

Augustan Conservatism

tracting secrets," he observed, "words are sometimes incautiously dropped which convey ideas of extremities in case of their failing in their expectation of redress."[34] Language, then, took on a life of its own in political contention, and so also did the emotional stakes of opposition protagonists: "It is too frequently the humour of popular assemblies when an act has been done or resolution taken with percipitate warmth; ... they think themselves engaged in honour to support it and obstinately adhere to it, tho' the impropriety thereof appear obvious to their cooler consideration." Bull believed that if he could dispense as much "lenity, moderation, and indulgence as could consist with the positive injunctions of the law" he could buy enough time for cooler consideration to prevail.[35] Events proved him wrong.

Attorney General Egerton Leigh, Bull's colleague in South Carolina, a quintessential Augustan bureaucratic operator, was not as surprised or as sanguine. "Are we so besotted and usurped in mercenary schemes of profit?" he demanded of Lord Gower in 1775, "to barter away our precious rights" to govern the American colonies? "Where is our national character, that virtue which has made us the admiration of the world?" Troops would be useless to reimpose British authority in the colonies, he argued; but a blockade of colonial ports and prolonged exclusion from British commerce would "bring the Americans to reason ... and settle these unnatural divisions." The core of imperial authority was the credibility of the language used by the Crown: "If this Kingdom speaks in a lofty tone at this juncture, the language will give a lesson to the European states as forcible as fleets and armies" and a firm, convincing threat to prosecute rebellious leaders for treason "will call men of property to reason and reflection, for at present the Americans are in a state of political enthusiasm bordering nearly on madness." Dealing with that malady meant drawing on the knowledge and understanding of royal officials who knew colonial behavior intimately. "I have lived twenty years among them," Leigh declared; "I know their genius, habits, customs, feelings, and powers. I am no stranger to their wants, their mutual jealousies, their daily necessities, and their absolute dependence on this country." Threatened on one side by Indians and on the other by slaves, "a circumstance of humiliating disgrace to these bawling sons of liberty," the colonists were like a newborn baby—"impotent and dependent." Cynicism, sophistication, and expertise were the sinews of Empire.[36]

The outbreak of the War of Independence did not silence defenders of British authority in the southern colonies. Instead it thrust

The Late Colonial Period

loyalist polemicists and advocates of imperial military vigor into situations of deprivation and danger either on the periphery of southern society or in British garrison towns. Sometimes shrill and desperate, loyalist outbursts about the nature of war and revolution were nonetheless firmly grounded in Augustan values about the reciprocal obligations of inferiors and superiors, constraints on individual volition, and distrust of political innovation.

Loyalists in the South saw limitless opportunities for the British to convert their enterprise and opportunism into military and political advantage. Anticipating in November 1780 an imminent British invasion of Virginia, the loyalist military adventurer, John Connolly, explained to General Henry Clinton how the upper Ohio valley could be reclaimed for the Crown by manipulating critical features in the social organization of the region. The population that had burgeoned in 1767 and in 1776, he reported, consisted of "adventurers allured by the prospect of an idle life" and former tenant farmers from the northern neck of Virginia "whose increase in children and desire to be independent" motivated them to become squatters in a frontier where "civil authority" was too weak to restrain their land-grabbing conduct. Overnight the region changed from a "rude wilderness" into a "sociable and tolerably well cultivated settlement." In order to protect their own interest in western lands, Virginia Revolutionary leaders encouraged settlers in the region to join in the rebellion in 1775 and "royal authority" gave way "to a confused democracy." Predictably the rebel leaders in this unstable setting overplayed a strong hand by imposing harsh taxation and militia fines. Alienated by these measures, "the great majority" of settlers, who are "valuable loyalists," "would be ready to shed their blood in support of the former constitution, yet, under their present embarrassments, their services are totally lost and we can expect nothing but their empty good wishes." With the loyalist majority entirely cowed, nothing stood in the way of rebel conquest of the Illinois territory. This would threaten Detroit and Niagara, cut off communications with Canada, and trigger new and more powerful raids down the Mississippi against West Florida.

Connolly emphasized the desperate quality of the situation because it contained the key to a miraculous British recovery in the west:

> from the description given, your excellency will perceive that many of the people—dispersed over that extensive country—are unencumbered

Augustan Conservatism

with families and their attendant cares, [or by ownership] of fixed property, accustomed to an erratic life, and ready for every adventure wearing the face of poverty. Abandoned to the influence of designing men,
their constitutional courage and hardiness have been prostituted to the
basest purposes and their arms opposed to their sovereign and their
own proper interests. Policy requires that this unprovoked ill-humor
should be turned from its present channel and directed to a proper
object of resentment.

By dramatically increasing the trade of the Ohio valley with Montreal
and Detroit, Britain could give its loyal allies in the region a compelling motive "to support that power from which they derived
such striking benefits." Simultaneously, Britain should mobilize the
Spanish-hating southern tribes for a massive assault on New Orleans.
Once in control of the Ohio and Mississippi valleys Britain could
invade western Pennsylvania and occupy Fort Pitt. All of this, Connolly admitted to Clinton, might seem an undertaking of "too considerable a magnitude," but he urged the general to trust him. "I feel
myself so firmly convinced of the practicability of what I have advanced that I would stake my salvation upon a favorable outcome."[37]
　Virginia loyalists felt certain that the same qualities of opportunism and desperation that fueled loyalist insurgency on the frontier
would be the undoing of tidewater rebels. John Goodrich proposed to
Clinton a pincer attack on Williamsburg, "the metropolis of infamy,"
from the James and York Rivers.

I know the genesus of the Virginians [he explained]; an example of
devastation would have a good effect, the minds of the people struck
with a panic would expect the whole country to share the same fate.
Offer rewards for bringing to justice the active rebels, let them be pro-
portioned to their rank and consequence ... , make proper examples,
countenance and protect the inoffensive and honest farmers. This
done, every rebel will suspect his neighbor, all confidence will cease,
the guilty in crowds will retire to the back country without a possibility
of removing provisions for their subsistence, hunger will make them
desperate and open their eyes, they will fall on their destructive leaders,
peace and submission, of course, must follow.[38]

The Connolly and Goodrich appraisals of British opportunity and
rebel vulnerability reflected their dependence on conventional Brit-

The Late Colonial Period

ish assumptions about the potency of imperial power and the destabilizing effects of mindless opposition to constituted authority.

Imbibing unnatural and untried doctrines about their obligations as subjects, the loyalists contended, the patriots became victims of their own desperation. "It was the universal and professed maxim" at the outbreak of hostilities with Britain, wrote the Reverend J.J. Zubly under the pseudonym "Helvetius" in the *Royal Georgia Gazette* in 1780, that "*if we succeed we will be called a revolution and deemed a rebellion if we miscarry.*" This "neck or nothing" frame of mind anesthetized the patriots from the pain of anticipating the "ruin and destruction ... coming on apace." "Helvetius" had even heard South Carolina patriots say, "we must not look to the consequences," as though the very possibility of defeat and punishment, seriously considered, would be enough to unnerve the radicals. "Upon no other principle than the prospect of success, and that success would abolish the criminality of the means," he concluded, "would men that have any regard for their lives engage in any desperate action." The rebellion not only ignored the truth and gloried in violence, injustice, and irresponsibility, it necessarily converted truth into falsehood and good into evil: "upon this plan ... men must place perjury in the room of a lawful oath, to murder must be no crime; rapine and violence hold the place of equity and justice, nor can any design be too dark or any action too villianous for men that expect to succeed in wickedness." By this circular morality, the Revolution became a self-justifying endeavor in which "success will sanctify ... all the measures made use of to obtain it."[39]

Bound together by their desperate flight from reality, by an abandonment of traditional moral norms, and by the perversion of the truth, the Revolutionaries had plunged their society into a moral and social morass. "Before the interruption of regal government [in South Carolina], plenty, affluence, and increasing prosperity seemed to combine to render the people happy, while poverty, wretchedness, and ruin characterize the era of democratick oppression," wrote "Drusus" in the *South-Carolina and American General Gazette* early in British reoccupation of the province. Yet pacification and submission to British authority were not yet complete. "Can any man be so absurd as to imagine that the inhabitants of this country were subjects to Congress?" If Congress could not provide protection and military security for the people living under British occupation, how could it claim allegiance? "Drusus" demanded. In theoretical terms, no confederation even existed until the Articles of Confederation were ratified. In practical terms, the disintegration of the insurrectionary administration in South Carolina was ample evidence of Congress's artificiality and illegitimacy. "If ... this MIGHTY STATE [i.e., South Carolina from 1775 to 1780] in possession of *legislative authority*" and an *"executive"* inflicting "vengeance and confiscation against the refractory and, exercising arbitrary and despotick power in violation of every principle of the constitution, could not prevent its DISSOLUTION, can it be reasonably supposed ... that Congress, aided by a few republican enthusiasts in this province will be able to re-establish its independency and participation in the union?"[40]

In their quest for a coherent understanding of the Revolution—for a reasonable way of dealing with capricious, illogical events—the writers of the loyalist press commented astutely on revolutionary behavior. They noted, as we have seen, the symbiotic union of moderation and radicalism in Whig rhetoric: a defense of the existing social order that magnified to fantastic dimensions the evil potential of British policy and heightened the moral drama of colonial opposition. The resulting tension within American society was excruciating, and the loyalists noted the release of guilt and desperation into every political transaction. Aware that this emotional energy needed to be channeled and conserved, some patriot leaders advocated Spartan discipline, and others struggled to construct and operate constitutional government. Unable to appreciate those corrective, self-denying measures by the Revolutionaries, some of the most thoughtful and knowledgeable loyalist polemicists believed that they alone lived in a world of discipline and constraint. "There are bounds to all human power," declared "Helvetius" in the *Royal Georgia Gazette*; "the doctrine of non-resistance has long and deservedly been exploded, but its opposite, like some powerful and dangerous medicine, ought to be handled with the utmost caution, lest it become a dangerous weapon in the hands of a madman." The history of modern Europe, explained Zubly—who chose the name "Helvetius" because he was a Swiss emigrant—showed that civility and maturity were the mark of people who did not resist every injustice or jealously guard every scrap of power. "The Swiss never revolted," and ever since the height of the Roman Empire they "pleaded, petitioned, and appealed" against imperial encroachments but "suffered" with grim dignity rather than "taking up arms or revolting." The Spanish Netherlands, "Helvetius" continued, did revolt against Phillip II, goaded to violence by the Duke of Alva's barbarous suppression of the Dutch Protestants; in marked contrast with the American Revolution-

The Late Colonial Period

aries who casually printed millions of dollars of worthless currency and boasted of their national greatness, the Dutch were tenacious, humble, and soft-spoken. Even courage and genuine patriotism, "Helvetius" concluded with a final example, did not guarantee success to a people fighting for their freedom. The Corsicans had fought bravely for more than forty years against their Genoese overlords only to have "the French, like true politicians, after weakening both parties at last make a conquest of it for themselves"—inflicting cruel atrocities on the Corsican patriots. The lesson of history was clear: "intestine commotions and civil wars are productive of such infinite mischiefs that humanity shudders at their approach.[41]

"Helvetius" skillfully arranged a series of quotations from Emmrich de Vattel's treatise on international law. This humane and rational commentary on the limitations of military power as an agent of change placed extremely narrow limits on the meaning of a just war. Vattel observed that while legitimate national interests were at stake in many wars, the passions and aggressiveness of particular rulers were more intimate causes of conflict. He underscored—in the passages "Helvetius" quoted—the futility of war as a means of achieving social change; war itself settled nothing, it only compelled a defeated nation to submit to negotiation. If peace settlements depended on "exact and punctual" compliance by all parties, no war would ever end short of the utter desolation and annihilation of the losing side. Because warfare itself spawned so much incidental injustice, a war was never an instrument of justice. The civilized way to end a war, Vattel insisted, was for both sides to strike an imperfect bargain and "extinguish differences by the most equitable" feasible arrangement. On the basis of these terms, the concessions proposed by the Carlisle Commission in 1778 conceded virtually every American claim short of independence. "Is it a just and lawful plea against generous offers of peace," he demanded, "that they cannot be accepted because those to whom they were made" are allied to France? Is fear of insulting an opportunistic ally a valid reason to perpetuate a dreadful war?

Ultimately, the unity of the moral order, which the Revolution had so savagely torn, depended not on history or philosophy but on God's final judgment. Looking forward to that vindication, "Helvetius" defined the Revolution in much of its complexity:

> The penalty due to obstinate rebellion in this life is a trifle not to be mentioned with what you must expect when all of the ghosts of the

Augustan Conservatism

slain, every drop of innocent blood you spilt, every act of violence you
concurred in or committed, all the confederates of your crime whom
you have forced or seduced, every injured widow's groan and every
orphan's tear whom you have ruined, the spoils of the honest and innocent whom you have robbed, every friendly warning which you rejected,
will at once arise in judgment against you and render you as completely
miserable as you have rendered yourselves distinguishedly wicked.

No single sentence in all of the loyalist press dealt so comprehensively
with the nature and impact of the Revolution. In a single spacious and
ominous image, Zubly juxtaposed the innocence, agony, spiritual and
physical isolation, virtue, and brutalization of the loyalists with the
destructive force and inner nature of revolution: the self-justifying use
of violence, the way coercion expanded outward until it overwhelmed
even the weak and helpless, and the patriots' determination to pay
any price, moral or material, to insure the permanence of their new
regime.[42]

Zubly's conceptual virtuosity was not entirely idiosyncratic. Conventional loyalist thinking in the South during the War for Independence could, under the right stimulus, explain in Augustan
conservative terms how the adept use of British power could still create a good society and how such a society might sustain itself politically. Just such a stimulus arrived in 1783–1784 when news reached St.
Augustine, East Florida, that Britain had ceded the Floridas to Spain
in the Peace of Paris. In their own writings and in appeals transmitted
to London for them by Governor Patrick Tonyn, the East Florida loyalists linked imperial vitality, and their own capacity to act virtuously, to
British predictability. "The principle part of the original planters,"
Tonyn wrote to Secretary of State for Home Affairs Thomas Townshend in May 1783, "after having expended large sums of money began to feel themselves in comfortable circumstances.... They were
happy in the full enjoyment of their native rights and privileges under his Majesty's auspices.... Amidst a general revolt" they "stood
firm." Then came 12,000 loyalist exiles confident of royal protection.
"This consideration ... induced them literally to lay out the wrecks of
their fortunes in building Houses and forming Settlements; ... they
were ambitious of this province ever remaining characterized for loyalty."[43] Yet these heavy-handed, melodramatic documents were the
quintessential expression of the loyalist perception of political reality.
Anonymous East Florida loyalists and Tonyn, who had a flair for trans-

The Late Colonial Period

lating their sentiments into the prose of official correspondence, did not invent new modes of expression, new assumptions about the nature of politics, and new rhetorical devices in 1783. These documents and characteristics of language represent an experience stretching back to 1775.

With ill-disguised attempts at subtlety and indirection, *The Case of the Inhabitants* argued deductively that as subjects they had during the course of the war no choice but "to hazard life, fortune, and all that is dear" in support of the Crown and to acquiesce willingly in the terms of peace including the cession of Florida: that, having lost all, their shattered lives could be restored in no other way than from the generosity of the British nation, and, therefore, Britain had no choice but to assume the cost of their resettlement and full compensation for the land, possessions, and slaves they had lost. The burden of responsibility for affirmative action was entirely on Britain; the East Florida loyalists had simply accepted their duty to fight against the American rebels and then to agree to the peace settlement that returned Florida to Spain. They were nothing but pawns in a world where allegiance placed absolute obligations to obedience and acquiescence on subjects and where rulers axiomatically protected the interests of their faithful supporters. "To admit a contrary idea," the document declared, "would be to assert that Great Britain hath lost all public faith": that she punished the innocent, disregarded justice, and forfeited her reputation for "probity, justice, and good faith," and "untied the strongest bonds that unites civil society.... That language may suit our northern neighbors," it concluded pointedly, but not the inhabitants of East Florida who have known Britain's "kindness and fostering hand." Belying the notion that allegiance required unquestioning acquiescence, it concluded, "we must not *as yet* complain."[44]

This helpless, immobile position provoked more than self-pity; it also prompted the East Florida loyalists to recall the whole range of emotions that had been brought forth by their experience and bad fortune. "Abandoned by that sovereign for whose cause we have sacrificed everything that is dear in life," a group of them wrote to the King of Spain in October 1784, "and deserted by that Country for which we fought and many of us freely bled," and "left to our fate bereft of our slaves by our inveterate Countrymen,... We ... are Reduced to the dreadful alternative of returning to our Homes, to receive insult worse than Death to Men of Spirit, or to run the hazard of being Murdered in Cold blood, to go to the inhospitable Regions

Augustan Conservatism

of Nova Scotia, or take refuge on the Barren Rocks of the Bahamas where poverty and wretchedness stares us in the face. Or do we do what our Spirit cannot brook ... renounce our Country?"[45]

This remarkable version of history depicted the empire as a place of opportunity and protection for venturesome men, where venturesomeness bred a "spirit" which made humiliation and a lack of options a galling fate. War had consumed economic opportunity and the terms of the peace had denied its replenishment. A certain naivete and unconcern for political power permeated these remarks. Tonyn underscored this attitude: "I am confident," he wrote to Secretary of State Townshend, "that our gracious sovereign will make liberal allowances for human frailties and that you will represent in the most favorable light spirited men laboring under difficulties and misfortunes which a steady adherence to the duty they owe their King and Country has accumulated upon them." They are "unacquainted with the great engines by which government is upheld," and therefore "have been led to think of themselves as aggrieved because [they are] unfortunate." The antidote Tonyn prescribed for this benumbed state of the "principle inhabitants" of the province was a still more apolitical faith in royal beneficence:

> nothing can give me greater pleasure than to find that you gentlemen— whom I have ever represented as well affected rather than [as] harbouring murmur and discontent in your present calamitous circumstances—[will] submit yourselves to the measures of government and rely upon the benignity of our sovereign, the justice of the nation, and the wisdom of His Majesty's ministers for a suitable provision to be made for you.

In April 1781, when the East Florida Assembly renewed its contribution to the support of the empire, Speaker William Brown wrote in just such a tone of calculating innocence to Tonyn, "we hope the present smallness of our quota may not be considered as a measure of our loyalty to the most beneficent prince in the world or our attachment to our bountiful mother country."[46]

There were centrifugal forces at work in the province, Tonyn acknowledged in a superbly analytical letter to General Guy Carleton, which wrought havoc with these civilized and gentlemanly British standards of conduct. Tonyn reported that he could not dismantle his administration until the treaty with Spain was finally ratified, and in

The Late Colonial Period

the interim "an abandoned set of men" in the Georgia and East Florida back country had

> committed several daring robberies and will certainly attempt to ravage this country and insult government in its feeble, disabled condition. . . . In this stage of impotency the settlements will be exposed and the Negroes plundered . . . and when His Majesty's daily bounties to the refugees cease . . . they will become exceedingly clamorous and impatient, and the worst is to be expected from the lower sort. In addition to these evils, the licentious, disbanded soldiers who have discovered intentions of rapine and plunder are most to be dreaded.

The logic of the situation was inescapable: "This ever loyal province, given up to accommodate the peace of the Empire, and the inhabitants thereby losing their pleasant abodes and property have, Sir, a just claim for every assistance and compensation which can be extended to them and indulgence in their choice of destinations to any part of His Majesty's Dominions." Only by adequate resettlement and compensation could the empire be true to its own best standards: a place where acquisitive, venturesome men could depend upon British reliability and predictability and receive, in addition to economic opportunity, just reward for risks and sacrifices in the service of the Crown.[47]

In wartime Savannah, Charlestown, and St. Augustine, and among the loyalist insurgents operating from those bases of British military power—at the outermost edges of an embattled empire—public philosophy was less firmly grounded in institutions than it was in Great Britain. Here normative judgments were harsher and more jarring and the ideological stakes much higher. Most impressive in Augustan conservatism, as it radiated outward and sought to provide a rationale for civility and order, was its consistency and plausibility. When the variety and complexity of conditions in the Empire taxed consistency, Augustan conservatism appealed to morality. When rebellion created implausible, grotesque conditions of disorder, morality became shrill and strident if nonetheless cogent. In situations where conservatives and evangelicals collided, or where their activities converged, the moral imperialism of Augustan conservatives appeared in its most audacious and vulnerable form.

Excursus I

Connections:
The Fabrication of Order
and the Social Uses of Religion

Augustan conservatism sought to hold society together with ties of subordination, self-interest, and metropolitan dynamism; British and colonial evangelicalism sought to redeem and meld together, from within, the lives of people caught in subordinate roles, blighted by their own selfishness, and fed corruption by the British economic and political colossus. That, at least, was the view from the perspective of the antagonism between the evangelical flock and the institutions and culture under which they lived. From within that culture and from the perspective of situations where antagonism did not intrude, evangelicals and conservatives could be seen locked together in the same social environment, each goaded and perplexed by similar difficulties.

Sometime around 1730, Arthur Dobbs, Anglo-Irish politician and future royal governor of North Carolina, wrote a treatise on the history and economic and social development of the British Empire. He began with a short history of European colonial expansion from the Romans to the sixteenth century, in which he contrasted "thirst for dominion" with the more mature appetite for trade and commerce. Dominion might trigger colonization but it too readily degenerated into self-destructive greed; commerce worked much better, but without a mature metropolitan economy to absorb colonial wealth and free institutions (especially churches) to channel the energies and desires of the colonial populace, even a trading empire would nurture within itself the seeds of its own destruction. For the British Empire, those seeds included the dispossession of the Indians and the exploitation of slaves. Left unattended, the despotic energies summoned forth by the process of colonial expansion would leave a legacy of havoc. Dobbs's remedy was clear:

We can by no other method justify our dispossessing the natives than by gaining their consent to it, by giving them an equivalent, bye in-

The Late Colonial Period

structing and civilizing them, and sharing the benefits of their country with them. Shall we who are Christians, who ought to be held up to the strictest rules of justice and morality, give them a just handle to oppose the religion we profess by practicing none towards them? Shall we, who by the precepts of our Lord and Saviour, ought to love our neighbors as our selves, . . . instead . . . pride our selves by our superior knowledge in arts and sciences and despise them as an inferior race, not worth reclaiming?

. . . All the ties of humanity and religion, all the advantages we possess from our learning and liberty, oblige us to exert our selves in relieving the distresses and promoting their happiness.

Dobbs further recommended that "methods should be taken and laws made to oblige the masters of Negroes" to provide slaves with religious education, opportunity to cultivate their own gardens, and discriminatory taxation of masters for their unconverted slaves. Only a massive program to Christianize the Empire, Dobbs declared, could harmonize and manage the energies and passions of its multiracial population.[1] Fifteen years earlier, Lieutenant Governor Alexander Spotswood tried to implement just that policy by making the conversion, education, and protection of Indians a cornerstone of royal administration in Virginia—to the outrage of the planters and Anglican Commissary, James Blair, who joined hands to secure Spotswood's downfall.[2]

Four decades after Dobbs wrote his treatise, the Anglican clergyman, Theodorus Swaine Drage, arrived in Salisbury, North Carolina, to assume his duties as rector of St. Luke's Church. Governor William Tryon appointed Drage subject to a trial period of two to three months during which the St. Luke's Vestry would indicate its satisfaction.[3] Drage's efforts to secure that approval were a fiasco. Dissenters—both separate Baptists and Presbyterians—turned the election into a contagion of disputed returns and intimidated victors.[4] Unable, for want of a functioning vestry, to secure installation as rector of the established church, Drage appealed to Tryon for support and was told by the governor that

I lament . . . that you have met with so unjustifiable an opposition to your establishment in St. Luke's parish. . . . The intemperate zeal of the dissenters, I am inclined to believe, arose from mistaken principles. Their seniors [i.e., leaders] must know their persuasion is a sect under the Act of Toleration. . . . This is even implied in His Majesty's Instruc-

Excursus I.   Connections

tions to me wherein "he commands me to permit a liberty of conscience to all persons (except Papists) who are contented with a quiet
and peaceable enjoyment of the same, not giving offence or scandal to
the government."

I confess I have a pleasure in acknowledging myself greatly obliged
by the Support the Presbyterians have afforded Government in my administration, and it will be a circumstance of peculiar concern to me to
have them Sully the Merit of their late publick Services, by pursuing
measures which are in manifest Violation of the Rights and Liberties of
their fellow Citizens by throwing difficulties and obstructions in the
way of the Maintenance and free exercise of a Religion Established by
the Laws of their Country. I would appeal to the reasons and judgment,
and not to the passions of those Gentlemen, how far it may prove im-
politic in the issue to the interests of their persuasion should they carry
any further their opposition to the Legal Settlement of a Clergyman in
St. Lukes Parish.

Tryon was one of the most energetic mid-century Crown officials
engaged in the task of reinvigorating royal authority in the American
colonies. Working with limited resources like the direction and sanction of Royal Instructions, and limited ecclesiastical patronage
granted the governor in 1765 by the legislative establishment of the
Anglican Church in North Carolina, Tryon sought to hold social disorder and opposition politics at bay long enough to allow the benefits
of subordination and harmony to develop a momentum of their own.
Tryon expected the grandeur of a new governor's palace in New Bern
to help create the right atmosphere for benign royal rule. The North
Carolina war of the regulation, sparked in part by Baptists angry that
their ministers could not perform legal marriages, brought Tryon's
transfer to the governorship of New York in 1771.[5]

His letter to Drage, however, expressed with exceptional candor
and insight the religious stakes in the North Carolina contest between
fabricated order and indigenous pluralism. Even if their leaders knew
better, Tyron explained, the Baptist rank and file were genuinely ignorant of the fact that they worshiped at the sufferance of English religious toleration, subject to the condition that they remain peaceable
and polite. "The frontier parts of this, and neighboring provinces,"
James Seymour, in Augusta, Georgia, wrote in 1772,

are over run by a set of ignorant preachers who call themselves (and
indeed not improperly) *irregular Baptists* [to distinguish revivalist Sepa-

The Late Colonial Period

rate Baptists from Calvinist Regular Baptists]; they travel from place to place and pretend to miraculous conversion and immediate inspiration. . . . These preachers have no appointment or ordination from any society of Christians whatever, yet . . . they presume to administer the sacrament of baptism to adults, often plunging their deluded hearers into the rivers and creeks in these frontier settlements.[6]

Presbyterians, in Tryon's eyes, functioned as a interface between dissent and orthodoxy. They had played a conciliatory role in the Regulator controversy, offering themselves as intermediaries between the governor and the rebels and emphasizing the importance of maintaining order. Tryon suggested to Drage that Rowan County Presbyterians could be handled by an appeal to their "interests" which by-passed the "passions of those gentlemen." Above all, Tryon saw himself as exercising finely calibrated political leverage. "I claim no concessions [specially granted authority]," he told Drage, "but the rights of the country as well as those of the Crown. It is my duty to maintain [that balance] as long as I am invested with such important trusts." He could not impose his will on the Rowan County dissenters, Tryon meant by this delicately phrased self-assessment; he could only utilize his limited religious powers to balance dissenter privileges against the stabilizing influence of Anglican worship. He advised Drage to take his case to the "next General Assembly" and offered to add some dependable Anglicans to the Rowan County Justices of the Peace prior to the next vestry election. He balanced that clinical political move with praise for "the temper, moderation, and good sense with which you have conducted yourself through this whole business," a blunt admonition that Drage not cause unnecessary trouble.[7] Drage apparently agreed for he soon departed for South Carolina where he served a parish in Camden until his death in 1774.[8]

Tryon believed in the reality of this calculated, rational, cynical, somewhat moralistic kind of political administration. His obituary in *Gentlemen's Magazine* in 1788 repeated what must have been a cherished family tradition: "Illustrious as a legislator [i.e., statesman], he suppressed the rising seeds of revolt in North Carolina. . . . Calmed to peace under his mild and beneficent sway, the people relinquished every other ambition than that of looking up with filial attachment to their friend and protector." Every objective detail of that account of Tryon's governorship was historically false; its governing assumptions and literary tone, however, expressed exactly what Tryon believed he had done.[9]

Excursus I.   Connections

The Dobbs and Tryon documents of 1730 and 1770 spanned the period of the Great Awakening and the origins of the American Revolution as well as the mid-century rise of pluralism, dynamic social and economic change, and cultural conflict in American life. They also spanned the appearance, first noted by Jon Butler, of two different religious movements in the southern colonies, nurturing, genteel *evangelism* and revivalist, demanding *evangelicalism*. The missionary activities, or evangelism of Anglicans in the early eighteenth century, as well as the increasing prominence by mid-century of Quaker, Huguenot, Presbyterian, Regular Baptist, Lutheran, Moravian, and German Reformed churches, Butler argues, "plowed and fertilized the spiritual soil later tilled so successfully by evangelicals."[10] While corrosive disputes between Anglicans and dissenters—between evangelists and evangelicals—sounded like those of bitter antagonists. Anglican evangelism sought through religious nurture to be a servant to political power, while dissenting evangelicals wanted to empower the powerless through a dramatic awakening of the soul.

As is often the case, the best insights came from a partial outsider, Joseph Ottolenghe, an Italian Jew converted to Christianity in England in 1734 and in 1751 sent to Georgia by Dr. Bray's Associates, an Anglican missionary organization, as a lay catechist to blacks. Three nights each week, "when their daily labour is done," he taught slaves how to pray, read the Bible, learn the catechism and Lord's Prayer. "In order to get their love, I use ... all the kindness and endearing words that I am capable of, which makes them willing to come to me and ready to follow my advice." The scandal of spiritually indifferent masters and slaves in dire need of salvation struck the innocent, conscientious teacher even more forcefully than it did Whitefield or Davies:

> I find upon examining them, which I do once a week, that by the blessing of God they daily improve in the knowledge of our holy religion. It is true that their masters, who think they should be great loosser [s] should they permit their slaves to learn what they must do to be saved, not considering that he would be a great gainer if his servant should become a true follower of the blessed Jesus.... Others ... from the West Indies ... alledge ... that a slave is ten times worse when a Christian than in his state of paganism, but they must mean such as practice Christianity as they do.[11]

Ottolenghe combined evangelical and rationalist phraseology when he yearned for slaves to "learn what they must do to be saved,"

The Late Colonial Period

but learning remained for him an exercise of instruction and an attainment of knowledge—albeit knowledge embedded in intimate personal experience. "Slavery," he wrote to the Secretary of Dr. Bray's Associates,

> is certainly a great depresser of the mind which retards their learning a new religion proposed to them in a new and unknown language, besides the old superstition of a false religion [Catholicism encountered by the slaves in the West Indies] to be combatted with.... Nothing [is] harder to be remov'd (you know) than the prejudices of education, riveted by time and entrench'd in deep ignorance, which must be overcome by slow advances, with all the patience and engaging means that can be studied, to make them fall in love with the best of religions, and so captivate their minds as to give all their very little leisure to the study of it, and I have so far gained this point, in drawing the Negroes to it with the cords of love.[12]

The line between falling in love, having captivated minds, and being drawn by cords of love and the freedom discovered in the new birth—the psychological difference between evangelism and evangelicalism—was tissue thin.

Closely related but ultimately distinct versions of religious sensibility represented one point of contact between evangelists and evangelicals. The two also shared a common dilemma—their discovery that the world would fiercely resist the gospel of love and their dim realization that as members of society they were implicated in that betrayal. The wounds of society which Anglicans sought to heal were ugly indeed; Ottolenghe wrote of slaves who were "loaded with hard labour and worse usages, ill fed, ill cloathed, cruelly corrected and barbarously treated, in so much that a dog and an horse are treated like humane creature[s] when compared with . . . these poor unhappy wretches, . . . robb'd of dear liberty . . . and . . . reduced to a most deplorable and cruel slavery!"[13] Anglicans also strived to give permanence to their fledging ministry of humanitarianism by calming the fears of whites, giving religious sanction to slavery, and upholding notions of rank and duty. When evangelicals attacked pride, sin, and arrogance in the southern colonies, they discovered that the culture early Anglican evangelists had bolstered was resistant to attack and resilient in the face of moral criticism. Before evangelicals could come to terms with the world they were called to be in but not of, a political revolution and the creation of a new republic would vastly complicate their task.

Part II.

REVOLUTION AND REPUBLIC

3.

Whig Conservatism and Republican Constitutionalism

The happiness of society ought to be the end and aim of all government, and that is most promoted by assimilating it to the tempers, pursuits, customs, and inclinations of those who are to be ruled. . . . The Constitution of Britain had for its object the union of the three grand qualities of virtue, wisdom, and power as the characteristics of perfect government. From the people at large the first . . . was most . . . expected, the second from a selected few . . . , and the latter from some one . . . to whom heaven had given talents . . . for sudden and decisive action. . . . Might not this or something like this serve as a model for us?

> William Hooper to the North Carolina Provincial Convention, Oct. 26, 1776, Paul H. Smith et al., eds., *Letters of Delegates to Congress, 1774–1789*, 5 (1979): 401.

The republican is the most ancient form because it is the most natural. . . . The tumults and distractions of republicks . . . generally arise from attempts to establish monarchical, or, its nearest kin, oligarchical governments. . . . The contaminating prison of these perverted forms occasions the natural decay and death of republicks.

> *Virginia Gazette* (Purdie), May 17, 1776

The rights of Englishmen together with the defense of liberty against tyrannical conspiracy combined to fuel the American Revolution. British and colonial history affirmed the rightness of the cause while libertarian ideology channeled fears and apprehensions that something terribly wrong was afoot in the Empire. Between them,

Revolution and Republic

both sets of norms—positive rights and imperiled liberties—made the Revolution conservative in its ends and radical in its methods.

While complementary and mutually reinforcing, the dynamics of claiming rights and thwarting despotism rested on different ideological assumptions and suggested different implications for the kind of politics Americans should adopt and practice. Political rights underlay the freedom of individuals to pursue their own interests and happiness; fear of conspiracy inhibited individualism and drew people into a fellowship of disciplined republican citizens. Rights harkened to Locke and libertarianism to Scottish moral philosophy, English opposition thought, and Florentine and Roman republican history.

The conditions of political life in the southern states from 1775 to 1783 inhibited conflict between these two strands of revolutionary zeal. The planter elite in Virginia, the Carolinas, and to a lesser extent in Georgia supported resistance and independence with a unanimity that retarded bickering over theory. One of the blessings of liberty the planters sought to preserve was the freedom to own and exploit slaves—a people whose bondage and misery dramatized to them the desirability of freedom. But as the task of writing constitutions and waging war progressed and threatened the cohesion of society, southern patriots found increasing consolation in republican pessimism. They sought during the 1780s for a way to stabilize their political credo and to harmonize optimism about rights and pessimism about the fragility of liberty. In 1787–1788 James Madison—and probably the example of his teacher, John Witherspoon—provided a compelling demonstration of how that stabilization and harmonization would, at a crucial moment, be effected.

Among the earliest people to perceive these tensions in revolutionary society were patriot leaders who had only recently emigrated to North America: Alexander Hamilton who saw energetic government as the guarantor of liberty, James Wilson who envisioned law as cement of political order based on consent, Charles Lee who proposed the republican uses of irregular warfare, Witherspoon who believed that virtue should be taught to people in a republic, and James Iredell who labored to discern the correct grounds for severing the imperial tie.[1]

Iredell emigrated from England in 1768 at the age of seventeen when his father, a Bristol merchant, suffered a paralytic stroke. Forced to make his own way in the world, Iredell had the good fortune to be a distant kinsman of Henry McCulloh, the wealthy North Carolina land

Conservatism and Constitutionalism

speculator and Crown official. Iredell's family connections were just good enough to secure him the post of Comptroller of Customs in Edenton, North Carolina. His arrival in the colonies in the late 1760s, his Crown appointment, his loyalty to and affection for his benefactor McCulloh were the very circumstances that should have made him a loyalist when the Revolution erupted in 1775. Iredell's experience emphasizes the crosscurrents of opportunity and risk that faced officeholders and functionaries in the patronage system of the British Empire. During his first seven years in Edenton, Iredell sent his Customs Service salary home to Bristol to help support his parents; he remained the grateful protege of Henry McCulloh; he ran the Edenton Customs house efficiently, and he covered for his immediate superior (and his patron's son), Henry Eustace McCulloh, who had far-flung business interests in the colony; he vigorously enforced the Navigation Acts, but despised the arrogance and venality of the new Customs bureaucracy headquartered in Boston. He became a close friend of Samuel Johnston, a wealthy Edenton lawyer and landowner, and he married Johnston's sister, Hannah, winning over a rival suitor, Sir Nathaniel Dukinfield, a member of the Royal Council who remained Iredell's close friend. In his spare time, Iredell read law and started an arduous legal practice.[2]

Probably in no other colony, except perhaps Georgia, could a newcomer have risen so rapidly both in service to the Crown and as a member of the local elite. The price of the rise was prolonged anxiety and painful euphoria. Henry Eustace McCulloh's exploitation of Iredell and his procrastination in securing Iredell a promised promotion in the Customs Office forced a year-long postponement of Iredell's marriage. "A rashness in promising and an indifference about performing," he lamented in his diary in 1772, "is a fault deserving severe censure." Seeking short-term advantage as a servant of the McCullohs and long-term advancement in league with the Johnstons generated severe pressures and discouragement for Iredell, but these difficulties seem to have instilled in him a perspective about success and striving. The news of the sudden death of a respected citizen of Edenton— perhaps a reminder of his father's ill health and financial reversals— struck Iredell with "the uncertainty of life and the instability of all worldly treasures" and the high risks that accompanied "an anxious solicitude to obtain unbounded wealth and dignity."[3]

Iredell's political education coincided with the last stages of the pre-Revolutionary controversy, and he wrote four long and revealing

Revolution and Republic

analyses of the issues in the conflict—pleas for the British to revert to traditional support for colonial liberties and also thoughtful affirmations of the rightness of resistance and independence. Without mentioning Locke by name, Iredell placed Lockean contract theory at the core of his interpretation of politics. "The Americans consider themselves equally entitled to Liberty with your British Subjects . . . ," he addressed George III in an essay actually written "to justify his own conduct to himself"; [4] "as Men, who have ever preserved their Freedom, they had a right to continue free; as Subjects of the Crown, they were guaranteed by . . . stronger obligations. *Our original contract* is in being. This stipulates Sovereignty on the one side; Liberty on the other."[5]

A reciprocal compact, he argued, was "happy kind of monarchy which reserves just enough power to the Crown to make it useful and respectable but not enough to enable it to despise the people whom it governs."[6] A government so engorged with power that it alienated itself from its subjects—"despised" them—was a regime that had transgressed the thin line separating legitimate rule from tyranny.[7] The duty of the ruler, Iredell contended, ran in exactly the opposite direction. "True liberty consists," he quoted Blackstone, "not so much in the gracious behavior as in the limited power of the sovereign." Liberty therefore gained sustenance from constitutional forms limiting power and balancing the necessary functions of government against the subjects' needs for space and psychological security. The British should have used the financial crisis of the East India Company as a time to repair the contract and readjust the balance between duty and liberty. "A kind of stagnating quiet prevailed. There were seeds of much ill-humor prevailing, but *little shewn*, and the peaceful exertion of . . . Government left room for tenderness and discretion to operate." The "great distress" of the East India Company was real enough, but "the Americans had surely a right to determine whether they would buy tea." Moreover, the colonists had a long and honorable record of peaceful opposition to revenue measures they considered unconstitutional. "No mobs, no riots, no resisting of its landing" had characterized in opposition to the old Townshend duty on tea.[8]

That restraint was part of the compact between the colonists and the Crown. Now "it was necessary to make a choice whether to return to the old and successful method of governing the colonies, or to persevere in the new, odious, and in all appearances impracticable one." Iredell found in the deliberations leading to the Tea Act a clear-

Conservatism and Constitutionalism

cut alternative between policy based on custom or one based on prescription. Respect for the contract and obligation to nurture implicit bonds of Empire when the opportunity arose to do so both underscored the value of custom and precedent as means of disciplining and regulating the aggressive proclivities of rulers. "The Connexion between Great Britain and America . . . depend on a system of Government which reconciled and healed the minds of Men and gave them no occasion of jealousy or alarm, no fear they were being treated with ignominy and dishonour."[9]

The emotional dynamics of the contract dominated Iredell's thinking. In a 500-word sentence in his untitled treatise on the causes of the Revolution, he urged "that the anxiety of the People in this situation ought to be considered" in its several dimensions:

"The *fear* that power would henceforth be exercised in a new and unconstitutional manner;

[and the] "*resentment*, natural to Men who see . . . their Protectors take a pleasure in browbeating them";

the real *danger* that "loose and disorderly" men would react violently and bring havoc and vengeance on the just and unjust alike; the *prospect* that "a whole People, Men, Women, and children" could thus be "consigned" to "misery";

the *indignity* of hearing a hostile Britain telling the Americans "the ridiculous tale of their being only constitutionally connected with Her";

and the *realization* that the relationship of Britain and her colonies had reached a new level of historical development "which ought to be judged by its own circumstances" rather than by "narrow, pedantic rules" conflicting with "*liberty*" of "a brave People."

This torrent of repercussions of a ruptured social contract—fear, resentment, danger, indignity, imminent change—had so aroused "the ardour of my feeling," Iredell paused to reflect, that it had "drawn these reasons to a greater length than I intended." And the end was not in sight. He plunged at once into a protracted analysis of the

Revolution and Republic

damage done by the Coercive Acts: "the fatal haughty System," "arbitrariness," "despotism," the suspension of a colonial charter that was "a *mutual compact* and of course not alterable but by the consent of *both* Parties."[10]

Iredell's grief over the destruction of the contract, his diagnosis of that process as an attenuation of costly experience and tradition in colonial history, and his chagrin at the irreversible psychic damage done by violations of trust and dignity all doubtless reflected his English background and pride in becoming "a British American," as he still called himself as late as 1777. His urgent search for grounds of reconciliation that did not infringe American liberty and were indeed rooted in the best traditions of British freedom has suggested to historians that Iredell was a cautious, fearful revolutionary. Viewed in the context of his forceful and consistent Lockean libertarianism, Iredell was simultaneously conservative and radical: radical in the peculiarly eighteenth-century meaning of that term as a person who saw abuses of power and the very nature of authority itself as moral issues; conservative in his conviction that coercion of the colonies was evil because it shattered the sense of security and order that people derived from their charters, from their traditional autonomy, and from their historic assumption that political and constitutional rights could never be unilaterally abrogated by Parliament or by the King. "We cannot divest ourselves of every vestige of freedom to please you [or] to make the business of government go on more smoothly," he wrote to "the Inhabitants of Great Britain" in September 1774; "a power of taxing and harassing us with cruel, oppressive, and inconvenient laws we will not give you because it is a novel claim and can never be exercised but to our destruction."[11]

The conceptual framework in which Iredell placed his passionate political fears and grievances was the familiar view of politics as a contract enshrined in Locke's *Two Treatises on Government*. The other great source of American revolutionary ideology was the republican civic humanism derived from Roman thought by Renaissance writers like Coluccio Salutati and Nicolo Machiavelli and revived in the eighteenth century by the writers of the country ideology and the moral philosophers of the Scottish enlightenment. Where Lockean contractualism was optimistic and personal, the republicanism of the country party and of the Scottish "Common Sense" philosophy was pessimistic and communal. Lockeans believed that the compact, properly honored and observed, protected society from human depravity and

Conservatism and Constitutionalism

contained ample nourishment for a healthy, functioning political system; republicans saw liberty constantly imperiled and virtue always in short supply. The Lockean requirement that the compact serve as the public conscience requiring periodic rededication of society to libertarian principles eventually evolved into a tenet of modern liberalism. Republican hostility to money and innovation was—as already emphasized—profoundly conservative, but despair and the sense of being a lost cause also made classical republicanism a radical impulse during moments of upheaval. The two ideologies were not necessarily incompatible, but they rested on different assumptions and produced different tendencies.

The Virginia planter and burgess, Landon Carter, illustrated particularly well how Lockean resistance prepared the ground for republicanism, then thwarted its advance, and finally acceded to republican imperatives. Like Iredell who scorned the conventional phraseology of British officialdom—"a few artful syllables" intended to "cheat... us out of our liberties"—Carter dismissed the "noisy Alehouse" language about the "protection" the colonies allegedly received from Britain. British protection was a code for restricting colonial liberty that aroused Carter to examine the claim aggressively. Considered in "its only valuable light," protection meant preserving the "Religion and liberties of the People." Here was a model of compact government in which a complex and integral set of guarantees and obligations guided British political life rather than dictated subordination in specific matters. "The Protestant Religion," Carter explained, was a blessing and benefit to the colonies but not something which could be embraced or jettisoned by individual volition. "How am I able to divest myself of that [religious] liberty?" he asked. For a slave, liberty of conscience might be separable from physical freedom because religion could comfort the slave while perpetuating his bondage at the same time. For a free people, protection and liberty were not just a legal condition but also a kind of political consciousness: "The Colonists... glory in their connection with that Country from whence they first derived their being and... have been hitherto preserved in the enjoyment of their Liberties, and Religion.... Nature and Justice must blush to think that Children could ever be entitled to less...."[12]

Fearful that a declaration of American independence in 1776 and the "adoption of this republican form which we seem to be hurrying into" would substitute one folly for another, Carter remained convinced that the traditional "mixed form" of popular, aristocratic, and

Revolution and Republic

monarchical government still stood the best chance of maintaining order and promoting virtue.[13] When independence came, he reluctantly but with gathering conviction found Lockean grounds for endorsing the new order: "every contract, especially about government, is reciprocal with conditions on both sides. Allegiance was mine and the condition for it was justice and freedom together with a paternal affection. If that is broken or denied me, I am absolved."[14]

The republican experiment into which Carter feared Virginia was "hurrying" was the adoption of a state constitution in June 1776. By that time, South Carolina had acted on the recommendation of the Continental Congress that the colonies create governments capable of protecting their liberty and approved its first state constitution in March 1776. Following the declaration of American independence, Maryland completed its new constitution in October 1776, North Carolina did so in December, and Georgia in March 1777.[15]

These documents broke decisively with Augustan political orthodoxy. "All power is vested in, and consequently derived from the people," a Bill of Rights declared at the opening of the Virginia constitution;

> magistrates are their trustees and are at all times amenable to them. . . . Government is . . . instituted for the common benefit, protection, and security of the people, nation, or community; of the various modes and forms of government, that is best which is capable of producing the greatest degree of happiness and safety and is most effectively securing against the danger of maladministration. . . . No man or set of men are entitled to exclusive or separate emoluments or privileges from the community. . . .[16]

That statement was a classic definition of the republicanism derived from Florentine humanism and from British opposition theorists; it rejected any hereditary principle in government, located ultimate authority in the whole body of the people, insisted on practices of consent, identified virtue as the life-force of the community available to be exercised by the wise and capable, and warned against the ever-present dangers of corruption, official privilege, and misuse of power.

Revolutionary state constitutions in the South joined these potent republican doctrines to familiar notions of contract and consent. "All men are by nature equally free and independent and have certain inherent rights," the Virginia Bill of Rights declared; "the com-

Conservatism and Constitutionalism

munity [a republican rather than a Lockean term] hath . . . an inalien-
able . . . right to reform, alter, or abolish" governments that violated
their own purposes.[17] The Maryland constitution fused the republican
and Lockean approaches even more closely: "All government of right
originates from the people, is founded in compact only, and [is] insti-
tuted solely for the good of the whole."[18] The North Carolina constitution used Virginia's language about the popular sources of authority
and emoluments and privileges; it also followed the suggestion made
by John Adams that a bicameral legislature was the best antidote to
the "fits of humour, caprice, passion, prejudice, hasty results, and
absurd judgment" of individual legislators, and stipulated, in agreement with Adams, that "the legislative, executive, and supreme executive powers of government ought to be forever separate and distinct
from each other."[19] In deference to instructions from Orange and
Mecklenburg county electors, the North Carolina framers provided
for popular election of both houses of the legislature, disestablish-
ment of the Anglican Church, and a Protestant religious test for officeholding. As in North Carolina, the planter-merchant elite in Georgia shared power with backcountry leaders and made significant concessions to them: an executive council in place of an upper house
with only limited legislative functions and a truncated appellate court
system. Declaring themselves to be representatives of the people,
"from whom all power originates and for whose benefit all government is intended," the members of the Georgia provincial congress
assumed the power to frame a new government in pristine republican
terms.[20]

The price of an entirely new conception of legitimacy in the
revolutionary South as a whole was the adoption of separation of
powers, bicameralism, and property qualifications for officeholding
as security against social upheaval, particularly in South Carolina and
Maryland. The low-country electoral districts in South Carolina had
126 of 202 seats in the Assembly with property qualifications for its
members of £1,000 free of debt. In Maryland a £500 qualification for
election to the lower house and £1,000 for the upper house limited
access to those offices to 10.9 and 7.4 percent of the state's population
respectively. In South Carolina, the low-country elite serenely assumed its ability to maintain political dominance, while in Maryland
conservatives like Charles Carroll of Carrollton were apoplectic over
"the detestable villainy of designing men who under the specious and
sacred name of popularity are endeavoring to work themselves into

Revolution and Republic

power and profit... to establish a most ruinous system of government" and determined to draft a constitution that would thwart that democratic danger.[21] A pessimistic view of the prospects of the newly independent states undergirded the entire republican constitutional enterprise. "In order to prevent anarchy and confusion," the North Carolina preamble declared, "it becomes necessary that government be established in this state; therefore we, the representatives of the freemen of North Carolina ... do declare that a government for this state shall be established."[22] Thus the formation of state governments incorporated both contractual and civic humanist language and assumptions.

More than politics and constitution-making, warfare and military activity were familiar and accessible forms of symbolic behavior in Revolutionary America. The War for Independence forced upon the southern states the realization of their fragility. What John Shy has called "the essential triangularity" of the war—the way British and American forces "contended less with each other than for support and control of the civilian population"—jeopardized the fragile cohesion of republican state governments and politicized the conduct of the military struggle. By shifting the focus of scholarship away from American victory and British defeat and toward the social impact of the conflict, the triangularity hypothesis brings coherence to a plethora of information about the war. Despite the best efforts of conservative commanders on both sides, the war spilled off the formal battlefield and into the surrounding society. The politicizing and brutalizing of noncombatants hurt both sides but did far more damage to the British because it mocked their pretensions as protectors of the King's faithful subjects and guarantors of order in the colonies. The dual task of holding society together while conducting a socially divisive war, moreover, involved Revolutionary leaders in desperate experimentation, much of which ran counter to their basically conservative predilections.[23]

On the eastern shore of Maryland, especially in Dorchester County, and in neighboring Sussex County, Delaware, a kind of tory populism prevailed among small farmers who defied the whig elites that had overthrown the Maryland and Delaware proprietary governments in 1775. Called "riots," "insurrections," and the work of "pirates" by contemporaries, this disaffection took many forms—seizure of valuable salt from a prominent whig official; rowdy disruption of a

Conservatism and Constitutionalism

Committee of Observation meeting by 100 armed men; taunting and shoving of an isolated whig official; an organized band of some 400 outlaws, led by the "backsliding Methodist" Cheney (or China) Clows, which operated from a swampland hideaway in Queen Anne County from 1778 to 1782; or a bizarre act of intimidation in which a group of tory refugees descended on the home of constable Robert Appleton in Bombay Hook, Delaware, and ordered him to read a Methodist sermon, destroy legal papers pertaining to loyalists, and submit to being whipped by a black man.[24]

The racial and religious references in the Appleton incident highlighted two intriguing features of Eastern Shore/Delaware tory insurgency. News of Lord Dunmore's appeal to Virginia slaves to join him in suppressing rebellion in 1775 reached the ears of Eastern Shore blacks and may have prompted fearful Maryland officials into overreaction; this may have alerted yeoman farmers to the tenuous authority of the Revolutionary regime. As the war progressed, loyalist activity became increasingly identified with the influence of Methodist preachers who seemed intent, as they did in Virginia, on building a new kind of spiritual order among poor whites, some slaves and free blacks and were oblivious to the patriots' presumptions to serving a divine purpose. [25]

At one level, these raids, insults, and acts of vandalism were militarily insignificant; they merely served to demonstrate that concentrations of loyalists and neutralists among the common people in isolated parts of Delaware and Maryland could defy civilian officials with impunity. Neither side dared nor desired to use terror against the other. The low level of overt violence, as well as its chronic and persistent nature, forced both government and insurgents to acknowledge each other's existence; this laid the basis for a subsidence of conflict after 1783. But at another level, that of potentiality, this regional conflict was grim warfare. "If Howe had proceeded up the Delaware River" in the summer of 1777 "and . . . had landed a few hundred soldiers in Sussex County," Harold B. Hancock speculates, "probably hundreds of soldiers would have flocked to him from all over the Delmarva peninsula" and possibly have given Britain control of the trade routes between Philadelphia and Baltimore. Even with scant British assistance, loyalists living in this region—probably a majority in 1776 and at least a large minority thereafter—posed a real threat to the political stability of two state governments. The limited

Revolution and Republic

violence perpetrated by the insurgents and the clumsy retaliation carried out by state officials made possible the absorption of the disaffected into the fabric of republican society after 1783.[26]

The same tension between official and popular justice developed in North Carolina. A vacuum occurred in the summer of 1781, when the government was exhausted by Cornwallis's invasion of the state and the suppression of the loyalists fell into the hands of individuals like Andrew Bread, "a person in the Practice of Shooting down peoples whom he is pleased to suppose disaffected to the... government," in the words of Thomas Cabune who nearly because one of Beard's victims. General Stephen Drayton saw events of this kind as part of a rough process of "convicting, reclaiming, or punishing of Tories" in which "our own imprudencies & irregular proceedings made more enemies than had ever become so from mere inclination."[27]

Both the Cabune and Drayton documents date from July 1781. Events in North Carolina during that summer provide a model for explaining regular and irregular warfare in the Revolution. Major James Craig occupied Wilmington in January 1781 and in July appointed David Fanning commander of loyalist militia already operating under Fanning's leadership. Craig and Fanning had finally learned how to fight irregular war in America. Fanning devised a new guerilla strategy based on what John S. Watterson calls "quickness, mobility, deception, and improvisation." Fanning's raids concentrated on freeing tory prisoners, capturing the most notorious persecutors of the loyalists, operating widely in eastern North Carolina under cover of darkness, "plundering and destroying our stock of cattle and robbing our houses of everything they can get." Fanning's men were disciplined, and violence was carefully targeted against key officials. Throughout Cumberland, Bladen, Anson, and Duplin Counties pockets of dispirited loyalists felt emboldened by Fanning's exploits.[28]

General Nathanael Greene and Governor Thomas Burke sensed almost immediately what was happening. In the face of frantic appeals for troops to protect people against Fanning, both men realized the futility of such tactics. They understood that the plane of the conflict had been tilted in Fanning's favor. With Continental troops tied up in Virginia by Cornwallis's march north, and North Carolina administration in shambles, Fanning's discipline, sense of the jugular, and secure base at Wilmington made it possible to demoralize an entire patriot populace and to move from one triumph to another—a process culminating in a raid on Hillsborough in September that bagged Governor Burke himself as prisoner. The only safe remedy was to hunker down and wait for events outside North Carolina to shift advantage away from the British irregulars. The use of retaliatory terror against known or suspected loyalists only played into Craig's and Fanning's hands, enabling them to present themselves as agents of justice for the oppressed and targets of barbarity. The Fanning-Burke duel in North Carolina in the summer of 1781 therefore pitted for the first time in the war adversaries who thoroughly understood military triangularity. Just as Fanning taught the patriots a lesson about the fragility of their political achievements, the shift in the fortunes of war in 1782 taught the loyalists how to recognize defeat and gave them time to make a choice between exile in Nova Scotia or taking their chances with Revolutionary justice in North Carolina.[29]

As North Carolina experience suggests, loyalist postwar reintegration arose not only from patriot victory or from a stabilizing equipoise but from violence itself. The fierce civil war that convulsed South Carolina from late summer 1780 until the spring of 1782 played out the memory of a previously learned lesson with frontier lawlessness in the mid-1760s and harsh repression later in the decade by the South Carolina Regulators. The savagery employed by both Whigs and Tories in 1781 and 1782 frightened and shocked South Carolina patriot leaders. General William Moultrie did not exaggerate when he found, in early 1782, a shattered society of brutalized, frightened, impoverished people for whom "a dark melancholy gloom appears everywhere and the morals of the people are almost entirely extirpated." Even moderate, self-critical leaders like Aedanus Burke had felt an almost uncontrollable rage against the British and their loyalist lackeys in South Carolina. Prior to the British evacuation of Charlestown the state legislature had compiled a list of more than 700 names of loyalist collaborators and had imposed harsh fines and confiscation.[30] Almost simultaneously, however, a kind of braking action set in, softening the impact of these penalties and restoring most of the accused to the body politic. Even vigorous pursuers of the loyalists found the work distasteful. These symptoms of moderation then encouraged Aedanus Burke to make a major public appeal for reconciliation on the ground that South Carolina could not afford the luxury of remorseless revolutionary justice: "the experience of all countries has shown that where a community splits into a faction, and has a recourse to arms, and one finally get the better, a law to bury in *oblivion* past transactions is absolutely necessary to restore tranquillity."[31]

"A plundering Whig is worse than a non-plundering Tory," declared Samuel Eusebius McCorkle, Presbyterian minister in Salisbury, North Carolina, and namesake of the early church historian. "It is in your interest to join with the [latter], if disposed to join you, [and] to support and execute the laws upon the [former], if indisposed to repent or restore," he instructed North Carolina leaders in the spring of 1781 in a sermon on "The Crime and Curse of Plundering." McCorkle equated plundering of helpless tories with the looting of "silver and . . . gold and vessels of brass and iron" by an Israelite soldier named Achan in the Book of Joshua, which "kindled . . . the anger of the Lord against the children of Israel." McCorkle's argument, in fine republican pessimism, held that individual enterprise and enrichment did energize society but also had a corrosive influence. No one had a right to injure the public good in the pursuit of private gain, and in war the line between rational self-interest and besotted greed and vengeance became perilously thin.[32] Constitution writing thrust whigs in the South into the republican experiment, and the military struggle revealed the fragility and precariousness of virtue in the new polity. Understood in these terms, republicanism was a set of imperatives and impulses badly in need of structure and process.

These political and military events occurred within a provincial society in which teachers and writers devoted a great deal of time and energy to making sense out of public events and educated future leaders of the new nation to think about, and to strengthen, the web of ideas and values holding the new culture together. A leader at the center of this educational activity, Benjamin Rush of Philadelphia, urged the creation of schools in which each "pupil be taught that he does not belong to himself but that he is public property." More than family or advancement or reputation, Rush urged, students in a republic must be inculcated with teaching about public duty, welfare, safety, and prosperity.[33] Through the oratory and historical writing of his protege, David Ramsay, Rush would influence a generation of young men in post-Revolutionary South Carolina. The most far-reaching and pervasive voice in southern higher education between the Revolution and the Civil War was that of John Witherspoon, president of the College of New Jersey at Princeton and teacher of a famous course on moral philosophy that provided a generation of Princeton students with an explanation of the self-governing, self-

Conservatism and Constitutionalism

critical qualities of human beings—a public philosophy. Witherspoon's students founded Washington College and Hampton-Sydney
College in Virginia, dominated the University of North Carolina during the early nineteenth century, and served as the model for colleges
in Kentucky and Tennessee and for Joseph Waddel's famous prepara-
tory school in Willington, South Carolina, where John C. Calhoun
studied before entering Yale.[34]

Witherspoon's republicanism was an improvised but attractive
mixture of Calvinist doctrines of depravity and civic humanist notions about virtue. He spoke of "the insolence, cruelty, and obstinacy
of Lord North, Lord Bute or Lord Mansfield," which required that
"we . . . grapple with the ignorance, prejudice, and partiality of human nature."[35] That pair of trilogies itself indicated Witherspoon's
willingness by 1774 to place the discussion of evil within civic, rather
than spiritual, categories; North, the power broker; Bute, the insidious
royal confident; and Mansfield, scourge of seditious libel, respectively
epitomized partiality, ignorance, and prejudice. To enable them to
understand evil of this kind, Witherspoon told his students, God had
"implanted" in human beings "conscience, enlightened by reason,
[by] experience, and [by] every way . . . we . . . learn the will of our
Maker."[36] This formulation was the very conception of human nature
that Witherspoon had condemned time and again in Scotland as
leader of the orthodox wing of the Presbyterian Church of Scotland
opposing the influence of Scottish moral philosophers, especially
Francis Hutcheson. In 1758 he scornfully dismissed enlightenment
Christianity in Scotland as "a pliant and fashionable scheme of religion, a fine theory of virtue and morality."[37]

Witherspoon's theological reorientation, following his installation as President of Princeton in 1768, has perplexed historians more
than it did his contemporaries. American Presbyterians knew little of
the ecclesiastical wars in Scotland, and the Trustees of the College of
New Jersey were attracted to Witherspoon more for his reputed erudition and eloquence than for his orthodoxy. Once in America he
sought to revitalize the finances and academic stature of the College
by nurturing a new consensus among American Presbyterians based
on Scottish moral philosophy as well as self-conscious piety. Mark A.
Noll further suggests that Witherspoon found the Berkeleian idealism, dominant among the Princeton faculty, an offense to his sense of
tangible, perceptible creation and therefore used Hutchesonian
moral philosophy as an intellectual weapon against Berkeleian me-

Revolution and Republic

taphysics. Whatever his motives, Witherspoon's lectures on moral philosophy, modeled on Hutcheson's textbook, had become by the early 1770s an integral part of this comprehensive reform of the Princeton curriculum and an indelible part of the education of a galaxy of early American clergymen, statesmen, and writers, especially James Madison, class of 1772.[38]

Though initially antagonized by the colonial whig lionization of John Wilkes, whom he considered a libertine and reckless defamer of royalty, he emerged between 1774 and 1776 as the leader of popular protest in New Jersey, a delegate to the Continental Congress, and a signer of the Declaration of Independence. This new status enhanced his prestige among American Presbyterians and won a telling accolade from John Adams: "Dr. Witherspoon enters with great spirit into the American cause. He seems as hearty a friend as any of the natives—an animated son of liberty."[39] Adams's verb, "seems," suggested a wariness about the Scottish divine that would be shared by nearly every patriot leader who encountered Witherspoon. He compensated for this emotional distance from his contemporaries by adopting the role of self-appointed moral theorist of American republicanism. In a series of writings between 1776 and 1778, he analyzed the appeal of toryism, concluding that the ignorant, the pretentious, and the socially marginal were most vulnerable to British blandishments. Only through knowledge, discipline, self-denial, and devotion to the common weal could Americans protect their revolution from betrayal to the disaffected and preserve the integrity of their political principles. Witherspoon's distrust of learning not grounded in personal virtue, his detestation of the way opportunism and greed ensnared individuals with shallow commitments to the public good, and his conviction that cultivated conscience and love of liberty alone would satisfy the human need for a sense of civic belonging all defined for him and his readers the problem of evil and its political containment.[40]

Witherspoon divided the whole of the public sphere of human life into two compartments. One he called "ethics," the inherited cultural values that made society possible. The other was "politics," the intrinsic human qualities that determined how people understood those values and enabled them to act as public figures. Ethics arose from "benevolence, . . . a calm and deliberate good will to all" and was a "dictate of our conscience" rather than a mere "extension of the private affection" felt for family and friends. Even more than love of one's "country," admittedly a "noble and enlarged affection," the "love of mankind, . . . wishing and doing . . . others . . . good in soul and body," had the highest claim on human action and commitment. Witherspoon's "politics" identified concepts of "justice," "mercy," "self-discipline," and "duty" as norms of civic responsibility. Because people had only imperfect capacity to observe these norms, politics was the flawed adherence to those standards. Self-discipline, for example, was a Stoic virtue, a "temper of mind" that "pain is no pleasure nor evil any good"—a sometimes "strained and extravagant" ideal but a moral achievement nonetheless. Likewise Witherspoon, himself a slaveowner, declared that "unprovoked" bondage was nothing more than an exercise of "superior power" and, on the other hand, "I do not think there lies any necessity on those who found men in a state of slavery to make them free to their own ruin," a delicate way of saying that a slaveowner ought not bankrupt himself just to liberate slaves he had not personally subjected to bondage.[41]

Ethics and politics in Witherspoon's moral philosophy assumed the interaction of vice (be it sin, weakness, corruption, or egotism) and virtue (a capacity for disinterested, benevolent, socially redemptive conduct). Encounters between intractable vice and evanescent virtue occurred repeatedly as Witherspoon's lectures progressed. In Lecture XII, "of Civil Society," he assayed the moral weaknesses of monarchy, aristocracy, and democracy. The "politeness and elegance of manners" in a monarchy most easily degenerated into "submission and obsequiousness." Aristocracy "narrows the mind" even though it had staying power when exercised on a small scale; democracy, "the nurse of eloquence, because when the multitude have power, persuasion is the only way to govern them," was nonetheless subject at times "to a savage and indecent ferocity." So did law and jurisprudence, Lectures XIII and XIV, conjoin human weakness and strength to form stable human enterprises. In the final analysis, Witherspoon concluded in his "Recapitulation," moral philosophy dealt with everyday life, had some of the characteristics of a science, drew its strength from the simplicity of virtue and the luminosity of conscience, and "is perfectly coincident with scripture."[42] "Eclecticism with a vengeance," Douglas Sloan writes of Witherspoon's mixture of moral philosophy, Scripture, Calvinism, and even the work of rationalist Anglican, Samuel Clarke.[43]

The purpose of his eclecticism as well as his distance from an Augustinian sense of human depravity and flirtation with what Mark

Revolution and Republic

Noll calls a "value-free science of ethics"[44] was educational. Students at the College of New Jersey and the larger constituencies of American Presbyterians, New Jersey patriots, and delegates to the Continental Congress, were leadership elites requiring knowledge and guidance. "It is of considerable consequence" in the training of such leaders, Witherspoon declared, for them "to be accustomed to decency of manners in the best company. This gives them ease of carriage and a sense of delicacy which is of great use in forming the deportment of an orator." By "orator," Witherspoon meant anyone with the professional and social credentials to shape the culture and direct the public affairs of American society. Imbued with this goal, Witherspoon's student, William Graham, class of 1773, a painfully shy teacher and a founder of Liberty Hall academy in Virginia, sought out a "preceptor" or teacher of gentlemanly deportment and devoted himself to "the polish of his mind and his manners," including "carriage and gesture," entering and leaving a room "without hesitation and in no ungraceful style." The lessons failed to take. "I do not believe that all the dancing masters in the world could make any alteration in your manners, " the teacher lamented; "we must let you go out as you are and make your own way through the world in your own way."[45] The very fact that an observer considered this behavior remarkable underscored the significance of Witherspoon's emphasis on mastery of social space. Witherspoon's republicanism was the process of instilling civility through participation in the life of the *polis*, nurturing the capacity of men to behave better in their public capacities then they could possible do in their private lives. With this concept, Witherspoon joined vice and virtue so closely that he could observe the moral sense guiding the ego.

Madison's analysis of constitutionalism easily adopted the framework Witherspoon had taught him at Princeton seventeen years earlier. Witherspoon's exposition of Scottish moral thought captivated Madison because it equipped him to approach politics as "a science . . . rather than [as] a business" in the tart opinion of his businesslike classmate, Fisher Ames.[46] Witherspoon's didactic "virtue/vice" and "ethics/politics" polarities were, to start with, spacious and subtle enough to provide Madison a framework for an elegant, persuasive political theory. The creative tension in Witherspoon's concept of virtue and vice was his paradoxical treatment of human action as an expression of virtue and yet the dependence of such action on divine grace. Whether or not he resolved his paradox by assigning the moral

Conservatism and Constitutionalism

sense a critical role in the work of redemption, or merely trusted that, in America, Providence would enhance the potency of virtue among sinful men, Witherspoon certainly did tighten the links between vice and virtue, thereby fashioning a kind of secularized Calvinism that filled a real need in early national political culture.

Madison made the most of this discovery. "As long as the connection subsists between his reason and his self-love," he predicted, "[man's] opinions and his passions will have a reciprocal influence on each other" with passions "attach[ing] themselves" in dangerous ways to rational thought. "The first object of government" was to protect society from destructive jealousies over material inequality especially fomented by organized groups or factions united by a common sense of deprivation. "The latent causes of faction," Madison concluded, "are sown in the nature of man." Thence arose disputes over religion and politics, rivalries between the followers of different leaders, the influence of demagogues, and the persistence of "frivolous and fanciful" dissatisfactions. "But the most common and durable source of faction has been the various and unequal distribution of property"—debtors and creditors, "landed," "manufacturing," "mercantile," and "monied" interests. These political actors, left to their own devices, would "clog the administration" of government and "convulse the society."

Madison's genius, of course, was to see the solution in the very bosom of the problem—what he called in *Federalist No. 10* "a republican remedy for the diseases most incident to republican government" and in *Federalist No. 51* making "ambition . . . counteract ambition." By dealing boldly with what they could control—"the extent and proper structure of the union"—the framers of the Constitution sought to remove the most prominent of the conditions: provinciality, isolation, and localized conflict, which encouraged "men of factious tempers, of local prejudices, or of sinister designs" to "obtain the suffrages and betray the interests of the people." "An extensive republic," recommended by David Hume, would enlarge the pool of talented, public-spirited candidates for office and focus public attention on issues of the common weal. Admittedly, Madison adroitly conceded, the creation of a spacious republic carried with it the risk of "render[ing] the representative too little acquainted with all" the "local circumstances and lesser interests" of his constituents. But, turning this difficulty to his own advantage, Madison reminded his readers that these were the very circumstances that encouraged narrowly self-interested behavior

Revolution and Republic

and made legislators "too little fit to comprehend and pursue great and national objects." Intrinsic to human society, according to Madison's formulation, was a kind of latent, moral inertia that could be overcome only by a quickened pace of moral stimulation and intellectual challenge. "The great desideratum which has not yet been found for republican governments," he told George Washington in the spring of 1787, "seems to be some disinterested and dispassionate umpire in disputes between different passions and interests in the state." Seven months later, in *Federalist No. 10*, Madison triumphantly announced the Constitution's solution: the counterpoise of latent localist vices and active national virtue in the federal allocation of "great and aggregate interests" to the protection of the national legislature and "local and particular" ones to the states.[47]

Conceiving of "great and aggregate interests" as a kind of social glue for the nation was the theoretical achievement of the tenth *Federalist*, and the capacity of the ego to stimulate the civic imagination was the theme of the fifty-first. The larger and more comprehensive the factions operating in an extended republic, Madison posited in his famous formulation, the more likely they were to be coalitions of related interest groups with goals compatible with the public interest. Article I, section 8 of the Constitution empowered the national government to discriminate between legitimate and illegitimate factional demands and thereby to tame and civilize ambitious and enterprising supplicants for official favor. "Take in a greater variety of parties and interests," he explained, and "you make it less probable that a majority of the whole will have a common motive to invade the rights of other citizens, or if such a motive exists, it will be more difficult for all who feel it . . . to act in unison with each other." And within the very bowels of government itself, Madison declared in *Federalist No. 51*, the same disciplining and civilizing processes could function—the same conversion of self-gratification and self-interest into socially redemptive behavior. How, he asked, could powerful, expansive, strategically situated officials be kept within the bounds of restraint without eviscerating their legitimate authority? "The defect must be supplied by so contriving the interior structure of the government . . . that its several constituent parts may, by their mutual relations, be the means of keeping each other in their proper places. . . . This policy of supplying by opposite and rival interests the defect of better motives" was intrinsic in all of "human affairs" where "the private interest of every

Conservatism and Constitutionalism

individual" operated as "a check" on every other individual. The concept came directly from Witherspoon, who declared in his lectures on
moral philosophy that "it is folly to expect that a state should be
upheld by integrity in all who have a share in managing it. They must
be so balanced that when one draws to his own interest or inclination,
there may be an over poise upon the whole" against which others will
instinctively react.[48] What Arthur O. Lovejoy called Madison's concept
of "counterpoise," and what Madison himself described as "the moral
relations" between "the claims of justice" and "the rights of humanity" that called for "moderation on one side and prudence on the
other," was simply the mixture of ego and constraint in every mature
political act.[49]

Disciplining this potentially subjective use of public and private
experience, in Madison's view, was the shared understanding of history. Republicanism had no other sources except knowledge of past
self-government and of the wise use of power by fallible rulers in the
past. Minos of Crete, Lycergus of Sparta, and Draco and Solon of
Athens—very different rulers and historical figures—all had responded to political crises by taking the opportunity to formulate new
constitutional arrangements. Madison viewed these figures with a
mixture of awe and suspicion. They had each seized the creative moment and worked with the available social materials. "History informs
us . . . of the difficulties with which these celebrated reformers had to
contend," he explained, "in order to carry their reforms into effect."
Compromise, indirection, a willingness to incorporate the "prejudices" or the "superstitions" of the people—these were the requirements of Greek statesmanship. At the same time, they were all
"single" lawgivers who violated the spirit of the law by arrogating
power to themselves. On this point, Madison found history more
opaque. "Whence," he asked, "could it have proceeded that a people
jealous as the Greeks were of their liberty should so far abandon the
rules of caution as to place their destiny in the hands of a single
citizen?"

The framers of the Constitution, in his view, deserved a respectful
hearing because they had modelled their work on classical examples,
had avoided easier and more thrilling recource to reform by a single
ruler, and refused to be immobilized by the ambiguity of historical
precedent. "If these lessons teach us . . . to admire the improvements
made by America on the ancient mode of preparing and establishing

Revolution and Republic

regular plans of government," Madison mused with disarming candor, "they serve not less . . . to admonish us of the hazards and difficulties incident to such experiments."[50]

History would judge the framers of the Constitution as it had the constitution-givers of the past; placing themselves before the scrutiny of yet-unborn generations of students of the past, the American framers laid their proper claim to historic fame. In his musings on the glory and shame of Greek constitution-making, Madison illuminated the ambivalence about power that formed the subtext of his political theory in *Federalist Papers* 10 and 51; power might be corrupting in the end, but the onset of imaginative and bold public leadership was a moment rich with possibility. And the devotion of the people to the best of their own traditions and social instincts could prolong the creative interval between the impulse to serve the community unselfishly and the inevitable final retreat into self-interested, self-protective conduct by a ruler.[51]

Madison's republicanism in the mid 1780s was an act of both civic faith and social perception. He beheld a society alive with unchannelled energies, rudimentary institutions, and a poorly cultivated sense of identity and purpose; he believed that the right configuration of constitutional arrangements and the proper articulation of civic values could bring coherence and wholeness to this inchoate situation. The most challenging moment Madison faced as a legislator applying constitutional solutions to societal disputes came in Virginia's debate over church-state relations, which lasted from 1776 until 1787 and culminated in 1785 and 1786. Many conservative, Episcopalian planters had sought in 1779 and again in 1784 to have the General Assembly enact a statute subsidizing Christian churches in the state on the ground that "the general diffusion of Christian knowledge hath a natural tendency to correct the morals of men, restrain their vices, and preserve the peace of society." Backed by Patrick Henry, the great localist leader whose powerful oratory and genuine love of the people had evangelical roots, the bill seemed assured of adoption. Then Henry's elevation to the governorship in 1784 removed him from legislative debate at a crucial moment. Madison seized the opportunity to rally opposition to religious assessment and, in its place, support for Thomas Jefferson's Statute on Religious Freedom, drafted in 1779.[52]

Madison's vehicle for this fight was a "Memorial and Remonstrance against Religious Assessments," which brilliantly combined

Conservatism and Constitutionalism

two different kinds of arguments. One was drawn out of scores of anti-assessment petitions from evangelical Presbyterian, Baptist, and Methodist churches in Virginia, and the other came from his own and Jefferson's reading in Enlightenment history and philosophy on the evils of state-sponsored religion. Official promulgation of religious observance and practice, Madison declared, "will be a dangerous abuse of power."[53]

Like Witherspoon before him, Madison saw religion and piety as useful means in the building of a functioning republican order. In the "Memorial and Remonstrance," therefore, he made philosophical arguments carry the burden of the case and used consideration of piety to run interference and expose weaknesses in the opposition. The first of fifteen numbered paragraphs in the document linked the whole issue of freedom and religion to Enlightenment experience. It quoted Article XVI of the Virginia Declaration of Rights (1776) that "the duty we owe to our Creator can be directed only by reason and conviction," and then paraphrased the language of Jefferson's proposed Statute on Religious Liberty by asserting that "the opinions of men, depending [as they must] only on the evidence contemplated by their own minds, cannot follow the dictates of other men." (Jefferson's bill declared that "God hath created the mind free" and "altogether insusceptible of restraint.") From these presuppositions, and probably from Locke's *Letter On Toleration*, Madison drew two crucial conclusions: first, that "homage" to the "Creator" preceded "both in order of time and in degree of obligation . . . the claims of civil society" and, second, that "religion is wholly exempt from" the "cognizance" of "civil society." A person entering into a political compact "must always do it with a reservation of his duty to the . . . universal sovereign."[54]

Madison devoted the remainder of the Memorial and Remonstrance to a blending of the secular and spiritual concerns. While his arguments were eclectic, the rhetoric subtly mixed evangelical fears of secular impurity with rationalist aversion to encroachments on private judgment. Thus he argued that the power to establish Christianity as the favored recipient of public financial support—adroitly equating assessment with establishment—enabled government to establish particular sects of Christians over others and to enforce conformity "in all cases whatsoever," echoing the words of Parliament's Declaratory Act of 1766. He exulted in the "primitive" Christianity that existed before the rise of ecclesiastical establishment and, in the

Revolution and Republic

same breath, incorporated Jefferson's charge that established churches "beget habits of hypocrisy and meanness." He reminded his readers that the avowed purpose of assessment was the instilling of a particular kind of self-control—"correct the morals of men, restrain their vices, and preserve the peace of society"—by denouncing the use of "religion as an engine of civil policy." In a still more pointed reference to the religious implications of assessment, he questioned whether a public official could be a "competent judge of religious truth"; no evangelical reader of the awkward, and narrowly Anglican, five-part definition of a Christian church in the 1779 assessment bill could fail to find that formulation theologically offensive.[55]

Equally distasteful to Baptists and Methodists was a well-meaning provision in the 1784 bill allowing sects without ministers— Mennonites and Quakers—to receive funds designated for them directly rather than through clergymen. Madison seized on this clumsy notion of church polity to illustrate dangers of allowing legislators to make religious designations. "Are the Quakers and the Mennonists the only sects who think a compulsive support of their religions unnecessary and unwarrantable?" Madison demanded; "can their piety alone be entrusted with the care of public worship? Ought their religions to be endowed above all others with extraordinary privileges by which proselytes may be induced from all others?" Nothing of the kind was intended by the provisions of the 1784 bill, nor did Mennonite and Quaker practice involve the stealing of proselytes. Madison did not let these facts stand in the way of scoring the telling point that legislation hinging on matters of internal church polity inevitably would arouse destructive jealousies.[56]

Madison's final paragraph was his most spectacular fusion of rationalist and spiritual considerations. Religion lay beyond the authority of the state, he declared, moving boldly in the direction of secular libertarianism, in the same way as did "all our fundamental rights," including trial by jury, freedom of the press, and the right to vote. Madison then astutely attached to that embracing concept of political liberty a prayer that the "supreme lawgiver of the universe" would "illuminat[e]" the minds of skeptical legislators with three distinct visions of a good and virtuous society. Madison wanted God to dissuade politicians in the first place "from every act which would affront his holy prerogative" and secondly from "violat[ing] the trust committed to them." Finally, he prayed that the Almighty would "guide them into every measure which may be worthy of his blessing,

Conservatism and Constitutionalism

may redound to their own praise, and may more firmly establish the liberties, the prosperity, and the happiness of the Commonwealth." Those three prayers respectively acknowledged the political potency of a Calvinist view of God, a Lockean sense of obligation, and a republican agenda for the fostering of social good. Madison knew exactly what he was doing; he even winked before pronouncing the benediction—"we . . . earnestly pray," he explained to readers not accustomed to seeking divine intervention, so "that no effort may be omitted on our part against so dangerous a usurpation."[57] If constitution-making indeed involved the use of available materials to construct a new order, Madison's contribution to the separation of church and state selected and fit together religious and philosophical materials with uncommon resourcefulness.

The constitutional thought and political experience of southern whigs, patriots, and republicans from the Stamp Act crisis to the ratification of the Constitution was a search for the *substance* of authority derived from the "tempers, pursuits, customs, and inclinations"[58] of the people. Constitutionalism and politics in the South were likewise a *method* for nurturing fragile republican practices sot that oligarchic and monarchical perversions did not take root in the soil of popular government. Where the search seemed headed in the right direction, it drew on the history of political consent and depended on the talents and convictions of individuals; where it seemed imperiled, this quest appealed to civic impulses and challenged politically responsible men to save the community.

Among the most impressive examples of southern constitutional and political discourse were Madison's contributions to *The Federalist Papers* and his "Memorial and Remonstrance." These writings drew on the Lockean substance of American tradition and experience to give both the government and the governed ample social space in which to follow their predictable, legitimate proclivities; they also employed republican methods for holding the multitudinous elements of the social order in healthy alignment.

4.

Evangelical Persuasion

As our Lord and Saviour has loved us and given himself for us, that he might deliver us from the curse of the law and the flames of devouring fire, and hath taken us from the wild stock of nature, made us to drink of the same fountain of his everlasting love, and so tempered our spirits as to unite us together ... by the sweetest bands of love and fellowship, declared us to be a select body by him chosen, and set apart from the world, it becomes our duty then to walk as people who are not of the world but chosen of God and bound for the heavenly Canaan.

"Circular Letter," Kehukee Baptist
Association Minutes, October 1800,
Baptist Collection, Wake Forest
University Library

As people experienced conversion, as they worshiped, prayed, established churches, maintained church discipline, read the Bible, listened to sermons, and faced the prospect of death, they performed in the life of their culture the same roles that constitution-framers and public officeholders did in the political life of the South during the early years of the republic. They sought for order and meaning in their experience, for standards of authority grounded in tradition and applicable to their own situation, and for language and narrative powerful enough to bind together people who shared in the building of the kingdom.

The prospect of converting not just isolated folk on the fringes of society but large, heterogeneous segments of the populace of the new republic called for religious language of unprecedented attractiveness and self-confidence. A *persuasion* is the language and rhetoric of a movement gathering momentum and confident of its power and validity. The natural outgrowth of a religious impulse focused on conversion, the evangelical persuasion sought to interpret the whole

Evangelical Persuasion

character of life in the new nation and to define citizenship in spiritual and moral terms.

At the onset of revolution, the design of the kingdom became, in advance of written constitutions or a declaration of independence, a justification of political action and a covenant of righteous rebellion. Throughout 1775 the Carolinas were divided between whigs, tories, and a sizeable portion of the population fearful of committing itself to either side in the conflict. In South Carolina powerful backcountry leaders, suspicious of the ambitions of the low-country elite that organized resistance to British authority, thwarted attempts by whig leaders in Charlestown to circulate defiant resolutions for signatures in the interior. Aware of the preponderance of religious dissenters in the backcountry, patriot leaders dispatched two clergymen, Rev. Oliver Hart, a Baptist and Rev. William Tennent, a Congregationalist, to the region to plead the case of American liberty and British tyranny. Outmaneuvered by backcountry loyalist leaders who had the support of the militia in the area, Hart and Tennent found little opportunity to change people's minds. Not until after a split in loyalist leadership and a brief outbreak of fighting in November 1775 did the patriots secure control over the interior of South Carolina.[1]

In North Carolina, the situation was much more fluid and more confused. The Provincial Congress enjoyed strong support in plantation counties near the coast, in the Neuse and Roanoke valleys, and farther west in Rowan and Mecklenburg counties. But the majority of the white population lived in a neutral belt of Scottish settlers in the upper Cape Fear valley, and in the upper Piedmont where there were many German and Quaker settlements and where farmers felt little kinship with low country planters. Guilford County, with its large German and Quaker population and involvement in the Regulator movement, was one of five counties that failed to elect delegates to the first Provincial Congress in August 1774. In early 1775, the former Regulator John Fields secured the signatures of 116 other of "his Majesty's most loyal subjects of the County of Guilford" to a petition expressing "open detestation to all illegal and unwarrantable proceedings against his Majesty's Crown and dignity."[2]

In this stressful and confused setting, David Caldwell summoned the people to the patriot cause by preaching on "The Character and Doom of the Sluggard."[3] "The slothful shall be under tribute," declared the text in Proverbs 12:24, and slothfulness in Caldwell's call to political action and Spartan discipline was the natural human inclina-

Revolution and Republic

tion to inactivity, unreflectiveness, and apathy, and to narrow and stupid concern with one's own comfort.

> The sluggard, as a worthless being, destitute of merit and doing no good to himself or any body else is as really an object of reprobation as the miser, the spendthrift, or the highway robber; and the blessings which he foregoes and the evils which he brings on himself here are but forerunners of the heavier losses which he will sustain and the more insufferable woes which he will bring upon himself hereafter, . . . bound hand and foot, and cast into outer darkness where no ray of comfort can cast even a momentary radiance over the gloom.

Personal slothfulness and political indifference were for Caldwell paralytic social forces that were "at the bottom of all negligence, disorder and bad management in business"—these words resonated with eighteenth-century fear of disorder and fixation with the human proclivity to slide into licentiousness. For, he explained, "these are not all the evils, or the worst evils to which the sluggard is subject; . . . those of a mental and moral kind are much more serious in their nature and consequences." Human beings who lost hold of moral sensibility and spiritual humility naturally allowed their psyches to become so encrusted with apathy, social indifference, and self-concern that these habits of mind choked off all capacity for virtue, civic action, and self-awareness. Physical deterioration then accompanied and aggravated the erosion of the will: "while he [the sluggard] is impairing his health and shortening his days by inactivity and sloth, he is gaining nothing in any other way and must therefore be chargeable with his own misery and ruin." Poverty, loss of economic prosperity, the resulting disintegration of the drive to creativity, the inability to impose order and system on his farm or occupation all compounded the effect of sloth until debt, ruined reputation, and shattered self-esteem completed the self-destructive process.

The political and social implications of these tendencies in human nature, for Caldwell, were ominous. Throughout history "sloth" as a state of mind and body and as a moral condition had tempted rulers to exercise tyrannical power. The slothful were people who seemed, to arrogant and unreflective rulers, to be fit objects of unbridled governmental coercion. The "ignorance, disregard of moral obligation, and supreme love of ease" of the groveling sluggard corresponded exactly with a tyrant's appetite and cynicism.

Evangelical Persuasion

> While [the sluggard] is spending or losing by his ignorance and sloth the inheritance handed down ... through a number of generations ... [of] his predecessors, ... the ambitious and covetous, those tyrants of the human race and pests of society believing that his ignorance will screen them from his notice and that his indolence will make him perfectly submissive, ... thus ... are encouraged to make their experiment, and they too often succeed.

Not only did the slothful encourage and facilitate oppression, their own "shame" and "sinking spirits," their own pitiful compliance and submission became self-made chains of slavery. The miraculous way in which God might intervene to preserve colonial liberty, Caldwell declared, would occur only as the Holy Spirit penetrated the encrustations of habit and lethargy and converted the soul, the conscience, the moral sense within the human frame into something graceful and swift and responsive.

Caldwell's sermon was an extraordinary performance. No other political sermon of the Revolution dealt so thoroughly with the psychology of commitment. The images of the human mind and body as a repository of sluggardly inertia, and of the spirit as poetic, free, and morally purifying, allowed Caldwell to infuse political commentary with religious radicalism. The advocate of order and moderation in the Regulator controversy only seven years earlier was confronted in 1775 with the spectre of the annihilation of political liberty by the British before the colonists could overcome their own caution and inexperience.[4] He therefore chose imagery that elevated conscience over the tranquillity of the whole community or even the preservation of social hierarchy. Unlike whig sermons in New England and the middle colonies that required, as Perry Miller has shown, national repentance as a precondition of divine intervention in the struggle against Great Britain,[5] Caldwell's words did not specify repentance as a distinct step in the forming of a commitment to the American cause. Nor did he suggest that the sinfulness of the people had provoked God to allow British oppression as a punishment. Rather his notion of benumbing sloth depicted sin in original Calvinist terms closely resembling innate depravity. This historic theological orientation, however, became the means of depicting sin in strikingly new terms—as a part of a process of moral decay closely linked to physical deterioration and aging, a process of dying in which all humans were involved.

Revolution and Republic

Addressing upwardly mobile, bookish Presbyterians, Caldwell pushed to the utmost the search for political truth in history and the Bible. Richard Furman addressed a different constituency when he joined Oliver Hart and William Tennent in appealing to backcountry settlers to close ranks with low-country planters in opposing British oppression.[6] In an anonymous manuscript address on liberty, signed "A Loyal Subject," and widely circulated in the backcountry in late 1775, Furman displayed less erudition than Caldwell but frankly groped toward an understanding of colonial resistance as a moral crisis. "This alarming occasion," he explained, "concerns great numbers; . . . their lives, fortunes (and what is much greater) consciences being called into question." Furman felt constricted by the very paralysis of will and intellect that Caldwell had described. Promising his readers he would speak from "a heart . . . influenced with the most tender and impartial concern for the good of the whole" society and that he would engage in "an impartial inquiry" into "the truth" behind "the unhappy disputes . . . between Great Britain and America," Furman nonetheless admitted "I find myself under difficulties (it is true) to go through this work because . . . so much [has been] called into question by people who have not the opportunity to inform themselves, who are prejudiced by false reports, carried about by men who wish well to neither King nor Country." "We are all liable," he warned, "to be imposed upon" by false, partial, and twisted information.

Trying to cut through misinformation and ambiguity, Furman allowed the very language of backcountry loyalists to define the issue: "if the above articles are believed by you, viz: the Congress being in rebellion against the King and designing to enslave and ruin the people, I shall . . . shew that they do not appear to be true." The truth, Furman countered, was the autonomy of individual conscience. "If a man tells me that he has a right to do with me or any thing I have got what he pleases, and therefore demands something of me, either of labour or of part of my estate, if I give it, I then submit to his unlimited power over me, and by my own consent he has a right to lay upon me what he pleases." That presumption to a power of intruding into the lives of all the colonists, Furman insisted, was the precise meaning of the Declaratory Act of 1766, the Tea Act of 1773, the military occupation of Boston, and the imposition of "Popery" on all of the northern side of the Ohio valley by the Quebec Act—all violations of "the principles of the constitution." Those usurpations of power, Furman

Evangelical Persuasion

warned, were a threat to the moral autonomy of every American. Acquiescence to them will "bind yourselves under the unlimited sway of arbitary power in the hands of men who, to make use of you for the accomplishment of their purposes, will smile upon you and promise you fair things, but once they have gotten their ends will make you and your posterity feel the heavy hand of their oppression."[7]

Furman's highly personalized version of evil—smiling hypocrites and tyrants pillaging all of a man's freedom and dignity—reflected the flinty individualism and combativeness, which in isolated instances made Baptists intransigent loyalists in the Revolution. One of them was James Child, a Separate Baptist in Anson County, North Carolina, who warned his parishioners in 1776 not to bear arms in the War for Independence "either offensively or defensively" and threatened to excommunicate those who did. "Shew him a man with half moon in his hatt and liberty rote on it and his hatt full of feather [informal patriot insignia] [and] he would shew you a devil," one informant testified about Child; "the poor men was bowing and scaping to them; they lead them down to hell and . . . he did not value the Congress or comitye no more than a passill of Rockoon dogs for he got his [commission?] from the king; the [patriot] field offessers got there commission from hell or the devil."[8] In his address Furman acknowledged the loathing of backcountry Baptists for the wealthy planters and merchants who led the Revolutionary movement. "Let it be observed," he wrote, "that the great men are the chief losers" should the struggle with Britain fail, "their estates being along the seacoasts, their houses in towns and cities liable to be burnt or knocked down by bombs and cannon."[9]

With biting language, Furman and Child recoiled from politics that violated spiritual privacy; with eloquence, Caldwell and Tennent decried the paralysis of the will that left people vulnerable to oppression. Facing and interpreting the ordeal of life in a shattered polity, these preachers in the revolutionary South constructed an evangelical theodicy, that is, an explanation of evil that exonerated the Creator from responsibility for injustice and suffering. Theodicy was the underside of evangelical persuasion. Reaching and holding an audience, melding together a message of love, and a recognition of the pain love was meant to heal, evangelicals came to religious maturity at a critical juncture in the development of southern society.

At close range and in the flash of personal experience, love and agony fused with searing immediacy. Evangelicals saw first evidence of

Revolution and Republic

this reality in the faces of the converted. During one Methodist revival in Virginia in July 1776, the preacher noted how, "after prayer, Benjamin Tyus, lately a great opposer" of the revival "jumped up and began to praise God with a countenance so altered that those who beheld him were soon filled with astonishment."[10]

During the late colonial period, Baptists and Presbyterians brought evangelical Christianity to the South; beginning in the late 1770s and 1780s, a new church, the Methodists, emerged as a major religious force ordaining preachers and creating churches. An offshoot of the Church of England, and founded and led by John Wesley, Methodism brought a simplified and warmhearted message of salvation to ordinary people. First arriving in the colonies in the late 1760s, Methodist preachers came to Virginia in 1773 when Devereux Jarratt, a revivalist, Anglican clergyman in Dinwiddie County, Virginia, invited them to join him in spreading the message of salvation.[11] Methodists popularized Christian theology in ways Calvinist Presbyterians and Baptists had been unwilling to. "Methodist doctrine," Donald G. Mathews explains,

> offered people an endless number of chances to receive God's grace, for although the doctrine emphasized that a person might be assured of final salvation, it also allowed for the real possibility of backsliding. Contradictory as these two positions might seem, they reflected the psychological need for ultimate reassurance and the practical experience of falling from the state of grace, subjective realities which orthodox Calvinism could not take seriously.[12]

Jarratt himself appreciated the utility of observing first-hand the subjective experiences of people apparently wrestling with and being overpowered by the Holy Spirit:

> A gentleman of this parish [also identified as a "rich" man] had much opposed and contradicted [revivalist preaching]; he was fully persuaded that all outward appearances, either of joy or distress, were mere deceit. But as he was walking to his mill ... deep conviction fell upon him. ... The Lord heard him, and set his soul at liberty, ... and the power which came upon him was so great that it seemed as if his whole frame was dissolving.[13]

At a "love feast" held by Methodists in Dinwiddie County in 1776, Jarratt exclaimed, "the power of the Lord came down ... like a rush-

Evangelical Persuasion

ing wind. . . . Many mourners were filled with consolation, . . . many believers . . . so overwhelmed with love that they could not doubt but [that] God had enabled them to love him with *all* their heart." When the doors of the meeting opened and persons waiting outside entered the room, they witnessed an amazing and varied scene: "the anguish of some, . . . the rejoicing of others" a contagious spectacle that filled these witnesses with "trembling apprehensions of their own danger. Several of them prostrating themselves before God, cried aloud for mercy."[14]

If prostrate bodies, or rapturous or anguished faces, were first features of the social environment that evangelicals saw, and responded to, the next observable reality with which they had to deal was that of social class—the amazing capacity of revivalism to cut across class lines and at the same time to reinforce and even create a sense of solidarity among poor whites. The same "gentleman" that Jarratt described as "dissolving" into rapturous emotion encountered redemption while walking to his mill—clearly an indication of substantially more wealth than the typical Methodist worshiper if still below the aristocracy. The fact that he was a great opposer and contradicter of Jarratt further signaled that he regarded revivalism as a subversive social activity, and the circumstances of his conversion indicated that the miller was so powerfully drawn to religious controversy that his defenses were down and that he had inadvertently enmeshed himself in arguing the merits of personal conversion. Finally, the fact that he regarded facial expression as hypocritical suggested that it was in face-to-face confrontation with individual evangelicals that his defenses broke down. The whole scene dovetails closely with Rhys Isaac's view of the dynamics of such confrontations:

> The ironic term "New Light" [Isaac writes] by which evangelicals were designated in common speech suggests . . . that what was at stake was the proper authority of ancient learning. The resurgence of an oral culture in the calling of semi-literate men to preach extempore . . . engendered great outpourings of the spoken word, uncontrolled by scholastic conventions, [which] induced among preachers and hearers alike unprecedently intense reading, study, and searching of the Scriptures.[15]

This new access to knowledge fostered a more intense social solidarity. Jarratt defined the process simply: "I formed the people into a society that they might assist and strengthen each other," he said of his

Revolution and Republic

parish in Virginia in 1770–1771. "The good effects of this were soon apparent. Convictions were deep and lasting, and not only knowledge, but faith, love, and holiness continually increased." Being "formed into a society" represented a wholesale reorientation of the lives of these people. Jarratt implied that the group jelled because the members shared a conversion experience, then assisted and upheld one another, and finally deepened their understanding of Christian faith and habituated their practice of piety and compassion.[16]

In a society where the planters flaunted a kind of competitive conviviality, humble evangelicals reversed the dynamics of social interaction. Gentleness and self-denial became the marks of initiation. John Leland, the Baptist itinerant in Virginia, passed by a farmhouse from which came sounds of fiddling and dancing in 1787. It was a wedding party, and the groom came outside and invited Leland to "drink sling with him." Leland instead asked what the noise was from within the house. Told it was a fiddle, he asked to see the instrument. The groom carried this request into the house and the music stopped. "I lighted off my horse and went into the house," Leland explained; "by the time I got in, the fiddle was hidden, and all was still. I told them, if fiddling and dancing was serving God, to proceed on." No one moved, and so Leland proceeded to bless the party "in my own way" by saying a prayer. A few days later the family invited him to return and preach to them, and "in the course of a few weeks," many of the family and neighborhood "turned to the Lord" and were baptized in a nearby stream. Factually sketchy, this account is symbolically rich. The episode created a new basis for family and neighborhood life. As Rhys Isaac explains, "the hiding of the fiddle showed that the people, though engaged in traditional forms of celebration, anticipated and responded to the preacher's disapproval. The awakening . . . radically altered the social orientation of their home; it would no longer be a center for convivial hospitality."[17]

As they saw family members and friends in a new light, as fit objects of serious and compassionate attention, evangelicals came to understand family life itself as bound together by obligations to God to bring children and siblings and even parents to Jesus. Usually this responsibility fell on parents to break the wills of rebellious children and prepare them, through discipline and admonition, for submission to the authority of their heavenly father. In all such family relations, Philip Greven has shown, evangelicals endowed human authority with awesome and terrifying scope.[18] In one unusual case an

Evangelical Persuasion

evangelical son chastised his secular father. The Virginia Methodist, Stith Mead, knew well the authority and power of his parent. "I am deeply concern'd for your soul and for the souls of your family, fearing you are yet in the gall of bitterness and in the bonds of iniquity," he appealed to his father, quoting Peter's rebuke to the rich, complacent Christian, Simon, in Acts 8:23; "I have dealt plain in writing to you. . . . To use this authority"—he scratched out the word "authority" and substituted "freedom"—"freedom goes hard with me. . . . The devil tells me"—again he crossed out words and this time substituted the slightly less presumptuous verb, "insinuates"—"insinuates if I write thus, you will disinherit me." But now personal grief had swept away even that compelling reason for silence. Mead had learned just three days earlier that his brother, Samuel, had died. "Oh my heart, my sorrowful soul, how I am grieved, my bro[ther] Sam[uel] is no more." Of all of Mead's siblings, Samuel had been "my greatest mate, . . . O how binding nature is."

What made Samuel's death an imperative command to confront Mead's father was, first, Mead's uncertainty about his brother's salvation and, second, their father's apparent complicity in Samuel's failure to seek the Lord. Mead's father, Colonel William Mead, was an Anglican vestryman in Bedford County, Virginia. According to Methodist tradition, Stith as a boy slipped away from the house to visit the slave quarter and listen raptly to blacks discussing heaven and hell— experiences that paved the way for his later conversion. In 1785 the elder Mead moved to Augusta, Georgia, where he too was converted.

As in Leland's experience, the critical occasion involved "the indulgence of fiddling and dancing." The last time the brothers had visited their father, Samuel had been "a penitent seeker of religion," but "there was a dance in your house where my brother was drawn off" and Mead darkly suspected that Samuel had unsuccessfully continued his search for religious peace after that interruption. "The indulgence of fidling and dancing has ever been your beseting sin," Mead bluntly told his father, "and I fear will be your final and eternal ruin; you continue to send your children to the dancing schools or indulge them to attend the balls? If so, you are training them up for the *devil* to make them an heir of *hell-fire*."[19]

Fiddling and dancing were evangelical fixations because they were at the center of a social world in which strong currents of impulsive conduct jostled and thrust people from one kind of self-display to another. An oral tradition, first written down in the 1870s and con-

Revolution and Republic

cerning the early life of James O'Kelly, Methodist schismatic preacher
in North Carolina and Virginia in the early national period, preserves
this sense of commotion and distraction:

> Mr. O'Kelly, naturally of strong temperaments, full of life, deeply im-
> bued with republican institutions, with the charming and lovely Eliza-
> beth Meeks for a wife, and a happy family growing up around him,
> affected with *kingphobia* as deeply as Mr. Jefferson, sharing in the hatred
> commonly felt at the time against the rapacious plunderers who
> ruled ... the state ... at that time [a reference to land speculators, per-
> haps an echo of Regulator rhetoric], [he] gave his attention to anything
> else but religion. A fine fiddler, he was indispensable to all the old time
> *frolics* as they were then called. He was inordinately fond of dancing,
> and none could surpass him in 'tripping on the light fantastic toes' or
> shuffling the reels, jigs, and breakdowns of ante [i.e., pre-] revolutionary
> times. As was quite common in those days, he could drink as much
> whiskey as any, tho' never to such an extent as to injure himself seri-
> ously. Of a fine sense of honor and quick to resent an insult, he never
> engaged in a quarrel, but usually gave the offender his ponderous fist,
> wielded by his stalwart arm, that usually sent the one who had the
> rashness to vex him sprawling in the ground. . . . In the highest moment
> of his rage and anger, and when under the influence of liquor, or
> worse, [it was] the lovely Elizabeth Meeks [who] disarmed his rage and
> anger and made him mild as a lamb. He would never gamble or horse
> race, things quite common in his day.

Not until 1775, when he was forty and his twelve-year-old son, William, wanted to become a preacher, did O'Kelly "turn his attention to
religious matters," become converted, and take up the work of lay
minister. "Immediately after his conversion everything irreligious was
abandoned. His iron will knew no half way ground; he deliberately
laid his fiddle on a huge fire and burned it up."[20]

This account preserves well the strongly pictorial quality of evangelical perception—the robust competitiveness of backcountry North
Carolina society in the 1770s, the use of music, dance, and drink (and
for many, horse racing and gambling) to regulate and channel the
rough energies and high spirits of individualist, anti-authoritarian
people; and the social approval bestowed on spontaneity, high-
tempered defense of honor, and the effective and not especially sadis-
tic use of one's fists, as well as on angelic feminine restraints as a
regulating device. The itinerant Methodist preachers who converted
O'Kelly's wife and son, and thereby caused a family crisis, wrenched

Evangelical Persuasion

him out of a mobile, fluid, superficial existence and confronted him with matters of eternal depth and seriousness. "Lord, I'm ashamed to say how I've refus'd thy grace, and twin'd my heart away from thine inviting face," declared one of O'Kelly's hymns, probably recounting his own passage from unbelief to salvation; "O strive with me, nor turn away they face; my soul is longing now for thee and thy refreshing grace."[21] The solemn act of placing his fiddle—an object of value, craftsmanship, and endearment—on a "huge fire" before a circle of glowing faces was a ritual act of deep resonance.

The task of seeing the world anew and acting on the basis of a spiritually sensitized perception of reality was a frustrating undertaking. "All socially constructed worlds are inherently precarious," Peter Berger explains: "Supported by human activity, they are constantly threatened by the human facts of self-interest and stupidity" as well as by inertia, human forgetfulness, and the rigidity of well established social practices. The world people create can therefore turn on its creators and threaten or dominate them. Two functions of religion, therefore, are to *legitimate* social practices that have the best claim to being the cement holding society together and to remind people that they are part of a *cosmic* universe, transcending this world, in which their puny lives have infinite value. Both legitimation and cosmic orientation of life help to maintain the world people had already constructed; the balance between constructing the world and maintaining one's integrity and volition within it, Berger insists, is always precarious, temporary, provisional—occurring in the shadow of death.[22]

The autobiographical sketch of Aaron Spivey of Bertie County, North Carolina, written shortly before his death in 1822,[23] opened to view the very process by which the prospect and certainty of death reached back into personal life and violently wrenched an individual out of one pattern of existence and into another. Spivey was born in Bertie County in 1763, the fourth of seven children.[24] Although he recalled that his parents had "strictly attended to . . . morals," he grew up in a cultural setting in which "religion was generally despised . . . by men of Character as they call them." Though sensing a need for personal "reformation," the need to support his young family "rationally appeared to be my duty" and he, like "the Prodigal Son thought I would put off the work a little longer untill a more convenient season." During the spring of 1787 an epidemic swept through the area, bringing death to "sum of my neighbors and near connections," and filling him, as he sat at the deathbed of a close friend with a mood of

Revolution and Republic

"gloominess and Horrour." The death of his friend, and the nagging sense of personal unworthiness, triggered a prolonged emotional crisis—a fear that his own death was imminent: "I returned home loaded with guilt . . . under dreadful apprehensions of the Justice of God being executed upon me for my accumulated crimes; now I began to think differently to what I used to think; now I began to think there was no time to spare, for the avenger of blood was pursuing me." For more than a year Spivey prayed, read the Bible, avoided sleep out of fear he would die before awaking, experienced and then doubted his conversion, and finally "was induced to believe the following system: Unconditional Election, Predestination, and final perseverance of the Saints through grace." Accordingly on December 13,1789, he was baptized by Martin Ross and joined the Baptist Church at Skewarky near Williamston, North Carolina. He soon felt a call to the ministry but resisted it until July 1794 when he was ordained minister of the Cashie Baptist Church.

The themes of death, conversion, and discipleship dominated Spivey's autobiography. His premonition of death was a wrenching personal crisis because it convinced him, to the very core of his consciousness, that he was himself dying spiritually as well as physically and that the agony and terror accompanying that discovery defined, in ways he could not avoid, his own personality and character. Witnessing death, being close to a dying person, created around Spivey an aura, a protective layer, of numbing pain mixed together with almost ethereal beauty and calm. Minutes before his friend had died in 1787, "a certain gentleman whose name I ever shall revere" took Spivey aside for a word of comfort and prayer. The words struck Spivey with their "fervency and zeal and showed such rackings for the happiness of the soul which in a few minutes made its flight." The whole experience, Spivey wrote, "filled me with amazement" and the two mean walked in silence broken only by Spivey's "groan" as his friend touched his shoulder and said "our friend is gone to a long eternity." He remembered at the age of thirteen or fourteen hearing the words of the prophet Joel, "Your old men shall dream dreams and your young men shall see visions" and hearing St. Peter's vision of the Holy Spirit reaching equally into the lives of Jews and Gentiles alike. At the time, these visions terrified him, filled him with "melancholy," and left him drained and unable to respond to these visionary pronouncements of the Kingdom of God. The particular form of that adolescent melancholy, he vividly recalled, had been the fear that he would die

Evangelical Persuasion

before he acted in response to the imperative expressed in Joel's and Peter's visions. Now, a decade later, the same awful foreboding returned in recognizable form.

This time, after several false starts and paralyzing sensations of inadequacy, he experienced conversion

> as I was riding the road the evening, I think the first Wednesday in July [1789], being under uncommon prayer pleading with God to show me how it was possible for my soul to be saved. Jesus Christ then for the first time was revealed to me as a sufficient Saviour. The Next inquiry was, is he my Saviour? My own heart with a dread replied no, tho I confess with joy I had some gleam of hope from a discovery I had of the blessed Redeemer as the Saviour of Sinners.

The gleam of hope was at first excruciatingly narrow; Spivey wept, felt "over-whelmed with grief," prayed again, and found "more patience" in his quest for spiritual certainty. Finally the gospel of Matthew, "Come unto me, all ye that labour and are heavy laden," convinced him that these were the words of the Savior saying "I, Jesus Christ [am] the inviter; the object invited are those who are labouring under a weight of their own guilt and condemnation and they who comes [those who come] must through [throw] themselves wholly on his will and mercy. . . . The words seemed inactly [exactly] sutable [suitable] to my care and [my] believing myself to be invited." With Spivey's previously constricted, emotional, spiritual consciousness now expanded, "this belief brought such glorious discoveries to my mind. They are beyond my expression." The process of conversion continued to unfold with deliberate care. With the Psalmist he wept all the night and experienced joy in the morning; he wondered if he would ever be tempted to sin again; he saw his family and friends and neighbors in a new light, "by nature they are the children of rath," but now he could see them with his spiritual eyes and "find my Soul more serene in the merits of my adorable Saviour."[25]

Disease and suffering, as well as lapses of morality and seasons of doubt, reminded the evangelical faithful that life was too short and quickly expended not to be invested in obedience to God's will. After describing symptoms of a high fever and massive nasal bleeding, William Piercy in Savannah wrote to the Countess of Huntington that

> in the midst of all my afflications the Lord has been exceedingly gracious to my poor heart. At the lowest ebb I never had the least appre-

Revolution and Republic

hension of my present dissolution but a full persuasion that this sickness, like that of his favorite Lazarus, was not unto death but for the glory of God. The Lord seemed to assure me that it should prove a fresh anointing and a fresh baptism for some greater work in these parts.[26]

Edward D. Smith, a South Carolina physician and member of a Congregationalist family with New England roots, did not join a church until the summer of 1810 when he was thirty-two years old. Then the sudden death of his young daughter, "who had been an idol with him," became the occasion in which "God was pleased to draw him to himself." But the tension between destructive willfulness of humans and their acceptance of their own mortality remained an integral feature of the human condition. "The trying vicissitudes of the last years," a woman in Virginia explained, "have not passed without their beneficial effects, altho' my rebellious will has too often suggested that, of all others, I have the most reason to despond." Or, as a South Carolina eulogist said of Smith, his "unremitting rectitude of conduct ensured his success in all his endeavors to restrain the extravagances of youth."[27]

Because evangelicals regarded life itself as a process of dying, and sainthood as the first stage of subsuming the self under the sway of divine authority, a Virginia Presbyterian minister declared, life acquired an urgency and a seriousness defined by an event beyond the grave.

> The main thing it [the scriptural text, unfortunately missing] drives at is to persuade men to be serious and to mind God and their souls in time and not to take their measures of men merely from the difference in their outward circumstances in this world, which death will quickly put an end to, but from their inward good or evil state which without respect of persons will end in happiness or misery, everlasting and irreversible.[28]

"We are hastening to an awful eternity as fast as time can move," wrote Richard Furman, and "must appear at the tremendous bar of the omnipotent and immaculate judge to undergo the scrutiny of infinite wisdom and justice, and are already informed that 'except a man be born again he cannot see the kingdom, . . . that if any man will be the disciple of Christ he must take up his Cross daily and follow him," and "that without holiness no man can see the Lord!" Those texts were a

Evangelical Persuasion

depiction of the reorganization of loyalty and commitment which the approach of death made imperative.[29]

For even the most pious person knew that holding together the elements of faith and consciousness in the last hours before dying was a supreme test of character—for the dying person and for the family as well. "Participation in the ritual of dying centered . . . on the death-bed," Lewis O. Saum has written; "to an almost unnerving degree, the imagination and emotion and memory of humble America hovered about that sacrosanct spot." The watchers hoped to give solace to the dying one, to witness "a calm and clear-eyed death," and to draw from the experience assurance that the departed loved one had died in a state of faith, safe in the arms of the Savior.[30] "In the beginning of October a change took place that was the death-knell to all our hopes for his recovery," a Virginia woman wrote of her father. He had told her that he desired

> to live some years longer with my dear children—then he added with a look and tone of acquiescence that could not be mistaken, "God's will be done—whatever it is—I am willing either way." The visits of his sister's minister were evidently a solace to him; indeed the visits of persons who showed him such kind attentions were received by him with pleasure and gratitude. . . . At times his agony of suffering was painful to witness. Several times in the midst of these paroxysms of bodily anguish, he seemed to be assaulted by the powers of darkness. . . . He said, "I fear I shall sink into despair!" One of his children repeated some promise of the Savior—saying, "do you recall these words of Jesus?" he replied, "I remember, dear, much of the Scripture, but cannot now recall it. . . . At another time, in piteous tones, he cried out, "My God, my God, why has thou forsaken me"—but this seemed to be the last conflict with darkness and fear, for from this to the end his "peace seemed to flow like a river."[31]

Such serenity was the supreme test of a well-lived life, what Stith Mead called "that tenor of heart and life which gradually and surely smoothed the terrors of death."[32] "Death had been to the subject of this memoir," Richard Furman once wrote of a friend, and expressing the same concern with the regulating continuities of sanctified life, "the theme of daily meditation"[33]—which for an evangelical was the innermost locus of introspective discipline. "I believe a sinner thus influenced [by a Calvinist view of depravity]," wrote an English evangelical in 1799

Revolution and Republic

being led to close in with Christ on the terms of the gospel and embrace him as his all in all, seeing himself thro' Christ forever absolved from sin and all its consequences, feeling the dire effects of it in his own soul, and seeing the extensive evil of it in the suffering Son of God, . . . will be led to cry out with the apostle, "O wretched man that I am, who shall deliver me from this body of sin and death?"[34]

In the same year, Robert Johnston Miller, an early Episcopalian and Lutheran minister in North Carolina, placed the same emphasis on the self-destructive proclivities of human beings.

If then we view mankind in this melancholy position: exposed to infinite sufferings and temptations; pushed on to sensual pleasures by strong appetites, not to be gratified with safety; violently averse to many difficulties which reason and honor forbid them to decline; liable to daily and hourly alterations, . . . destitute, afflicted, tormented; and all without the notice of any other state or the support of a compensation to be made hereafter; where shall we find a creature more truly pitiable?[35]

While sin and mortality would always be the companions of the living, the gospel could draw out the sting of the melancholy and the pitiable. Conscious of Christ's "agonies of a lingering and tormenting death and pouring out his blood as the atonement for our guilt," Robert Buchan urged in a sermon in Stafford County, Virginia, quoting Hebrews 12:1, "let us lay aside every weight and the sin which so easily beset us and let us run with patience the race before us, looking to Jesus the author and finisher of our Faith who, for the joy that was set before him, endured the cross, despising the shame."[36]

The evangelical conception of death as a progressive destroyer of life and, at the same time, a model of life-enhancing devotionalism grew out of the larger tension between action and contemplation. The world consisted of shared practices, but the maintenance of the values inherent in those practices in the face of human rigidity, pride, irrationality, and narrowness required a suspicion of social reality. "The same human activity that produces society also produces religion, with the relation between the two always being a dialectical one," Berger explains. Religious experience may be a response to social needs or social needs may be inspired by religious insights; either way, according to Berger, religion "derives objective and subjective reality from human beings who produce and reproduce it in their ongoing

Evangelical Persuasion

lives."[37] The precarious tension between the evangelical view of their world, on one hand, and their obedience to their maker, on the other, made their existence painful and filled it with vitality. As they created institutions designed to serve religious purposes, and as they reformulated the belief system they had inherited from the leaders of the first Great Awakening to serve the needs of a new, republican culture, evangelicals in the South sought in concrete ways to stablilize the precarious balance between their desires and their duty, between their capabilities and their limitations. In many concrete activities— among them church discipline, worship and hymnology, the use of scripture, and the management of revivalism—evangelicals in the South sought secure ground between the extremes of hubrus and self-denial.

On January 8, 1801, the Session of the Fishing Creek Presbyterian Church in the Chester District of South Carolina met to consider "a complaint . . . lodged by David Carr, a member of the Session . . . that Agnes Carr," apparently his daughter-in-law "had probably been guilty of the crime of intoxication at her own house on a Lord's day morning in February last and at sundry other place[s] at other times." In agreeing that the accusation was "of such a nature as to call for a serious attention," the Session acted as an arbiter of behavior and resolver of conflicts over morality that its members could not handle privately or informally. The resulting proceeding was explicitly called a "trial" with witnesses for both sides, a formal plea of guilty or not guilty, a verdict, and a sentence. Mrs. Carr admitted that sometimes she drank "more than was for her good" but as to the specific charge of drunkenness on a Sunday morning in February 1800, she emphatically asserted her innocence. Even these preliminaries contain fascinating clues to the personal and ethical stakes in the dispute. The fact that a year had passed between the most serious infraction and the complaint, and that there had been unspecified recurrences of drunkenness, possibly indicated that only on the Sunday morning in February had there been witnesses and overt conduct about which they could testify. Probably friction over Agnes Carr's conduct had been building for some time. And as the testimony would make clear, she had been, on at least this one instance, a very troubled person.

The difficulty arose on the Sunday morning in question when some travelers on their way to Georgia stopped in front of the Robert Carr home. While they were there Nancy (as Agnes Carr was apparently known) went into the house and "took a bottle of whiskey off the

Revolution and Republic

shelf, and handed it about the company." Later in the morning, a Mr. Ramsay arrived with a bottle of his own from which "she drank and gave the children some"—an act repeated from a Mr. Cain's bottle still later in the morning. By this time she was showing signs of not feeling well and "sat down upon a chair before the fire,... put her hand behind her haunch" and complained of feeling sick; "her head began to hang to one side—the tears to run from her eyes." Two of the women present, one of them her mother-in-law, Margaret Carr, then tried to put Nancy to bed but she writhed violently and had to be restrained. She got up and laid down on the cold hearth, complaining of the cold but refusing cover. At this point the testimony revealed that Nancy Carr was pregnant; she began to talk wildly of her fear of a miscarriage and her belief that the child in her womb had been dead for a month. "She rolled and tumbled about and would not be held by us." Someone brought her a cup of tea and she seemed to revive. Without warning, she grabbed Margaret Carr "and said 'Mother, I'll shake you limb from limb, I'll leave you limbless.' "

In cross examination of the two women who testified against her, Nancy accused Margaret Carr of telling her the tea was spiked for medicinal purposes. "I said no such thing," Margaret retorted. "Did you not say my pains were the worst you had ever seen?" demanded Nancy; "I said I thought [you were] the maddest I ever saw," came the reply.

Other witnesses said they saw Nancy in bed that morning, they even bent over to comfort her, and smelled no liquor. The Session found her guilty and gave her a month to show repentance. There is no record to show whether or not she did so. Fragmentary though it is, and strangely clinical in the detail of its observations, this account is rich with implications about the larger phenomenon of church discipline. Like other surviving records, this one stresses the reconciling, healing role of discipline. The case did not arise until a pattern of drunkenness throughout the year 1800—if we are to believe David Carr's complaint and her admission that she had a drinking problem—had come to alarm members of the family. The direct knowledge of witnesses arose from their initial efforts to help a person who was obviously distressed and in pain. The occasion of this drinking is also intriguing—a Sunday morning when travelers on their way to Georgia and some neighbors accompanying them invaded the privacy of the Carr household. The entire assembled group of visitors did not depart, one witness testified, because the horses

Evangelical Persuasion

pulling the travelers' wagon refused to budge. It was during this confused visit that bottles had been freely circulated. Isolation, drink, difficult pregnancies, quarrelsome relations between neighbors who needed one another but resented intrusion into their privacy—all of these social conditions, which bulk large in the Fishing Creek Church record of the Nancy Carr dispute, were endemic social conditions throughout the rural South in the early nineteenth century.[38]

Church discipline in the early nineteenth century was an intimate and flexible system of local social control that supplemented law enforcement and dealt with antisocial behavior that lay just beyond the reach of the law—drunkenness, gossip, shady business practices, illegitimacy, adultery, and abuse of slaves. There is some evidence that well-to-do figures in rural areas used church discipline as a way of keeping their poorer neighbors in line,[39] and other indications that discipline served as an early form of education in morality and self-control that was supplanted eventually by Sunday Schools as the place to inculcate virtue.[40] Church discipline was deeply rooted in the evangelical sense of community and in a desire to create a culture rooted in otherworldly compassion. "A member was expected to restrain his natural tendency to lust after the careless pleasures of the world," Donald G. Mathews explains; "evangelicals believed that the individual left alone was likely to lapse too easily into worldly association."[41] The need for intimacy, for loving direction of each other's lives, and for an orderly approach to the disorderly business of living were all involved in evangelical discipline. Echoing Virginia Baptist phraseology of a generation earlier, a North Carolina Baptist church covenant of 1790 repeated the words of the 1761 Mill Creek (Berkeley County) Virginia Baptist Church that "we desire to walk together in the fear of God . . . humbly submitting to the gospel. . . ." [42]

The same intense communalism—linking discipline to self-denial—pervaded another North Carolina Baptist covenant, this one in Wake County sixty years later: "we . . . covenent and agree to keepe up disseplen of the church whare we are members in the most brotherly affection towards each other . . . and not be whispering and back biting each other."[43]

Containing within their own walls the seeds of contention, lacking institutional means to constrain internal dissension, and conscious of their own calling to foster harmony, evangelical churches stood at the vortex of conflict. Article 4 of the Constitution of the Mill Creek (later Brick Union Lutheran) Church in Botetourt County, Vir-

Revolution and Republic

ginia, written in 1796—dealing with the conduct of church council meetings—proscribed behavior that must have been widespread in backcountry communities and described tensions that lay just below the surface of church life:

> We shall be... impartial in giving advice [and] modest in behavior; when a matter is brought up... we shall diligently pay attention, ponder the matter silently and seriously with an impartial heart. When it is one or another's turn to speak, he shall state his opinion distinctly and openly...; he shall not advise anyone either out of favor or rancor; not quarrel but with modesty and not always have the first word nor want to demand that everything must go according to his desire, even though he in his opinion might mean it well. Thus we want to ponder the matter together,... but... to avoid all tumult, disorder and confusion, only one shall speak at a time, and that without violence, not in anger, not in love of power, nor like the quarrellors and impetuous ones.

Striking in this analysis of the dynamics of small-group conflict was its sensitivity to internal hierarchies of energy, ambition, and self-confidence within the church and the use of decorum as antidote to these human proclivities to speak first, most fully, and without emotional reserve. At stake in the Brick Union church was also a democratic compact and republican polity that must have been in tension with hierarchies of wealth and prominence within the parish: "no one shall presume special privilege for himself even though he be older, richer, or more distinguished." Bringing social ranks together within a common polity was a comprehensive pietism reflecting the Lutheran and German Reformed backgrounds of this "union" church. Citing Paul's injunction to "put away from yourselves" the "fornicator,... covetous,... idolater,... railer,... or a drunkard," the Constitution required the church officer to bring to the pastor's attention "anyone in the congregation" who "leads an objectionable life or lives in obvious sins and vices such as: quarreling, fighting, envy, gluttony, drinking, dancing, wild cavorting,[44] gambling, lying, cheating, whoring, adultery, false oath taking, swearing, cursing, disregarding the Sabbath."[45]

Increasingly, evangelical churches in the post-Revolutionary period came to regard the family as the chief line of defense against disorder and moral license. "Our duty to our family," the 1800 Kehukee Circular Letter declared, resembled the work of "prophets, priests, and kings" who should "teach," "pray with," and govern

Evangelical Persuasion

spouses and children; "a family should not be governed by passion; justice should be tempered with judgment and mercy." Remembering the disastrous consequences of Eli's coddling of his sons in First Samuel, or Solomon's regrets about his neglect of parental discipline, the letter warned that "after giving too great a loose to the the reins of our children's lusts, we shall find our reproofs to be in vain."[46] Henry Pattillo, Presbyterian minister in Granville County, North Carolina, published in 1787 a manual on family and household management that considered thoughtful, planned, systematic discipline essential to the spiritual and mental well-being of the family, and equated the wisdom and virtue of the nation with the "spiritual health and religious prosperity" of its families. Accordingly, Pattillo's *Plain Planter's Family Assistant; Containing an Address to Husbands and Wives, Children and Servants; With Some Helps for Instruction by Catechisms; and Examples of Devotion for Families; With a Brief Paraphrase of the Lord's Prayer* knitted together pleas for productive work, devotional piety, and zeal for political liberty as the moral economy of southern agriculture.

Acting in the manner increasingly typical of southern evangelicals, Pattillo dealt with slavery by equating Christian fellowship and consolation with human paternalism. In queries #39–41 of "The Negroes Catechism," he asked: "Q. 39 Which do you think the happiest person, the master or the slave? [and] Q. 40 Do you ever think you are happier than he?" The prescribed answers were that when he rose on a "cold morning" or labored "on a hot day" the slave considered the master happier, but that when he thought of the master as tossing in his sleep, burdened with responsibilities, "then I bless God that he has placed me in my humble station . . . and feel myself happier than he is. Q. 41 Then it seems every body is best, just where God has placed them? A. Yes: The Scriptures say . . . every true Christian is Christ's free man, whether he be bond or free in this world."[47] This passage assumed, without defending, the morality of slavery and mirrored Pattillo's notion of "spiritual prosperity"—acceptance of the world as an orderly moral environment in which no one's situation was perfect and in which obedience and inequality were consistent with the reign of a benevolent God.

During the last quarter of the eighteenth century, evangelicals in the South responded to a revolution, to a new wave of revivalism, to racism and slavery, to death and dying, and to their own weaknesses and deviance. At work in each of these encounters was an acute sensitivity to conscience, to the demands of Scripture, and to the disci-

Revolution and Republic

plines of a new life in Christ. Those were painful tests to endure. The evangelical theodicy was no mere formula; rather it was a troubled, troubling attempt to resist despair.

The Circular Letters of the Chowan Baptist Association in the Albemarle Sound region of North Carolina—a Calvinist competitor of the more revivalist Kehukee Association—articulated effectively a view of the secular world as a throbbing, disturbing reality. "We are surrounded with many temptations, evils, and dangers while in this wilderness," the 1806 Circular Letter declared; "for in this golden and enlightened age, when religious characters are caressed by men of the world, we need to guard against too great a conformity to the vain amusements thereof." Now threatening and ugly, now alluring and reasonable, the conditions of society called for Christians to display constant discipline and vigilance. Yet something still more was required—a vitality, a sense of concentrated purpose. "It is a fact too demonstrably true to be denied that many professors of religion (and real Christians too) have and may leave . . . their first love and through the imbecility of human nature and the allurements of the world, in conjunction with the temptations of the Devil, fall into a supine and lethargic state." That psychological condition, lurking just beneath the surface of life in a rural, isolated environment, was a terrifying malady. Commenting on late eighteenth—early nineteenth-century preaching, Daniel Calhoun notes that "the sermon was hardly . . . the work of the professional man acting alone; it was produced by the people and the practitioner together," an observation that explains the urgent clinical quality of these circular letters.[48]

The external world not only placed individuals on the defensive; it thrust its charms and terrors on humans in ways that exploited their every weakness. The whole natural scheme of society tended to subdue human beings to the dictates of the world—to turn the believer into a "backslider": "the first signs are mental," explained the 1806 letter; "faith, hope, and love for God and his glory begin to be inactive. . . . Then follows a cold indifference to the relative duties in religion—a more than ordinary solicitude after the profits, honours, and pleasures of this vain world." Resistance and reformation were doomed from the outset, the sermon continued, for even if "his conscience whips him sometimes to the meeting house where the word of life is exhibited, his heart is callous, his mind wandering, and zeal languid, and does not often complain of a short sermon." Finally his devotional life of family prayer, Bible reading, and meditation deterio-

Evangelical Persuasion

rate, and the victim of the world sinks into a total spiritual stupor. There was no earthly remedy for this benumbed state of existence, the 1807 letter explained, because God Himself used human folly to chastise and humble His people: "we must expect, beloved, in the present world to endure *afflictions, and from the hand of God.* At such times *passion* would murmur and rebel, like Jehoram, who in the time of famine flew in the face of God saying *'this is the evil of the Lord. Why should I wait for the Lord any longer?'* " Even more common than divine chastisement of the believer was *"injurious treatment* from the hands of men." Escape from the whirlwind of suffering and evil in the world was impossible; only "patience" rooted in a total reliance on God's protection could counteract the chaos of the world, [and] "still the mind, restore its tranquillity, and preserve it in order even in the midst of distressing circumstances."[49]

God's capacity to heal and restore—His merciful intervention into human affairs—met human beings at the level of their need. He enabled them to perceive the world in what evangelicals considered to be objective and rational terms. God instilled into the patient yet suffering believer the critical ability of "bearing affliction without murmuring—enduring injuries without revenge and waiting for suspended favors until God sees fit to bestow them."

Here evangelical theodicy held that nearly all of life was a test of endurance, and that for the Christian sufferer the pilgrimage of pain brought him closer to victory over a sinful nature:

> Tribulations disturb the calm of life and trouble its waters, but patience will still the mind, restore its tranquillity, and preserve it in order, even in the midst of distressing circumstances. It is the opposite of passion. It is that by which we hold the reins of our spirits, or as the Lord expresses it, possess our soul.

God's intervention in the life of a believer was therefore both curative and instructive. God taught people to understand "the powers and passions of our minds, and organs, appetites, and faculties of our bodies" and made the dynamics of body and mind a regulating device. "Intemperance," explained the 1810 leter, "is obviously discoverable in the exercise of our faculties and appetites of body . . . ; it is an evil in ordinary cases to exercise ourselves beyond our strength to the injury of our constitutions" and "no less an evil . . . to be indolent or inactive."[50]

Revolution and Republic

Confronting the world with realism, faith, and humility therefore became an activity that defined the individual. "Experience," Jeremiah Ethridge explained in 1823, "conveys the idea of knowledge obtained by practice," and "Christian experience is that religious knowledge which is obtained by any exercise, employment, or suffering of body or mind. . . . The design of religion is not only to furnish the understandings of men with a regular system of truth but also to affect the heart and quiet the mind." For Ethridge, "experience" was more than the superficial impression conveyed by events, more than a narrative of activity. God dealt with people by strewing fragments of reality in their path—reminders of His intentions for the world, reminders of the potentialities of redeemed human beings.[51] But these fragments competed with "the indignant frowns, the contemptuous sneers and the fascinating charms of the world" as well as "with the allurements and buffetings of sin and satan." Only a person intentionally and consciously dependent on God's protection could avoid those hazards and continue "heaven-directed" in "paths of virtue." For the Christian pilgrim, happiness and security remained problematical—not because of any defect in God's care but because the world itself was unknowable and God's plan necessarily inscrutable. "The Christian, fixed and steady in his purpose," Ethridge explained,

> meets with a variety of things which give to hope and fear an alternate dominion over him—God, for wise purposes, sometimes hides his smiles in his pavilion of darkness, so that the Christian's providential duty may well be said to be sometimes clear, then cloudy. . . . In all this variety of enjoyment, suffering and exercise of body and mind, the judicious Christian collects a stock of useful and important knowledge; and this is what we call Christian knowledge.[52]

Ethridge's language was vibrant and compelling. Sermons in premodern society were virtually the only polished, persuasive discourse most people ever heard, and they therefore had a unique claim on the hearers' attention and feelings. Eighteenth century preachers developed two strategies, according to Daniel Calhoun; an older one was "calculating" and called for sermons of stark simplicity and thematic unity, and the newer approach was a "personal" style that projected the charisma of the preacher. The exegetical notebook kept by the Rowan County, North Carolina Presbyterian minister, Samuel McCorkle, shows how the calculating style laid the groundwork for, and

Evangelical Persuasion

fed into, the personal projection of the preacher's own self. Mc-
Corkle's notes reveal two abiding preoccupations, first, what he called
"the limits of human and divine agency"—agency meaning innate
capacity—and second a fascination with the Book of Job, the drama
of the situation in which salvation occurred and the narrative of a
faithful, suffering pilgrim.

The contrast between human and divine agency had compelling
resonance for McCorkle because it painted a picture of cosmic reality.
McCorkle wanted his listeners to envision three elements in that
scene: grace, providence, and the Holy Spirit. His cryptic notations
under these headings provide a rare insight into the way a backcountry preacher read the Bible and explicated a text. McCorkle started
from the premise that humans are created beings and that "every
happy circum[stance] is from God, and if being on the whole is happier than not being, it is from grace." Second, McCorkle reminded
himself and his parishioners that human understanding of this created condition was limited to an appreciation of Providence, the unmerited and inexplicable flow of favor from the throne of grace into
the lives of individuals. Notations on the nature of Providence spilled
across the page: "parents, bond or free and no more in choice than
Adam['s] seed, talents, reason, seasons, rank, the sac[raments], rel[i-
gious] priv[ilege], a Bible Sabbath, spread of the gospel" and then the
critical point, "all out[side] of [our] choice or power." His third head-
ing defined the power of God to heap blessings on His creation as an
irresistible Holy Spirit that "has come unasked, is free—blows where
best or when asked to Christians, Eph[esians] I, 18." That passage
spoke of "the eyes of understanding, . . . the hope of his calling" and
to it McCorkle added another powerful image, Ezekiel's assertion that
God "break[s] up the fallow ground."

This picture of God intervening in human life and transforming
the world prepared McCorkle to move from the calculated design of
salvation to personal advocacy. The transition began with phrases depicting the drama of salvation: "magnify law, unite mercy, justice, bear
penalty, . . . conquer death and rise again into eternal bliss." Here
again the terminology tumbled forth before reaching a conclusion,
three terms and a reference requiring close attention. They were, "silence, Socinians—enforced atonement" and "Gal[atians] I, 4." Soci-
nianism was the heresy that denied the divinity of Christ, and the
Galatians text its direct refutation: he "who gave himself for our sins
that he might deliver us from this present evil world. . . . " In that

context "enforced atonement" would be the Socinian view that God sacrificed a human Jesus with cavalier dispatch. But what did "silence" signify? Probably, McCorkle wanted to emphasize that God's omnipotence held the drama of salvation together and that human efforts toward the same end were utterly insignificant, a situation for which profound silence would indeed be an apt metaphor.

In June 1786 McCorkle preached on his favorite text, Job 14:14— "If a man die, shall he live again? All the days of my appointed time will I wait, till my change come"—which allowed him to fuse theological analysis and personal conviction. Living before Kierkegaard, McCorkle saw none of Job's anguished doubts about the consistency and predictability of the Creator or the reality of life after death. Instead he saw emblazoned in that text a trilogy of the stages of faith from its onset to its fulfillment, which he labeled "belief," "waiting," and "change." He dealt with belief quickly. It was the "power" associated with the nature, name, and office of God and God's willingness to suffer for humanity. Citing darkness and light imagery from First John, [53] McCorkle declared that God creates belief "as a bridge across the gulf of death." Belief further meant repentance, what McCorkle called "mixt grace" in which the spirit flooded into the consciousness of the penitent and triggered the response of "waiting," a faith-like activity.[54]

"To wait is to desire [the] event, Job VII," McCorkle noted. Waiting was an action fraught with potential emotion. Job described the onset of Job's suffering—sleeplessness, "flesh clothed with . . . clods of dust, my skin . . . broken and . . . loathsome"—and its temporal dimension: "How long wilt thou not depart from me nor let me alone till I can swallow down my spittle. . . . And why dost thou not pardon my transgression and take away mine iniquity?" Waiting was to be engaged in, and affected by, the wearing out of physical existence, and in the meanwhile it also meant "to be active." Here McCorkle cited Paul's exhortations to Titus for sober, conscientious behavior, Second Timothy on the "crown of righteousness" awaiting the faithful, and Revelation on "rest from their labours."[55] At its deepest level, waiting meant "fortitude" in the face of immediate or eventual death. "I will not blaspheme a master I served 80 years," McCorkle quoted Polycarp, the early Christian martyr who died with these words on his lips and Justin Martyr, who faced his death saying "let fire consume my flesh, nerves shiver, twill but send me home."[56]

Evangelical Persuasion

Just as "mixt grace" was the hinge between belief and waiting in McCorkle's scheme, fortitude was the hinge between waiting and "change." In a still developing, pre-modern society, change was no commonplace concept but rather an urgent prospect. The most elaborate of his three stages of faith, change occurred first in the body, then the body and the mind, next in the world of the spirit and the afterlife, and finally in inspiration, the "media by which the mind sees objects." It was inspiration that drew the sermon to its conclusion and answered Job's question about life after death. "We will not be unclothed, II Cor. V, but clothed upon," McCorkle's notes explained; [we] will be some medium, see I Cor. XIII, tongues of angels. . . ." The juxtaposition of these two Corinthians chapters emphasized McCorkle's platonic understanding of the soul. Second Corinthians, V, used the image of clothing to explain progress of the soul toward perfection. The "tongues of men and of angels" in I Corinthians, XIII which could speak corruptly, and the gift of prophesy and knowledge which could be empty vanity if the speaker and knower had no charity, together gauged the distance between the actual and the ideal. Paul's "now . . . through a glass darkly but then face to face" was the ultimate change in spiritual reality that began with belief, continued through repentance, gained shape and coherence in fortitude, and would come to completion only beyond the grave.[57] It was within this cosmic scheme, McCorkle concluded, that life and death, suffering and exultation, the unpredictable brevity of human existence and the eternal scope of divine creation all could be understood. Now at last, McCorkle was ready to move from exposition to personal zeal: "Go then, try the world, cast around your arms and hug it to your bosom."

In evangelical cosmology, the universe embodied order and disorder, purity and impurity, and spirit and flesh in a grand web of connectedness that only divine revelation could explain and reconcile. Conceiving of existence as a sacred order, evangelicals believed that fallen and imperfect beings—once in a state of grace—could transcend their insignificant state and attain a spacious perspective on their place in creation. The "knowledge possessed by a spiritually-minded man and the affections or graces which exercise his soul," William Jordan declared in the Chowan Association Circular letter for 1825, endowed the believer with five dimensions of self-consciousness: first, a sense of "our own depravity" and of "the ignorance and enmity of the natural heart"; second, "our condemnation

Revolution and Republic

as sinners"; third, a sense of "the spirituality of the law, its truth, holiness, and justice" and its role as an instrument of God's vengeance; fourth, the "infinite holiness, wisdom, and power of God"; and finally, "the Gospel" in which "love is its own law and holiness is an indispensable evidence of grace."[58]

In Jordan's moral universe, the depravity of man, God's wrath and judgment, and the healing process of sanctification formed a patterned, structured way of confronting disorder with order and of recognizing what Mary Douglas calls "the potency of disorder." "We submit the following remark to distinguish the backsliding of a true Christian and the final apostacy of the false professor," declared the 1806 Circular Letter in a vivid demonstration of the power of both evangelical faith and the forces of darkness: "The [backslider], when chastised for his misconduct, 'whereof all children of God are partakers,' is humbled and brought again into a path of duty; but the [false professor] murmurs, repines, and remonstrates in his heart against the dealings of providence and generally returns to the sinful practices of the world like some dog to his vomit and the sow to her wallowing in the mire."[59]

Evangelical discipline dealt severely with the backslider because he was capable of regeneration and because the struggle for his soul had already been won. For the "false professor" of Christian faith and other unregenerate folk, discipline and admonition would accomplish nothing; only a terrible demonstration of God's wrath would being such people to a point of spiritual crisis. But for those within the household of faith, the struggle against temptation was never-ending and all-consuming. "WATCH AND REMEMBER," Elder Martin Ross implored his readers in 1809;

Watch against a spirit of dogmatical arrogance and bigotry; remember you are far from infallability or perfection in knowledge and others have an equal right of private judgment with yourselves. Watch against a spirit of boundless curiosity and fond love of novelty; remember you are warned not to affect to be wise above what is written; but at the same time watch against a lazy indifference to a progressive acquaintance with things of God, and remember that the Bible contains an inexhaustible mine of human knowledge which you have not explored. Watch against all notions which flatter human pride and encourage the idea of merit in a sinner, and ever remember that the design of God in the gospel is to abase all the naughtiness of man.

Evangelical Persuasion

These sinful tendencies were the sources of pollution within the community of believers, and Ross's call to "remember" expressed well the evangelical strategy for dealing with evil: intellectual humility, a recognition of the infinite and largely untapped wisdom of Scripture, and a patient, meditative willingness to perceive "Christ's design to bring apostate creatures back to God" as a comprehensive antidote to the presence of evil within the community of faith.[60]

The drama of "watchfulness" within the evangelical fold reenacted the struggle to tame and subdue—but not suppress—the energies of individualism. "We contend," Ross declared, "THAT A MAN IS NEVER WELL INFORMED OF THE TRUTH UNTIL HE IS CONFORMED TO IT. For fallen man is God's natural enemy. And as long as this hatred and opposition to God remains, 'tis midnight with the soul."[61] The urgency and depth of that message was the core of the evangelical persuasion.

Excursus II

Convergences:
Toward a Christian Republic

The construction of a republican polity was an exercise in persuasion, the securing of consent, intellectual competition, and the application of theory to practice. Accordingly, political arguments about education went to the core of the republican experiment and occasioned the earliest intermingling of evangelical belief and republican ideology in the life of the new nation.

The opening of the University of North Carolina in 1795 triggered such an encounter of politics and religion. It involved a dispute over curriculum and governance between two of the University's first trustees, William R. Davie and Samuel McCorkle. McCorkle, the evangelical, stressed the classics and a strict student regimen of piety, prayer and religious instruction, whereas Davie placed the classics on an even footing with the sciences, history, and moral philosophy. To clerical criticisms that the University was "a very dissipated and debauched place," he tartly responded that "nothing . . . goes well that these *men of God* have not had some hand in."[1] The Trustees adopted McCorkle's rules in February 1795. They required a reading knowledge of Latin and mastery of Greek grammar for admission and an additional year of Latin and two of Greek for graduation. Although McCorkle included mathematics, science, history, and moral philosophy, these subjects remained subordinate to the classics and to religious instruction in the life of the school. Through mandatory morning prayer, divine service on the Sabbath, and Sunday evening examinations on "the general principles of religion and morality"; prohibitions on gambling, drinking, association with "evil company"; and a rigid schedule of recitation, lecture, and study, leaving only the hour following breakfast for amusement, McCorkle's regulations promoted discipline, subordination, and reverence.[2]

Though he probably voted to adopt McCorkle's rules, Davie soon concluded that they were gravely deficient, and in December 1795 he persuaded the Trustees to adopt a broader and more flexible course of study. He added French to the foreign languages, made foreign

122

Excursus II. Convergences

language study optional at the request of a student's parents, and created a degree in science with no foreign language requirement for admission or graduation. Mastery of the English language, he emphasized, was the primary objective, and the "other languages" were "but auxiliaries." Although McCorkle soon thereafter left Chapel Hill, Davie's ambitious plans never went into effect, and the presidency of Joseph Caldwell (1804–35) confirmed the classical and Presbyterian character of the institution.

The clash between Davie and McCorkle involved more than opposing egos or differences over curriculum; the two men represented different understandings of republicanism. In Davie's view, the country desperately needed political and social leaders steeped in Enlightenment philosophy, eloquent and persuasive in the use of language, and imbued with lofty, nationalist ambitions. The first "professorship" in his plan for the university was to teach "moral and political philosophy and history" through the study of constitutionalism, national law, Enlightenment, legal and social theory (Paley, Montesquieu, Vattel), and the skeptical and critical historical writing of Hume and Priestley.[3] McCorkle, also a Princeton graduate, saw the training of leaders for society as a moral enterprise and the destiny of the nation as a spiritual mission. Reason, scientific curiosity, and useful knowledge were meaningful for McCorkle because they enhanced man's understanding of the Creator.[4]

The two men had very different assumptions about the relationship of a university to society. Because people were the source of law in a free government, Davie expected them to receive an education that would enable them to formulate the law within the existing constitutional framework. Davie believed that his curriculum would produce "useful and respectable members of society." McCorkle, on the other hand, wanted to instill into students a sense of awe and exhilaration at being part of a chosen people. All history, McCorkle declared, proved that the United States was a specially favored nation—singled out by God for blessings and responsibilities as no other people had been since the Old Testament Israelites. Because churches that shared this sense of God's will were the most influential and effective institutions in the state, and because particular laymen and clergy—especially Presbyterians—were among the most assertive and confident of North Carolina's social and political leaders, McCorkle believed that the University should become a repository of and a rallying point for Protestant idealism.

Revolution and Republic

One evangelical schoolmaster found the process of inculcating virtue to be an especially compelling calling. "In order to be virtuous," Henry Allason, a self-educated Methodist teacher in Maryland reminded himself in 1807, "a man must resist his propensities, inclinations, and tastes, and maintain an incessant conflict with himself," that is between the guidance of the "heart" and the demands of "ambition" and public expectation. Learning to work through such experiences, Allason believed, required teachers who could "preside" over a schoolroom, "men well recommended, not given to intrigue and hence to loss of virtue. We should not ask if he is a wit, a bright man, a philosopher, but is he fond of children, does he frequent the unfortunate rather than the great?" Such a teacher would remember that the only punishment appropriate in a republican culture was exclusion of an offender from the company of other students, an "exile" proportionate to the seriousness of the offense and administered in a manner respectful of the student's personal dignity. Echoing the Renaissance humanist antecedents of republicanism, Allason here followed the ideal of the gentle schoolmaster set forth in Roger Ascham, *The Schoolmaster* (1570).[5]

Tying these standards and assumptions together was Allason's belief that

> nothing is durable, virtue alone excepted. Personal beauty passes quickly away, fortune inspires extravagant inclinations, grandeur fatigues, reputation is uncertain, talents, nay genius itself are liable to be impaired. But virtue is ever beautiful, ever diversified, ever equal, and ever vigorous because it is resigned to all events, to privations as well as to enjoyments, to death as to life, happy . . . [am I] if I have been able to contribute . . . toward redressing some of the evils which oppress my country and to open some new prospect of felicity.

Education for a republican like Allason was decidedly more public and shared than personal and private; happiness and virtue could only be known in civic activity. Allason felt this ideal constantly slipping away, retrievable only by recurrence to first principles of self-discipline and comradeship with others. Those first principles, Enlightenment philosophy taught him, were the product of prolonged historical experience. The Abbé Raynal convinced him that England's movement "from monarchy to tyranny, from tyranny to aristocracy to democracy, and from democracy to anarchy" had habituated English-

Excursus II.   Convergences

men to instability and change, and Locke's concept of consent explained why a prolonged history of political flux instilled self-reliance
rather than anxiety into British public life.[6]

In these examples of republican education, Davie conceived of
virtue as a faculty activated through learning and service; McCorkle
insisted on a regimen of piety and discipline to ward off moral and
social vices; and Allason took the middle—or perhaps the more
advanced—ground that to be a republican was to seize the day and
live out a credo of public service and unselfishness before evanescent
favorable circumstances evaporated.

An early test of these prescriptions for the moral nurturing of the
new republic occurred in 1785 when Methodist Bishop Francis Asbury and his English counterpart, Thomas Coke, circulated in the
Virginia Methodist circuits, and submitted to the Virginia General
Assembly, a petition against slavery. As we have seen, Methodists were
a suspect group. Because of Wesley's outspoken denunciation of the
American Revolution and because Methodist preachers during the
war for independence appealed to blacks and poor whites on the
fringes of society who resisted being mobilized into the struggle,
Methodists in the 1780s still bore the taint of toryism.

Now they were apparently at it again. Declaring "that LIBERTY is
the birthright of mankind" and "that the body of Negroes have been
robbed of that right," the Methodist leaders urged the "justice" of
restoring those "rights." The petition dismissed justifications of slavery based on paternalism, racial inferiority, and prudence. It recommended emancipation of blacks in order "to bind the vast body of
Negroes to the state by the most powerful ties of interest." Asbury and
Coke carefully circumscribed the religious justification for emancipation, but in ways that must have appeared flamboyantly aggressive to
Virginia slaveowners:

> [the] deep debasement of spirit, which is the necessary consequence of
> slavery, utterly incapacitates the human mind (except in a few instances)
> for the reception of the noble and enlarged principles of the gospel;
> and therefore to encourage it, or to allow of it, we apprehend to be
> most opposite to that catholic spirit of Christianity which desires the
> establishment of the kingdom of Christ over all the world.

Coke and Asbury inserted the words "except in a few instances" to
deflect anecdotal rebuttals about particular pious slaves and deftly

Revolution and Republic

limited their writ to the kingdom of Christ to be conciliatory, but their technical religious terminology, "deep debasement" and "utter incapacita[tion]," were, to the uninitiated, strident and, worse yet, presumptuous.[7]

That nearly eleven hundred slaveowners in six Virginia counties signed petitions condemning the Methodist attack on slavery was less surprising than the mixture of social and Biblical arguments they employed. Emancipation threatened not only a labor system and white supremacy but rather the whole moral economy of the Old Dominion:

> It is . . . ruinous to individuals and to the public. For it involved in it, and is productive of, want, poverty, distress, and ruin for the free citizen; neglect, famine, and death to the helpless black infant and superannuated parent; the horrors of all the rapes, murders, and outrages which a vast multitude of unprincipled, unpropertied, vindictive, and remorseless banditti are capable of perpetrating; inevitable bankruptcy to the revenue and consequently breach of public faith and loss of credit with foreign nations; and lastly, ruin to this now free and flourishing country.

Four of the five versions of these petitions cited Leviticus 25:44–46 about "bondsmen" and I Corinthians 7:20–24 on the duties of the "servant" and "freeman." What is interesting about those citations is the vast historical argument required to bring them to bear on the issue of slavery. "*We have reason to conclude*," declared two hundred and sixty-one Halifax County petitioners, that "this permission to possess and inherit bondservants" in Leviticus "was continued through all the revolutions of the Jewish government down to the advent of our Lord, and *we do not find* that either he or his apostles abridged it." Moreover, the use of the Corinthians text suggested that slaves had a direct calling from God to remain in bondage after their conversion. The proslavery petitions moreover sanctified the revolutionary compact that brought an independent Virginia into being in a stunning fusion of Lockean, providential, and martial imagery: "we risked our lives and fortunes and waded through seas of blood. Divine providence smiled on our enterprise and crowned it with success. And our liberty and property are now as well secured to us as they can be by any human constitution or form of government."[8]

The issues of human slavery and Christian freedom had joined. Over the next half-century, Christian proslavery would move beyond

Excursus II. Convergences

manipulative proof-text argumentation in search of more ingenious ways of treating slavery as a kind of stewardship, and evangelical abolitionism in the South would atrophy though never cease entirely. James O'Kelly, who for a time following his conversion in 1775 was a Methodist circuit rider in North Carolina and Virginia, / published in 1789 an *Essay on Slavery* declaring "that slavery is a work of the flesh, assisted by the devil, a mystery of iniquity that works like witchcraft to darken your understanding and harden your heart. . . . Can anyone . . . suppose," he demanded, "that in order to give us carnal pleasure in indulging our idleness, feeding our pride, like fed horses, . . . that God would ruin and butcher so many thousands of our inoffensive fellow creatures?"[9]

Mark Noll, Nathan Hatch, and George Marsden have argued vigorously that the new republic was not, and could not have become, a Christian nation because Christian discipleship, especially that of evangelicals, is too stark, personal, and consuming to accommodate itself to civic humanism. Discipleship and republicanism could and did unite, however, in specific, momentary situations like O'Kelly's question about idleness, pride, and gluttonous appetite for dominion. Republicanism prompted churches and ministers to channel the uncompromising demands of Scripture into a few interstices of society. "Let us ransack the sweet bowels of Christ for arguments," O'Kelly concluded his attack on slavery:

> let us persuade the Lord to conquer our people by the power of religion and not give them up to the curse of judicial blindness. Let us never distrust the Almighty.
> Lay all your shoulders to the mountain of slavery. I believe I am leaning on the main pillars on which it stands. If God would give me my power, I would bow till my heart broke, so it would be to the destruction of this bloody oppression.[10] (Judges 16:30)

Eventually, a later generation of abolitionists believed, something like that happened to destroy slavery. In his time, O'Kelly insisted that only as people gained through faith and discipleship direct access to the ear of their Savior, and allowed all distinctions of rank and privilege to fall away, could they claim citizenship in a Christian republic.

Even if evangelicalism did not become an instrument of reform or a consistent prophetic voice in the South, it did provide a resilient interpretation of how republicanism could survive and perpetuate

Revolution and Republic

itself. David Ramsay, a Presbyterian, South Carolina patriot leader, physician, and historian, grasped this didactic opportunity with more learning, imagination, and dexterity in supplanting Calvinist realism with republican pessimism than any of his contemporaries. "Industry, frugality, and temperance are virtues which we should eminently culti-vate," he proclaimed in a fourth of July oration in 1794;

> these are the only foundations on which a popular government can rest with safety. Republicans should be plain in their apparel—their enter-tainments, their furniture, and their equipage. Idleness, extravagance, and dissipation of every kind should be banished from our borders. The virtues now recommended are those which prepared infant Rome for all her greatness.[11]

Not only was this a pure version of republican ideology rooted in the classical *polis*, celebrated by Machiavelli, fashioned into prescrip-tive political vocabulary by eighteenth-century opposition polemicists in Britain, and put to work in the creation of the American republic; it also reflected Ramsay's personal situation and political experiences. Born in Lancaster County, Pennsylvania, he graduated from the Col-lege of New Jersey in 1765—three years before the arrival of his future father-in-law, John Witherspoon—and studied medicine at the Col-lege of Philadelphia from 1770 to 1773. With its burgeoning com-merce and self-conscious elite, Charlestown, South Carolina, seemed to him a promising place to establish his career. In 1775 he married Sabena Ellis, who died the following year, and in 1783 he married Frances Witherspoon, who also died after less than two years of mar-riage from scarlet fever following the birth of a son—events that would deeply affect his political and social outlook.

The slaveowner mentality in South Carolina offended the young Ramsay deeply. "White pride and avarice are great obstacles in the way of black liberty," he wrote his mentor, Benjamin Rush in 1780. "Riches are not a blessing to a people," he had noted a few months earlier; "they induce an effeminacy of mind as well as of body. Why cannot a man live happy under the loss of a brigade of negroes and of a few thousands [of money to the British] when what remains is more than he can ever enjoy?"[12]

The 1790s saw an eclipse of his political career—perhaps a back-lash against his earlier anti-slavery opinions or because of his chronic financial embarrassments—he and his third wife, Henry Lauren's

Excursus II. Convergences

daughter, Martha, struggled to raise eleven children on a physician's income. Marriage into a South Carolina family made him a slave-owner and prompted a retreat from his earlier radical racial views. Just two years after his marriage to Martha, he wrote to a friend in Massachusetts that "you speak feelingly for the poor negroes. I have long considered their situation.... Experience proves that they who have been born & grow up in slavery are incapable of the blessings of freedom."[13]

Ramsay's religious beliefs and Stoic resignation may have insulated him for a time from the materialism and hubris of the South Carolina elite, but his evangelicalism primarily mediated between his leadership aspirations and his view of human and social intractability.[14] His most explicit testimony on this point—a long letter informing John Witherspoon of Frances's sudden death—is slippery to interpret but nonetheless revealing. Ostensibly a letter about his departed young wife—about her piety, orthodoxy, and serenity in the face of death—and probably contrived to make the appropriate clinical, consoling impression on its recipient, Ramsay's letter to Witherspoon also transmutted private agony into public virtue in good republican fashion. "Had I been skeptical about... the great doctrines of religion which I have always been taught to revere... or about the gospel plan of salvation through the imputed merits of a Saviour," Ramsay confessed, then Frances's ordeal "would have convinced me of their reality." Her vulnerability and fragility taught him public fortitude and protected him from despair. Her completion of "the important business of life" reminded him of the existential and immediate requirements of personal virtue. The healthy condition of Frances's newborn—named John Witherspoon Ramsay and baptized in the presence of both parents just twelve hours before his mother's passing—prompted Ramsay to pray that "heaven may preserve his life and raise him up to *usefulness in his generation*."[15] The son's *vitae* echoed the soundness and precariousness of those aspirations: A. B., M. A., College of New Jersey, 1803, 1806; M. D., University of Pennsylvania, 1807; physician in Prince Edward's Parish, South Carolina, 1807–1813; sired a son; died in 1813.[16]

The peculiar mix of social imperative and individual volition in evangelicalism stimulated discourse in a republican culture. In 1816, Conrad Speece, an Augusta County, Virginia, Presbyterian minister, carefully copied and calendared his essays, poems, and letters from various newspapers and magazines; they were models of republican

Revolution and Republic

admonition. The first, and longest, was a eulogy to George Washington given at Hampden Sydney College on February 22, 1800. It emphasized the qualities of Washington's "bravery," "fortitude," "perseverence," "patience," and "invincible love of country," which by example entered directly into the consciousness of his contemporaries and shaped the malleable collective moral character of a generation. "He deliniates with a masterly hand the true interests of America," Speece explained; he "demonstrates with incontestable clearness the essential dependence of social order on private virtue; and points with the nicest precision the path to national prosperity, glory, and happiness."[17] Eleven years later Speece still brooded over the connection between private virtue and social order. "A Letter to a Young Friend who . . . Lately Made a Public Profession of Religion," warned that republican virtue continually decomposed as it came into cultural contact with self-regarding human heedlessness: "We are lamentably prone to unbelief, to ingratitude under the reception of innumberable benefits, and to wandering from God, the only source of true rest and peace, and after a thousand triffles lighter than air; we are liable to be entangled with those vanities which we have again and again renounced."[18] Visiting the United States two decades later, Alexis de Tocqueville would find exactly this kind of psychic rootlessness, "a bootless chase of that complete felicity that forever eludes" Americans, the most persistent feature of life in a democracy.[19]

Part III.

THE ANTEBELLUM ERA

5.

Sanctification
and Consciousness

I now [in 1815] felt afresh that I was a new creature, created in Christ to good works, ... buried with him in the likeness of his death, ... risen with him to walk in newness of life.... Not only was a new song put into my mouth, but a new impulse was given to my whole nature.

> Samuel Cornelius (Presbyterian minister in Pennsylvania and Virginia) to his son, January 25, 1860 (Detroit, 1860, privately printed), p. 21.

The Reverend Cornelius ... is well named for he appears to be the centurian of his band—a bold soldier in the cause of Christ.

> Judith Lomax Diary, April ?, 1819, typescript, Virginia Historical Society.

Evangelicalism was a journey into a world of new possibilities; it was also a contemplative inward pilgrimage and a process of personal sanctification. Each of these kinds of submersion into the sublime—conversion, living in but not of the world, and fashioning a life of obedience to one's maker—prompted strong autobiographical impulses. "I can remember things that was done comparitively speaking when I was nothing but a very small child," wrote Fields Cook in 1847, in the only surviving autobiography written by a slave while still in slavery;

and one of those instances is I recorlect that I was the pet of my mother and indeed of all my family. My mother being busily engaged in getting the breakfast she took me out of the bed and placed me in one corner of the kitchen where she had a large kettle of water on boiling to make coffee which by some means or other got up set.... I could not get out of the way so I got myself despertly scaulded.

A few lines later he was in older childhood: "I never knew what the yoke of oppression was in the early part of my life for the white and black children all faired alike and grew on together highfellows." One of his white friends, "for whom I had often fought with as much ambition as if he had been my brother," as he grew older began "to feel ... like the peafowl in the midst of a brude of chickens" and "raise his feathers and boast of his superiority ... over me." Here he saw the motif of his life, the key to his essential nature:

of these two great misfortunes, which appeared the worse to me, rejection or scaulding, I can not at this time tell and I must here remark for the sake of justice to myself and to be candid before an eliten community that if there be anything in the world that is hertful to one ... it is ... that after one has formed a real attachment to an individual that they should after wards appear to have forgotten all friendship and kindness and treat you with contempt.

Fields Cook was living in Richmond, Virginia, when he wrote this ten-thousand word untitled autobiography that he characterized as "my own observations" of "things ... I have seen and heard." "As I wish to see how the world go while I am in it," he explained "I have come to the conclusion to notice a few of them for my owne benefit." For Cook, there was always a tension between his own experience and the larger realities surrounding his life. "I am ... giving a scetch of my own life," he later apologized, "but these things [conversations he had had about life after death] come in on me so fociable that I sometimes forget what I have undertaken to write." As his detachment from the "world" and interest in the afterlife suggest, Cook was an evangelical Christian, and his account of his conversion and the process of discipleship that followed it dominated his autobiography.

It had all started one day when he and his young friend—the same friend who later treated him with contempt and was probably his owner's son—were talking about "a very great revival of religion in that part of the country where we lived." Though religion had made such "a very great impression upon most of the people," it seemed to Cook and his friend that anyone as "small" and insignificant as they could not presume to speak up for themselves before the creator of

Sanctification and Consciousness

the universe. Nevertheless, Cook later realized, "there is a spirit in man and the inspiration of God giveth an understanding." "One day as I was walking about the yard and midataing [meditating] on the subject of religion my friend came out of the house and addressed me with these words—'Fields,' says he, 'I can tell you there is a great many people getting religion and I think we ought to begin to think of our souls'." Fields replied that he had just had the same thought. So they tried jointly to devise a prayer,

> and it was right funy to have heard our prayers for you may be sure they were a composition of our own make, which was bad enough, I can tell you, but as bad as they were we were like the old woman . . . who could say nothing but January and febevary which she continued to say until her soul converted, and so it must be with all who will bow themselves at the foot of mercy with a broken heart and a contrite spirit.

Cook was unusually well educated. In the tense months following the Nat Turner uprising, he recalled, "a colored person could not be seen with a book in his hand, but all the books I had, had been given me by my owners and therefore I kept them though many a poor fellow burned his books for fear." But his strongest facility was certainly his ear and ability to recall whole sentences and blocks of dialogue. His account of his own conversion—like Aaron Spivey's—went through numerous stages of near completion, then set back, then fresh awakening, but unlike Spivey's was filled with wit and endearing self-deprecation. Perhaps Cook was writing for himself, as he claimed, but he also spoke directly to an unidentified audience he variously called "you" and "an enliten community." More plausibly, Cook like other black evangelicals experienced in salvation a sense of liberation from fear and anxiety of entirely different order from that of white Christians.

Cook's "observations" on his spiritual condition moved through a labyrinth of anecdotes, conversations, and remembered rumination. His pilgrimage to conversion contained nine stages: (1) a vision he had of simultaneously seeing "heaven and hell" and "departed souls . . . laid out on the gridiron broiling"; (2) a spiritual inertia in Cook and his friend as they became "some what nagligent about our prayers"; (3) with "firmness" of "exspression" his friend quoting "that old mama who was his grandmother—says he, she says 'who ever seek me early shall find me saeth the lord [Proverbs 8:17]' "; (4) at that point his friend, who had moved away, was converted and summoned Cook to visit him and hear about "this precious jewel" he had discovered, an invitation that seemed eerily like the voice of God speaking to Cook in the same way that he "did to our forefather in the garden of eden"; (5) like Adam, he could only respond that he heard God's voice but was "afraid of thy presents"; (6) in spite of his friend's compelling testimony, "I gave the notion out altogather as a bad Job"; (7) but God did not leave him in this resolution, "oh, how differently was I made to feel when concientes began to work with in me which brought me back to a sense of my duty"; (8) in this troubled state, he went to a dance "and while I stod on the . . . dancing . . . floorer, I all at ounce felt such a gilt and shameful feelling come over me" that he stood there "paralized"; and (9) while nothing happened immediately the painful memory had a lasting impact—"I did not stop dancing at this fright but all ways after had a dread on my mind about every thing I had done wrong"; and finally what brought this dread back repeatedly was "my fonness" for "the female sex, . . . of being where they were and of chatting with them" which "was a very hinderance to me in doing that work which god had called me to do."[1] This account of Cook's conversion corresponded closely to what Karl J. Weintraub calls the Augustine model of autobiography in which "the stress lies very heavily on the . . . inner necessity of the steps whereby the perversely willing creature, resisting the guiding hand of an ununderstood divine will, is being turned in the direction of the creature's true fulfillment."[2] Cook's explanation conforms exactly to this model:

> like the great rock fish [striped bass] that is hung by the gills and runs off with the line untill he is over come by that power which is above him and then is taken into the canoe, so we are the instruments of god's grace; when we fought against him all we know how he at last conquores us and brings us into his sheep fould that we may see what we are . . . and enjoy by yealing to his will.[3]

Cook's life after conversion was a series of episodes reminding him anew that, as a child of God, he was living a protected life. A recalcitrant "grey mare which periodically refused to be ridden" illustrated this conviction. After a half-mile gallop one day, the mare suddenly turned into an orchard, "right under a limb and struck my head right smack dash against it" knocking him to the ground unconscious. He regained consciousness to find the horse standing triumphantly

Sanctification and Consciousness

over him; "it was gods mercy she did not kill me." That close call reminded him of his boyhood fear of dogs and one instance in which, after being chased for a quarter mile, he was badly bitten by a dog— "the second event in the history of my life which I beleave that the hand of god did preserve me from death." He was seriously injured unloading pine rails; his recovery prompted him "to say within my own heart, with peter, this must be the lord." He recounted in great detail his "courts ship" of his wife, Mary, and her conversion and baptism at the First Baptist Church in Richmond. His autobiography concluded with an explanation of his own education, which began when a white playmate taught him to spell and others began to notice that he "was one of the aptes children that ever took a book in hand." Here too his conversion transformed the meaning of his experience. "I thought I knewd enough and stop learning untill after I was a man grown and after I was converted, I then just saw what I stood in kneed of when I was almost too old, as I thought, to learn any more."[4]

How much more Cook learned is not known, but by the 1870s he was a successful minister in Alexandria and Richmond, a medical doctor with a large library, and a prominent conservative political figure in Reconstruction politics. His political career after emancipation bore out the impression given in his 1847 memoir of prudence and confident association with whites. A strong champion of black voting rights and political action, he was also conciliatory in dealing with conservative white Virginians. He was a prominent delegate to a black political convention in Virginia in August 1865 and received an anonymous threat: "Beware! beware! Fields Cook, you and other negroes will die before the autumn leaves fall upon the unavenged graves of the many Southerners . . . buried through our land. . . . Slavery . . . was Virginia's only anchor. Beware! you are all doomed." Cook defiantly told the delegates to ignore the letter, that he would willingly sacrifice his life. The convention then joined in singing "My country 'tis of thee, sweet land of liberty, of thee I sing . . . ," as moving an evocation of spiritual and racial solidarity as "We Shall Overcome" would be a century later.[5]

Cook's struggle to make his own way as slave and freedman, and the way in which his evangelical beliefs undergirded and directed that quest, were strikingly similar to the experience of another prominent black leader in Reconstruction, James Thomas Rapier, of Alabama. "There has been a great revival here," he wrote in 1857 to his older brother, John, living in the Minnesota territory, "and it is still going

The Antebellum Era

on." "By the help of God, I have made peace with my Savior, which you and all men must do if you want to see His face." Several points in this confession, which opened a letter seeking to proselytize his brother, call for attention. Deliverance came to Rapier only with the *help* of God; it originated in an act of emotional volition—making peace with the Savior. Conversion, moreover, divided humanity into mutually exclusive spheres—those who could "see His face" and those who could not. Rapier's theology, as one would expect in nineteenth-century Canada—where Rapier, a free black from Alabama went for his schooling—was thoroughly Arminian, and his conversion united into a coherent whole the warring fragments of his youthful experience. Conversion caused a turning away from youthful passions of drinking, cursing, fighting, and wenching. It was from the weight of these sinful burdens that he felt delivered.[6]

His insistence that John Rapier should follow his example echoed the influence on both brothers of their father whose letters to them were replete with admonitions to "settle debts," "save money," "stay away from liquor," and "say nothing but is right." When James explained to John that "your sins are almost without number," he made it clear that he was not just talking about innate depravity; "they are much more than mine," he emphasized sternly, "but you will [read] in Paul's letter to Timothy [I Timothy 1:15] where he says Christ came to this world to save the chief of sinners of whom Paul was the chief." Little wonder John snorted in reaction, "Letter from James.... Professed Religion. Damned Fool."[7]

Rapier's letter to his brother contained several other Biblical references emphasizing both the direct action of God and the imperative duty of the believer to practice strenuous moral and spiritual discipline. He cited Ezekiel 33:11 and the ninth Psalm as evidence that "the wicked shall be turned into Hell." Both passages depicted a God actively concerned with the choices people would make: Ezekiel reporting God's message to Israel that "I have no pleasure in the death of the wicked" and desire only that "you turn back from your evil ways, for why will you die, oh house of Israel?" and Psalm 9:16, "the Lord has made himself known. He has executed judgment"; verse 5, "thou hast rebuked the nations, thou hast destroyed the wicked," all leading in verses 19 and 20 to a vision of salvation: "Arise O Lord. Let not man prevail. Let the nations be judged before Thee. Put them in fear, O Lord. Let the nations know that they are but men." Rapier's citation of John 3:3 ("You must be born again") came from Christ's

Sanctification and Consciousness

injunction to Nicodemus to "enter" the Kingdom by new birth in water and spirit, and his appeal to II Corinthians 5:17 cited Paul's assurance that believers are "new creatures." Both underscored the sense of conversion as a transforming experience.[8]

That experience occurred for Rapier in a world of disorienting confusion and evil. "I think the 56 chapter of Isaiah says there's no peace, says my God to the wicked," he told John in an accurate quote of Isaiah 57:21, a verse that reminded Rapier of his proclivity to cursing, always a dangerous exercise of temper and anger for a black man in a white community. And Romans 8:9, which Rapier paraphrased as "without holiness no man shall see the Lord" is even more stark in the King James: "They that are of the flesh cannot please God." Rapier's sensitivity to scriptural depictions of an alien world devoid of humanity corresponded with a vivid self-image: "I am merely a stranger and a pilgrim on the long groundless sorrow. My home is in heaven."[9]

This sense of being a pilgrim, like Fields Cook's feeling of being drawn by God along a course in life that he could not fully comprehend, revealed to Rapier that personal sorrow was to be part of the pattern of his life. Never marrying, and with no close personal friends, he told a cousin in 1872 that "the days of poetry are over with me and I must settle down to the stiff prose.... I have been surrounded by no one who cared for me or for whom I cared...." His political career during Reconstruction demanded all of his energies and emotional resources. "I am at my office nearly all the Time. Sleep there," he explained; "my breast appears to be innocent of all those social feelings necessary to make our life happy." His deepest satisfaction came from remembering his teacher and mentor in Ontario, a Presbyterian minister named William King, whose "lively interest in me as well as in all the boys who attended the log house and church in Buxton" had decisively shaped his initially buoyant approach to political combat in Reconstruction Alabama and his conception of politics as a form of service to others.[10]

Cook and Rapier added autobiographical depth to the historical record of evangelical Christianity among black people in antebellum and Reconstruction southern society. They embraced the same theology as white converts: Rapier's commonplace but nonetheless vivid vision of "see[ing]" the face of Jesus, and Cook's more venturesome recognition of a common "spirit in man", which divine inspiration could richly interpret. But like other blacks, they arranged the elements in the evangelical belief structure in ways that enhanced their

The Antebellum Era

own sense of dignity and spiritual autonomy. Salvation freed Cook
from "hertful" rejection at the hands of whites and supplanted subjection to his—admittedly—permissive master with a summons to under-
take "that work which god had called me to do." Rapier's frequent
citations to Scripture identified texts depicting God's discipline of
believers, the very quality he considered essential if blacks were to
persevere in their search for freedom. The "long groundless sorrow"
he found at the core of experience was the ultimate discipline. It
echoed and probably paraphrased the Psalmist's lament, "I am a
stranger in the earth, hide not thy commandments from me. My soul
breaketh for the longing that it hath unto thy judgments."[11]

The proclamation of liberation and the discovery of ecstasy in
the midst of suffering received special priority and emphasis in the
testimony of black evangelicals. This quality was particularly striking
in the preaching of black women like Zilpha Elaw, a free black born in
Philadelphia around 1790, who was converted at a Kentucky camp
meeting in 1817. Without a license or other authorization she became
a lay preacher in New Jersey. In the spring of 1828 she spent several
weeks in Maryland and Virginia in real danger of arrest and enslavement. "The Lord who sent me out to preach his gospel ... in these
regions of wickedness," she recalled, "preserved me in my going out
and my coming in ... during my sojourn on the soil of slavery." Psalm
121:8. A memorable experience was delivering a sermon in a Methodist chapel in Mt. Tabor, Maryland, to the white "proprietors" of the
church, who filled the seats, and slaves crammed into the gallery. Her
text was Luke 2:10, "and the angel said unto them, fear not; for be-
hold I bring you good tidings of great joy which shall be to all people," a passage of particular vibrancy when spoken by a woman. Her
account of what transpired kept its focus on the totality of the event
but also caught the racial variations in the response of the people and
the political and sexual dynamics of the situation involving the regular minister, Mr. Beard, herself, and the people under the influence of
what she was sure was the Holy Spirit:

> All were alike affected. Mr. Beard requested the congregation to restrain
> the expression of their feelings, but the powerful operation of the Holy
> spirit disdained the limits prescribed by man's reason and bore down
> all the guards of human propriety and order. The presence of the Holy
> Spirit filled the place, and moved the people as the wind moves the
> forest boughs. Mr. Beard's cautions were unavailing; the coloured peo-

Sanctification and Consciousness

ple in the gallery wept aloud and raised vehement cries to heaven; the people below were also unable to restrain their emotions; and all wept beneath the inspirations of the Spirit of grace.

In characteristic evangelical fashion, Mrs. Elaw specified the stages of sanctification at work in this tumultuous scene: "mercy, love, and grace . . . streamed . . . into our little earthly sanctuary to staunch the bleeding heart, remove its guilt, reform its character, and give new impulse to its powers."[12]

Evangelicals distinguished between autonomy and freedom—between the role a person played in society and the integrity one brought to dealings with others. Many slaves thereby acquired what Albert J. Raboteau calls "a sense of personal dignity and an attitude of moral superiority to their masters."[13] A striking example is a letter written in 1821 by an unnamed North Carolina slave to his former owner and minister, a Presbyterian named John Fort. "Master John," it began, "I want permation of you pleas to speak A few words to you—I hope you do not think me too bold Sir. I make my wants known to you because you are, I believe—the oldest and most experienced that I know of." The concerns the slave called his "wants" came in the form of a series of penetrating questions: Why had Fort turned his back to slave worshipers and ignored their spiritual needs? Was there more financial gain in preaching to whites? Did white people know or even care about the salvation of blacks? How could the prayers of whites for the redemption of the world be answered, much less offered, when tainted by greed and racism? These questions were all the more thunderous for their calm, unacrimonious tone. And like an Old Testament prophesy, the letter ended with a "thus saith the Lord" announcement of moral and ethical imperatives: "I now leave it to you and your aids to consider on. I hope you will read it to their church if you think proper. It is likely I never will hear from you on this subject as I live far from you. I dont wish you to take any of these things to yourself if nothing is due. do your god justis in this case and you will doo me the same.

Your Sirvent Sir"[14]

Cook and Rapier, explicitly, and Elaw and John Fort's sometime parishioner, implicitly, affirmed a widespread nineteenth-century evangelical assumption that human life contained a series of phases over which the individual had little control but that were significant

The Antebellum Era

parts of the context within which sanctification occurred. This conception made youthful encounters with both temptation and divine guidance moments of high drama and peculiar fascination. Anne Randolph Meade Page recorded such an episode in the 1820s involving her young children, Francis and Mary Frances. Francis accidentally struck his sister in the eye. Mrs. Page and her sister first scolded the boy for his careless roughness and then noticed that Mary Frances "sat sullen and mute." When asked to kiss her brother in order to "pacify his penitent grief," she angrily refused: "*No*, I *patted him* and he knocked *me*. I can't kiss him. I can't love him." The more the two women commanded the girl to embrace her brother, the more adamantly she refused. "I thought her state of mind shewed so dangerous a temper of implacability," Mrs. Page explained, that "I determined to devote myself to its investigation and, by the direction of our divine guide, to its removal." The dual purposes of human investigation and divine assistance did indeed frame the transaction that followed. Initially a subject of the investigation, the boy soon sensed the benefits of more active participation. "His aunt and I tried by caresses and every argument we could think of to quiet his sorrow," and failing that, they turned their attention back to the girl: "in vain we begged Mary to kiss him, and love him, which seemed from his manner, of our attending to our addresses to her, . . . the dear little fellow thought needful to his peace." The mother argued with the girl, then pleaded, then quoted the words of a hymn, "deal with one another as you'd have &c.," and all the while "*he* kept his eyes towards her."

Exhausting these preliminary psychological remedies, the Page household came to the hard crux of the problem of human willfulness. "I told her the danger of her thus obeying Satan, instead of . . . God—hardness still remained unsoftened." If warnings of dallying with the devil only reinforced the girl's defiance of parental, moral authority, it was time to use stronger, more intimate suasion: "I told her that instead of laying in my arms when she awoke in the night, I should refuse her approach and keep her at her distance in her own corner of the bed. Still she was inflexible." Systematically peeling away the layers of motivation and self-interest, Ann Page had laid bare the theological issue raised by Mary Frances's intransigence. "At length it struck me to present to her the sins she every day committed," and with them the theology of forgiveness: Jesus had "suffered a great deal" to secure her forgiveness for the hostility she was then showing her brother; she could only receive that blessing if she first forgave

Sanctification and Consciousness

her brother, and that as difficult as that step might be for her to take, the ability to take it was a gift of God which by faith she could invoke—"if she would only *try*." That categorical demand could be softened by setting it in context: "her saviour loved her so well," the mother assured the daughter, "that he would surely help her and . . . and then she would be happy."[15]

This tangle of theological and emotional considerations, Mrs. Page recognized, was only adding to the problem, and good evangelical that she was, she determined to get the theology of the problem straight even at the cost of plunging into its complexity. "Some time in the course of the evening, I reminded her how grateful she ought to feel to that good God who had sent out of her heart the dreadful feel[ing?] that she knew old Satan had burdened her with . . . It was God who gave her success when she tried." The issue of human versus divine agency—the most important area in which evangelicals broke new theological ground—finally ended the impasse between mother and daughter. " 'Yes', she said, 'but I did *some* myself.' Here was an opening," Mrs. Page exulted, "to explain the under agency, needful on her part, and yet press (from her inability to do what she knew was right at first) the *truth* of God's unseen power giving her success." The whole mysterious process of divine agency undergirding and empowering human capacity seemed to flow into the girl's mind with startling emotional impact:

> the state of her mind was of full animated enjoyment till bed-time. She went to sleep quite happy and in the night, on turning to me between sleep and waking, as usual to find her arms around me impressed my mind extremely by her slow, emphatic pronunciation of these words, "*Mama*, I wish you wou'd teach me what is *ne ces* sa *ry* for me to do" [broken italics indicating pronunciation]. I was so struck with the manner of her speaking that I asked her, "what did you say my dear?" and she repeated every syllable . . . with the same slow emphatic voice.

Within this occasion of bonding—mother to daughter, child to savior—Mary Frances had passed through a critical transition in her life, one peculiar to childhood and possible only in an evangelical household.[16]

The breaking of Mary Frances's willfulness, through successive appeals to her duty, sympathy, reason, need for physical affection, and piety, was typical of evangelical childrearing practices. "It is the duty of the parent," explained Francis Wayland, the Baptist President of

The Antebellum Era

Brown University in 1835, "to eradicate ... the wrong propensities in his children. He should watch with ceaseless vigilance for the first appearances of pride, obstinacy, malice, envy, vanity, cruelty, revenge, anger, lying ... and strive to extirpate them before they have gained firmness by age or vigor by indulgence." Wayland's litany of childhood vices began, significantly, with "pride." The conquering of pride was the supreme test of religious maturity for child and parent alike. "I have been thinking of you O, so often (once a day is my rule; but spontaneously, I mean)," Anne Meade Page wrote to Mary Fitzhugh Custis shortly after the birth of Mrs. Custis's first child; "your babe ... is a continual warning to your heart to rejoice with trembling—to remember what a momentous trust you are in possession of—and not to allow yourself to dwell too much on its present deliciousness." Stern duties lay ahead, as did unavoidable sorrows. "If the Lord's servant, *Job*, was afflicted ... , who am I not to have sore dispensations permitted me also? Let no mother therefore be deterred ... from a constant devotedness of all her child's powers to God." No amount of care and self-scrutiny exerted in these duties was excessive, Mrs. Page wrote, for "what if my child is the present captive of Satan?" Neither mother nor daughter were safe from the evil one: the joy of having a child and the responsibility of raising offspring were both gifts of the creator but were enjoyed "in so much unworthiness, so much short-coming in every way that I am to be shewn all this in its true colors by the temporary ill-success of my commission." Against all her desires to be a pious mother, sinfulness meant that "the service of her [the child's] maker and redeemer were made abhorent to my soul."[17]

These themes of unworthiness, of potential alienation from God always lurking in the corners of thought and conduct, and of duty to combat the evil one with repeated scourgings of abasement, defined in much of its complexity the phenomenon of pride. Pride was awesome because it was so pervasive in the antebellum South. In a society where the boundaries separating acceptable from antisocial behavior were blurred, in which the untrammelled judgment of the individual bore the brunt of dictating behavior, and where strength, virility, integrity, self-assurance, and hostility to external control were hallmarks of virtuous conduct, pride was a positive value and moral imperative as well as source of sin and cause of moral downfall. No problem so vexed southern evangelical clergy, therefore, as how to deal with pride in a proud culture. One solution was to envelop it in a larger value system: the defense of honor.[18] Evangelicals believed that pride could

Sanctification and Consciousness

be managed and even tamed through an appeal to honor—the human passion superceding sensual gratification and ego fulfillment. "Leaving argument and testimony out of view," the Presbyterian minister in Richmond, Virginia, William Jessup Armstrong, explained in an elegant formulation of the concept, "no man ... without doing violence to his own feelings, ... can deny his obligation to love God, nor can any reflecting person feel innocent or safe under the charge of being destitute of love to him." Honor, as well as pride, meant respecting and responding to one's most elevated feelings, fulfilling deeply felt obligations, and preserving the innocence of emotional bonds to superiors—especially to God. There were, of course, extreme cases in which honor had lost control of pride—Armstrong attributed them to "impenitrable obduracy which is the sad symptom of a seared conscience and the fearful presage of impending ruin." But for most people, even those "whose whole conduct declare that their hearts are alienated from him," there remained a healthy tension between self and conscience, between what Armstrong called "loftier pretension" to piety and actual confidence of being, like the children of Israel, "a peculiar people of GOD."[19]

In a sermon preached in New Jersey and Virginia during the 1820s on Hebrews 9:28—"Christ was offered to bear the sins of many"—Armstrong made the tie to honor still more explicit. The "vicarious sufferings which he endured on our behalf ... constituted a real and efficacious expiation for sin. Sin is the transgression of the law. When a law is transgressed, its honor is stained, its authority is destroyed." The theology was conventional but the language summoned forth images that were powerful and compelling to antebellum southerners: "vicarious suffering" by a brave, solitary, male figure; law transgressed, honor stained, and most telling of all, authority destroyed. The honor in which the law was held by its observers was for Armstrong a matter of delicacy and high drama, for when it was violated the honor of the law itself was called into question, "it brings his authority [i.e., the authority of the promulgator of the law] into contempt and encourages all who please to trample upon it." But sure and certain punishment reversed the process, "averts these consequences, ... magnifies the law, and makes it honorable." Only by keeping this view of divine justice clearly and fully before the eyes of human beings, could God vindicate "the offering of Christ" as "a real and efficacious atonement for sin." The crucifixion was therefore the supreme exhibition of honor in human history, and Armstrong's ter-

The Antebellum Era

minology again presented it in terms familiar to anyone who had ever seen a southern gentleman: "the transcendent dignity" of Christ's acceptance of unmerited punishment. And integrally linked to this vindication of the power of honor, was the lesson of God's authority: "let us learn from this subject," Armstrong concluded the sermon, "our obligations to be devoted to the service of Christ."[20]

The measured appreciation of the sanctifying process was an even more demanding evangelical exercise. It drew deeply on nineteenth-century romanticism with which it shared an impulse to relate and fuse all of reality into a single celebration of being. A young woman in the Valley of Virginia used the experience of climbing a mountainside with three companions on a "sultry" summer afternoon in 1831 as the occasion to examine her feelings about this phenomenon. Upon reaching "the summit," she recounted to a friend some months later,

> we were indeed presented with a scene of extreme... beauty; the mountain on which we stood steep and rocky, while all around rose woody hills whose bold and towering trees, sometimes nearly meeting and then receding, disclosed the picturesque outline of the luxuriant plantations which lay within their sheltering grandeur. The lengthening rays of the departing sun, glancing obliquely upon the landscape, rendered the scene still more lovely. A soft mist arose and enveloped the lower part of the hills. A dewey freshness now pervaded the air which was doubly welcome to *us*. All nature seemed hushed in silent pleasure.

This description was integral to the writer's own religious sensibility. "I viewed the scene with a feeling of pain and delight," she continued,

> which I did not understand and which I was afraid to express lest I should incur the ridicule of Scott [a companion], of whose superior powers I at that time stood much in awe. Those feelings, however, made a deep impression on me. My mind felt so dark, so confined amidst such splendid displays of—nature, I was going to say. But... why should we substitute a mere idea in room of that glorious Being who had created such profusion of magnificence and beauty and who has formed in the human heart capacity to feel so deeply what is magnificent and beautiful? Why, by ascribing this glory to a vague idea, separate ourselves still farther from its real and ever present author who so powerfully solicits and demands our affections and claims even the first

Sanctification and Consciousness

place in our hearts? Now I understand why my mind was so bound, so confined upon viewing such scenes.... I find it is because love is the natural consequence of admiration that we feel a kind of oppression in our feelings when we intensely admire the glories around us without raising our hearts to their author.[21]

This kind of ecstatic self-examination generated its own undercurrents of anxiety. "You have discovered the difference between the religion of the imagination and that of the heart and understanding," she congratulated her friend: "you are convinced that the former has no value and . . . the last is absolutely necessary." The dilemma of that faith was that the understanding is weak and the heart rises in "opposition to the strict and spiritual doctrines of the New Testament." Only by deeper and deeper submersion into a Christocentric sublime could the believer know "the purest, the most exalted happiness" arising from "our only Savior, our strength, our light, our peace, our *all*." Imagination, in this dichotomy, was a thing of the flesh, a corrupt human yearning to be given up through the obedient stewardship of a receptive heart and a sanctified understanding. The process was not easy or simple:

> With much reluctance I yealded up my long cherished hopes of happiness from the created things of this world and often, when I have thought them quite overcome, they would return with tantilizing influence. Indeed, I required more than ordinary means to wean my affections from objects of time and raise them to a source of felicity which the world cannot claim or give. The rod of affliction was applied by the judicious hand of a physician who would not err, and at last I was able to say it was well to be chastened and humbly kiss the rod of correction.[22]

When evangelicals spoke of chastisement and the rod of correction, they were talking about education in its broadest sense as the shaping of character within a prevailing culture. Before we can appreciate the searing experience of evangelical education, we need to examine the quest for knowledge and understanding in the larger culture of which evangelicals were a part. Two North Carolina student notebooks, kept in the 1820s, reflected that larger culture. Neither was a wholeheartedly evangelical document, but both were tinged with evangelicalism and illuminate the hazy borderland between evangelical and nonevangelical Protestantism.

The Antebellum Era

One was kept by Louisa Lenoir, a student at the Moravian school, Salem Academy, in North Carolina; it lacked the evangelical focus on conversion and the new birth but its Moravian devotionalism and fascination with faith as a tamer of the heart paralleled evangelical sensibility. The other copybook belonged to William S. Pettigrew, grandson of the first Episcopal bishop of North Carolina and himself a future Episcopal priest and planter. The Pettigrews scorned revivalism and Protestant sectarianism but had a lively fascination with the vagaries of human nature and sense of God's omnipotence in a sinful world closer to dissenter than episcopal theological taste.[23]

Lenoir's copybook contained nineteen essays, probably paraphrased from assigned readings, on topics like devotion, temptation, idleness, modesty, and timidity; the Pettigrew book contained some one hundred and fifty maxims, each written typically between five and twenty-five times as handwriting exercises and moral indoctrination. Predictably, Lenoir's education trained her in the creative use of introspection, Pettigrew's in self-confident interpersonal behavior, respectively befitting the needs of genteel women and men in the early nineteenth century. What the two students shared in common was a schooling and family upbringing Philip Greven has called "moderate," and aimed to discipline the self, to be wary of human weaknesses, and to regard self-control as a threshold of creativity.[24]

Lenoir's copybook entries fell into six categories:

1. Basic assumptions. These included her definition of devotion as "intercourse betwixt us and God," and a Goethe poem in translation entitled "The Divine"—"Hail to the spirits! the unknown sublime, revealed by faith alone. . . . "[25]

2. Human nature and its transcendence. Her discourse on human weakness linked to a perfect Creator concluded with the injunction to "content thyself with deserving praise and thy posterity shall rejoice in hearing it."[26]

3. Specific sources of moral downfall. Here appeared discussions of the temptress, selfishness, vanity and ostentation, idleness, and timidity.[27]

4. Patterns of moral downfall. These passages warned that folly and shallowness and an untamed ego led inevitably to the dissipation of human effort.[28]

5. Imperatives. These admonitions extolled moderation and aesthetic accomplishment.[29]

Sanctification and Consciousness

6. Strategies of moral combat. These included exhortations to duty, industry, female education, study, and modesty, "sanctioned by truth and justice ... as the means of exposing sophistry."[30]

The largest number of Pettigrew's copybook maxims prescribed behavior modification, for example: "Diligence is industry and constant application in work";[31] "Love the society of your parents and receive good advice";[32] and "Love your studies."[33]

Other Pettigrew maxims called on young men to emulate authentic moral behavior in others and to think of themselves as future role models for the young: "Friendship and honesty are the strongest ties of good breeding";[34] "Let innocence and prudence accompany all your diversions";[35] "Be zealous in the dissemination of virtuous principles";[36] "Purity of intention is required of all the sons of men";[37] and "Contend not for honours destitute of merit."[38]

At a practical level, many of the maxims set forth a style of interpersonal relations: "Question no man about his profession of religion";[39] "Unavoidable misfortunes should excite our compassion";[40] "Deal justly with all persons black or white";[41] "Give to everyone his due and pay all honest debts";[42] and "Questions on deliberate subjects require deliberate answers."[43]

Finally, as one might expect in a culture permeated with Scottish Common Sense moralism, the Pettigrew maxims argued that society itself consisted of a web of shared perceptions and obligations: "Temperance, industry, and economy are avenues to wealth";[44] "Public and private utility should excite one to action";[45] "Friendship and honesty are the strongest ties of good society";[46] and "Nothing is so beautiful as constancy, truth, and charity."[47] Presented graphically (figure 1), these two modes of middle-class moral education moved, in Lenoir's case from general to the specific conduct and in Pettigrew's from the concrete observations to a mature understanding of reality.

The education of women in this model, then, began with spiritual guidance and culminated in strategies for virtuous, pious behavior while the moral training of males started with direct observation of social reality and moved from that point toward a mature understanding of the functioning of the culture.

Evangelicals did not frown on moderate admonitions, but they framed the problem of knowing and being very differently. They inhabited a world in which temptation and impulse constantly bombarded the individual. Replying to charges that he had slandered a

The Antebellum Era

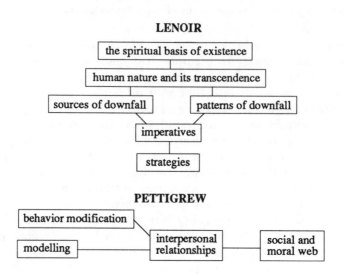

Figure 1. Lenoir.

political candidate, Jesse Mercer of Grantsville, Virginia, declared that "I never indulged myself in such expressions in the days of my vanity, and since I have been a professor of religion, I have never made any such virulent expressions." What he had done was to ask his friends not to support a candidate simply from motives of "goodwill" when doing so would "gratify the resentment" of bitter and censorious people toward his opponent. "I did this from the purest sentiments of friendship and to accomplish what I thought also to be a political *good*."[48]

Induced by experience and training to regard the human heart as unpredictable and constantly in flux, evangelicals made their wonder at its creation the locus of thought and desire. "I thank my stars that I differ so mutch with him [her husband] with regard to contentment," a woman in Missouri wrote to her sister in Virginia;

I have been taught in the Scholl of affliction of the impropriety of placing my affections on enjoyment that is soon fleeting. I do not wish

Sanctification and Consciousness

for you to infer from this resentment that I have lost all affection for my kindred far be it from me for I often think of them but am a ware that in case I was with you all that I could not enjoy myself as I yous [used] to do, and even if I could the same afflicting could reach me their. And when I reflect on the goodness of the Lord I am induced to put my trust in him for he surly has been mindful of me, circumstances that I thought I never could support under them, yet he has been my safe refuge.[49]

Instead of gauging progress in self-mastery over time, as in the dominant culture of moderate, personal discipline, evangelicals felt pinioned between a corrupt, personal past, in which time lay blighted along with the human spirit, and a fleeting future on this earth. "We have but a short period upon earth to make peace with God," an Alabama man wrote,

and upon that inch of time, eternity, distressed or eternity happy, depends. A longer probation would probably not be beneficial to man, for the sinner whose days extend beyond seventy years will be beyond all calculation sinful and poluted. On the other hand, the Christian in three score years and ten has sufficient trial for the steadfastness of his faith, for his growth in grace, for the exercise of supreme love to God in this imperfect world.

The care and exactitude of that assessment of stewardship and definition of sanctification were clearly intentional, for they preceded an important announcement: "Strange as it may appear to you, I am now a member of the Methodist Church . . . , not that I believe the Methodist church pirfect or even containing my views of theology, for it is of human origin, administered through human agents, and, of course partakes of their infermities; but I believe that all the different branches of the christian church do enjoy the means of grace."[50]

The concession that the Methodist, like other churches, provided access to God's grace while it also partook of human infirmity was a characteristically Methodist attitude. The Methodists grew between 1784 and the 1840s from a radical offshoot sect into the largest denomination in the United States. Circuit riding brought Methodist preachers into the vast rural hinterland of the new nation and its expanding western frontier, and the warm, uncomplicated, optimistic theology they preached triggered an outpouring of allegiance. Still more important, Methodists found in towns and cities a loyal follow-

The Antebellum Era

ing of professional men, merchants, and prosperous landowners, especially self-made men of wealth.[51]

Once in positions of influence in churches in the southern states, these laymen demanded and secured modification of the Methodist rule excluding unrepentant slaveowners—that is masters unwilling to initiate eventual manumission proceedings—from the communion table. Methodist compliance with proslavery sensibilities did not occur without anguish and struggle;[52] James O'Kelly's courageous denunciation of slavery had expressed the convictions of scores of early circuit riders in the South. O'Kelly soon left the Methodists because he rejected the authority of bishops and superintendents, and by 1815 the antislavery itinerants had lost the fight to proscribe slaveowning among communicants.[53] But that defeat was not a simple triumph of hypocrisy over moral idealism. Methodists in the South by the 1820s and 30s convinced themselves that, if they were to convert slaveowners, their church would have to divest itself of its abolitionist reputation. They also concluded that to fight sin within slaveowning families, the church must foster household devotions where masters, wives, children, and slaves would join together in prayer and Bible reading. In return, a Methodist manual, *The Home-Altar: An Appeal in Behalf of Family Worship* (1850), predicted "peace, happiness, and successful labor" would bless the farms of Christians. As Methodists touched a deeply responsive chord in southern society—as they became guardians of the sanctity of sectional values—Methodism found itself awash in the individualistic, acquisitive, self-assertive mores of the people.[54]

These attitudes quickly intermingled with the piety and moral earnestness of the white populace. With good reason some slaveowners wanted the opposite to occur: piety and moral earnestness to permeate the self-assertiveness and energy of their slaves. The minister of the strictly Calvinist Associate Reformed Presbyterian Church (ARP) in the Abbeville District of South Carolina, and sixty-one slaveowning church members, petitioned the state legislature in 1838 to repeal an 1834 Nullification era statute prohibiting the teaching of slaves to read:

We do not desire you to open the way for us to give our servants a *liberal education*, but we pray you to allow us the liberty, if we think proper, to teach our servants to read with so much fluency and correctness that

Sanctification and Consciousness

they may be able to peruse the word of God and other religious books with pleasure and profit to their souls.

With unusual candor and detail, this document articulated that the slaveowner's duty was one of spiritual stewardship over his household, a belief held strongly by the members of this small denomination of theological traditionalists.

The petitioners implored the legislature not to dismantle the Christian and republican mechanisms for inculcating virtue in the state. They pointed to Article 8 of the South Carolina constitution allowing "free exercise of religious profession and worship" so long as religious activity did not promote "licentiousness" or appear "inconsistent with the peace or safety of this State." That reservation was, of course, an enormous potential infringement of free exercise of the very sort that Madison had with difficulty dissuaded Virginians from adopting in 1785. But the Abbeville ARP petitioners argued vigorously that nothing licentious or contrary to public safety could possibly emanate from slaves' reading in Ephesians God's injunction to be obedient to their masters "with fear and trembling in singleness of heart as unto Christ." If the quiet reading of Scripture was so dangerous, then why did the state not prohibit slaves from attending worship services where the Bible was read aloud, the petitioners demanded to know, and for that matter why did not the state exclude slaves from the far more contaminating influence of Fourth of July celebrations and militia musters? Set beside the whole range of social outlets for human energy and potential traps for the morally unwary, the petition argued, Bible-reading classes for slaves ranked very high as means of cultivating virtue and protecting public order.

Christianity had a unique capacity to protect society from the worst proclivities of human nature, the Abbeville petitioners declared, because Scripture was the word of God and, moreover, because "experience fully proves that those servants who live in religious families and have been taught to read and understand their duty from the word of God are, as a general rule, more trusty . . . than those . . . whose souls have been entirely neglected." To thwart the work of creating enclaves of peacefulness and piety within families and churches was to violate the public good and represented an *unwarrantable interference* of the State in church affairs." What was most unwarrantable—literally, most presumptuous in substituting human for divine authority—was the sanction the law gave to "common informer [s],"

The Antebellum Era

the "most degraded of all characters," to spy upon, report, and cause to be prosecuted those persons who conscientiously taught their slaves to read the Bible. The petition came close to promising that the law would be broken, for the missionary principle in Christianity made efforts to convert the "heathen" an absolute imperative for believers; "to enact laws excluding that glorious light from a portion of our households" blighted the affection the petitioners had for their slaves, and affection was an impulse of the heart wholly separate from the "mere mercenary considerations" that were an unavoidable part of slaveowning.[55] The Abbeville petition was not memorable for its moral grandeur, nor was it an apology for slavery. Rather it declared the mission of families and communities to throw a cloak of devotionalism over their corporate selves.

The onrush of evangelicalism into the center of southern culture not only imbued the religious impulse with the characteristics of the dominant white, middle-class society, it also slowed the momentum of the evangelical movement. Evangelicals sought to accelerate anew the tempo of growth by rooting the sanctifying process in the richest of all known spiritual soil: revivalism. Mid-nineteenth-century revivals aimed less at converting the unchurched and more at backsliders who had grown weary in the way of the Cross. This routinizing of revivalism from the 1820s onward may appear to have been a less authentic religious activity than Whitefield's services in the 1740s or Methodist and Baptist revivals just past the turn of the century. What *was* authentic about later southern revivalism was the recognition of the dependence of evangelical proclamation on human contrivance as well as divine sanction. The relationship between the two was a mystery and a spur to action. "Religion with us is at a low ebb," wrote Samuel Benedict, a free black in Savannah preparing to emigrate to Liberia in 1839.

> We have with us this year as Pastor a Mr. Pierce, son of the celebrated Dr. Pierce of this conference. He is certainly a very smart and pious young preacher, but so far his preaching has not been *blessed*. But we continue to pray that the Lord may in the midst of this spiritual drought visit us and send a refreshing shower from above which may produce a plentiful harvest.[56]

Crowds ranging from a few hundred to some five thousand came to a week-long Methodist camp meeting near Warrenton, Virginia, in

Sanctification and Consciousness

mid-August 1822. The organizers cleared a hilltop of underbrush, and on the stone- and leaf-covered ground constructed rough benches, an altar and pulpit, and nearby tables for serving food. Forty to fifty families brought tents, some "very commodius and quite elegant" and pitched them next to the worship and feeding area. In an adjoining field young people who did not attend the services milled about socializing and enjoying refreshments. Everywhere the camp police with special insignia in their hats strode about officiously. A team of preachers took turns speaking. "One got up (as evidently as vain of his beauty as could be)," reported one critical but not unsympathetic male witness, and "launched out into a most passionate and affecting oration; about mid way of which, the gate of the altar was opened, and all who were desirous of entering were invited to do so; a number of persons both male and female immediately crowded in and fell upon their knees when three or four priests descended from the pulpit and commenced the most pompous and affecting prayers." Repeatedly invoking images of dead parents waiting to greet their children in paradise against a background of "screams and shrieks, . . . horrid and awful," and ministers were even amused at this spectacle and could be seen

> laughing in their sleave at the effect they had produced. . . . But amidst all this hurly-burly and mockery . . . I observed, as I thought, *one* sincere and real penitent. He had turned his back to the crowd and was kneeling, with his face concealed under the preachers' stand. . . . With hands closely clenched and a trembling frame, he poured out in palsied accents the most earnest supplication, . . . convulsive sobs and the streams of large and manly tears.[57]

Competition from Methodist and Baptist revivalists cut deeply into southern Lutheran congregations. Accordingly, the Lutheran accommodation with revivalism underscored the capacity of ritual abasement and searing emotional release to reach deeply into the lives of individuals and communities and to mix adaptively with older evangelical practice. "We have reason to believe that during the last Synodical year many have experienced the power of renewing grace and are now rejoicing in the hope of the glory of God," the secretary of the South Carolina Synod, Reverend George Haltiwanger, wrote in 1833.

The Antebellum Era

Some of our legalists have been convinced of the truth of the word of God that by the deeds of the law no flesh shall be justified. Some of our formalists have been convinced by happy experience that the Kingdom consists not in meats and drinks, i.e., forms and ceremonies, but that it consists in Righteousness and peace and joy in the holy ghost, yea many who have long been sitting in nature's darkness and in the shadow of death have emerged from the same to the glorious light and liberty of the gospel of the Son of God.... Vital Godliness begins to be more sought for as the one thing needful to prepare us for the enjoyment of the world of glory.[58]

The injection of such evangelical language into southern Lutheran discourse required difficult adjustments. Benjamin Kurtz, evangelical editor of the *Lutheran Observer* in Philadelphia, chided the Seminary of the South Carolina Lutheran Synod for its failure to teach students the "new measures" of revivalism fashioned by Charles G. Finney—the anxious bench for potential converts, protracted prayer and revival meetings, and vigorous support for temperance and missionary programs. Ernest Hazelius, Professor at the Seminary, had inadvertently provoked Kurtz's scorn when he had expressed his desire to attract students "who do *not* believe in the power of the anxious bench for the conversion of sinners, but in the power of the Gospel of the Saviour whether preached by old or new measure men." "Now I want ALL THE WORLD to know," retorted one anonymous correspondent to the *Observer*, that TWO-THIRDS of the Synod of South Carolina are decided NEW MEASURE MEN" some even "within calling distance of the Theological Seminary."[59]

The controversy produced an exceptionally detailed account of a "new measures" revival that took place at St. Michael's Lutheran Church near Columbia, South Carolina, where George Haltiwanger was pastor, in July 1843. Here the emotional rhythm of the services and the pent-up needs of the worshipers meshed in just the way that the revivalists advocated and yet within the context of Lutheran practice. The South Carolina Synod had recommended that the last weekends of five-Sunday months be used for special services. Only a few attended on Friday but more came on Saturday to hear Hazelius, Rev. Jacob Moser, and Rev. Michael Rauch deliver successive sermons— "simple yet moving and servicable." Then on Sunday a prayer service and two more sermons prompted fifteen new members to come forward (ten white and five black). More than 100 took communion in celebration of this breakthrough.

Sanctification and Consciousness

The people were then dismissed for about 20 or 30 minutes and then reassembled in the church to hear another sermon, after which they who felt an interest in the prayers of God's servants and were anxious to obtain a living confidence in the atonement of Christ, so as to have rest and comfort to their souls, were invited to draw near the altar and occupy the foremost seats [the anxious bench]. The congregation commenced singing a few verses and immediately there were some moving to press forward and seemed to come in earnest with loud sobs and to the throne of grace, crowding around the altar of the Lord, manifesting a deep contrition of soul. There were several prayers offered up to the throne of grace for them but their conviction [of personal guilt] seemed to strike deeper and we had no token of relief. Some indeed were powerfully wrought on.

The cathartic triumph of the aching human frame pressing against and finally piercing unseen psychic barriers was the essential achievement of a revival. Events on Monday built toward such emotional climax of the event; an "instructive, impressive sermon" by Hazelius, who then departed for the Seminary, was followed by another sermon by Haltiwanger on the nature of revivals that summoned "those anxious to obtain pardon for their sins, longing to have rest and comfort for their souls." Then came prayers, which unlike those of the day before reached to the depths of feeling and desire. People caught up in "united strong wrestling at the footstool of mercy" for help and freedom strained every tissue to bring on a collective and individual state of submission to God and release from sinfulness. The remaining clergy—Moser, Haltiwanger, and Rauch—moved out into the congregation speaking softly to individuals "in every pew"; "a mighty fire began to kindle, it spread instantly, ran not only through the congregation in the church but laid even hold on some who were looking on from the outside through the windows until some were struck with a religious awe, . . . forced to cry from the utmost of their very soul, so loud you could have heard them from a great distance, 'O Lord, have mercy on my poor soul'."[60]

The Rev. John Bachman, pastor of the most genteel Lutheran church in the South, St. John's, Charleston, was skeptical of the value of revivalism; he told members of St. John's in Charleston who asked for a "mourner's bench" to facilitate conversion experiences in the church that such seating arrangements "would not be in accordance with Lutheran teaching and usage which relied on the Sacrament of Baptism, catechetical instuction, the rite of Confirmation and com-

The Antebellum Era

munion as all-sufficient." Nevertheless, his sense of the conservation and concentration of emotion and volition in conversion shared the evangelical understanding. Witnessing the conversion of his desperately sick daughter he wrote.

> It was my duty to instruct her and guide her in her search after perfect peace. Fervently we prayed together and long wept. Still she desired more light, greater assurance of forgiveness, and stronger evidence of God's mercy. Our prayers have now all been heard; . . . four hours yesterday she spoke of the past, the present, and the future. Her eyes were bright and her mind clear; her perceptions keen and her judgment strong; her words were submissive and her prayers fervent. Her whole soul was so full of the love of God, and the mercy of her Saviour, that she seemed almost to forget her sufferings."[61]

Looking back to Lutheran revivalism in the South a decade later, Haltiwanger depicted it as a reorganizing and reorienting process; "a revival of religion wakes up the slumbering energies of a Church," he explained, "causes her to throw off her lethargy, prepares the membership for more extended schemes of usefulness, opens the heart to respond to calls of benevolence, brings lost sinners to the foot of the cross for mercy, and furnishes our Theological Seminaries with pious young men." Keeping these functions in equilibrium and harmony and preventing the revivalist impulse from dissipating itself, he concluded, posed the supreme challenge to the ingenuity and judgment of the clergy. "The great difficulty," he explained, "is to lead these seasons of grace to a happy termination. In carrying on, managing, and controlling them, we should never lose sight of the unalterable nature of man. If we preach entirely to the intellect, and never awaken the passions within his bosom, we will fail to enlist man's sympathies in the cause of God. If we play entirely upon the passions of his nature, while there may be much show for the time being, it will soon pass away."[62] The dilemma was a real one. Like the countervailing balance between legalists and formalists that he wanted the church to foster in 1833, bringing revivals to a "happy termination" meant paying close attention to the turbulent side of human nature and to the limited but crucial role of reason in sanctifying the lives of believers.

For David F. Bittle, pastor of St. Michael's Lutheran Church in Rockingham County, Virginia, in 1838–1839, and later President and Professor of Moral and Intellectual Science at Roanoke College, the new measures were an integral part of nineteenth-century progress

Sanctification and Consciousness

and enlightenment. "As the sciences advance, literature becomes universal, governments become more tolerant—and improvements in the arts are continually making—is it not reasonable to suppose the facilities for propagating the cause of the redeemer will be increased and the new measures will hence constantly arise?" Church history, Bittle demonstrated, going back to Jonathan Edwards, to Wesley and Whitefield, to August Francke and Phillip Jakob Spener, the founders of German Lutheran pietism, to Huguenot preachers, Guillaume Ferel and Pierre Veret, to the preaching of St. Paul, and to Pentecost was filled with precedents for protracted revivals, anxious benches, and prayer meetings. Their use by Christians in the 1830s only reflected the power of history to direct human affairs. The new preoccupation with a specific conversion experience, Bittle contended, was controversial and troubling only because conversion itself—involving as it did self-knowledge, volition, self-consciousness in the face of eternity—was a complex, and awesome, dimension of human experience.[63]

The revivalism that evangelical Lutherans in the South imported from the North was part of the modernization of American life during the antebellum era; modernization was the use of newly invented organizational techniques to set the direction and quicken the pace of social change. What was happening in the churches paled in comparison to the invasion of the South by market forces of the capitalist revolution in business that had been building since 1815 in the United States and for a half-century longer in industrial Britain. Capitalism, James Oakes argues, transformed slavery from a rural labor system into a high stakes investment game by making slaves and the agricultural products they raised increasingly profitable. Christianity, he further states, acquired a new spiritual and social role as pious planters sought relief from their economic anxiety and their uneasiness over rampant materialism. "From the growing love of wealth which seems to be the all-devouring passion of our country and from the sins and corruptions which this is sure to bring in its train," Oakes quotes a Virginia Methodist, "unless . . . repented of and abandoned, God will bring this nation also to the dust." "I am more and more perplexed about my negroes," a planter lamented; "I cannot just . . . sell them though that would be clearly the best I could do for myself. I cannot free them. I cannot keep them with comfort." This realization closely resembled the nagging apprehension that one's repentance and new life had been tarnished by sin and needed renewal. In this way evangelicalism, and the state of mind of perceptive slaveowners, mutually sustained an ambivalence that was troubling but also "attended with *great conveniences*." One close observer caught this mixture of social and religious apprehension when he observed that slaveowners "tremble when they look into the future. It is like a huge deadly serpent which is kept down by straining every nerve and muscle" and "someday will burst the weight that binds it and take fearful retribution."[64]

In one hundred fashionable urban pulpits in the antebellum South, studied by E. Brooks Holifield, the sustaining of sanctification amid human inertia required intellectually rigorous and stylistically pleasing preaching that drew heavily on Scottish Common Sense realism. Extraordinarily conscious of a critical laity and of ambitious clerical colleagues, the genteel and largely evangelical preachers in the Old South's finest churches strove to "be far wiser and better than persons imagine—to surpass the ideal of the vulgar mind and attain to heights to which they are wholly ignorant." The key to this seemingly effortless superiority was a homiletical "method" stressing "order and system, precise discriminations, tasteful language, irresistible logic, and elocutionary dignity."[65]

That method performed well the task of presenting intellectual, defensible "evidences" of "the reasonableness of faith" to congregations who had heard enough rationalism and skepticism to be troubled and defensive. "The claim which the Scripture addresses to us, to be the one authentic and authoritative revelation from God," Robert Lewis Dabney, professor at Union Seminary in Richmond, told his students, "is addressed to our reason.... The evidences of inspiration must ... present themselves to man's reason.... He who says he believes, when he sees no proof, is but pretending, or talking without meaning." Thomas Reid's *Inquiry into the Human Mind on the Principles of Common Sense* (1764), became a staple of southern ministerial reading because its distinction between sensation and perception in learning elevated abstract conclusions like religious belief to the summit human achievement while grounding such supernatural insights firmly in sensual experience.

The converse of Dabney's argument for the reasonableness of faith was the rationality of even inexplicable workings of Providence. "God himself being a God of order," Thomas Smyth, Presbyterian minister in Charleston postulated, "everything that is must be established within certain relations, consequences,... rights and obliga-

Sanctification and Consciousness

tions. These are founded in nature and are necessary and inflexible. We are therefore required to observe this order and act in accordance with these relations, subject to inevitable retribution." Every human disappointment and trial served to instruct people about the order of creation and the sequence of events that lay in God's hands; "duty... requires us to accept God's arrangements, to acquiesce in them, to act in harmony with them, and not to fall behind or to go beyond them until... God opens or shuts the door."[66] In the pews of fashionable urban southern churches, a Calvinist sense of divine omnipotence had become thoroughly imbued with Arminian moralism, with a pessimistic, romantic perception of doors closing on human happiness, and a peculiarly southern social conservatism concerning the duty to acquiesce in an apparently sinful status quo.

While characteristic of southern antebellum evangelicalism, social conservatism and convenient theological improvisation were not unique to the South. Most northern evangelical Protestant leaders shied away from attacks on slavery lest they alienate laymen who valued order, thus jeopardizing the allegiance of followers in the border states. The bulk of evangelical Protestant clergy in both the North and the South lived within a web of constraining assumptions and practices, which C. C. Goen summarizes as "an over-emphasis on individualism, an inadequate social theory, [and] a world-rejecting ecclesiology."[67] Individualism made sin an entirely personal matter; it also fostered a conception of society as an atomistic collection of separate persons who neither benefited from nor bore responsibility for sins that were part of the corporate life of society; in such a society, the church excluded from its purview any controversial political, social, and ethical question on which agreement was thought to be impossible as beyond the competence of church bodies to discuss.

The difference between northern and southern evangelicalism lay in the kinds of purists in each region who chafed under the dominant moderate consensus. In the North, discord took the form of an almost anarchistic condemnation of institutionalized oppression; in the South, intransigence expressed itself as reverence for the constituted order.

The northern groups that broke away from major denominations to attack slavery—the "come-outer" sects—considered every degree of proslavery thought, including especially moderation in denouncing slavery, as unacceptable moral pollution.[68] The defenders of a purely southern, proslavery evangelicalism saw the same kind of contamina-

The Antebellum Era

tion in the "blind impulses and visionary theories" of those who would "pull down the fairest fabric of [ecclesiastical] government the world has ever seen, rend the body of Christ in sunder, and dethrone the Saviour in His own Kingdom."[69] For Christian abolitionists, freedom belonged to all God's children; for Christian proslavery apologists all that God offered was "the dominion of rectitude, . . . the emancipation of the will from the power of sin, the release of the affections from the attraction of earth, the exemption of the understanding from the deceits and prejudices of error."[70]

6.

Proslavery Conservatism

> The slave ... is an actor on the broad theater of life—and as true
> merit depends not so much upon the part which is assigned, as upon
> the propriety and dignity with which it is sustained—so fidelity in this
> relation may hereafter be as conspicuously rewarded as fidelity in more
> exalted stations.
>
> James Henley Thornwell,
> *The Rights and Duties of Masters:*
> *A Sermon*
> (Charleston, 1850) p. 44.

During the summer of 1805, the Virginian agrarian political philosopher, John Taylor, looking for a place to educate his son, wrote to
Timothy Dwight, President of Yale College, inquiring about curriculum, expenses, academic calendar, and "other information" Dwight
might regard as appropriate. "Permit me to say," Dwight replied after
briefly summarizing the factual information Taylor sought, "that I do
not think it would forward your design to send your son to this college." With only two exceptions, the dozen Virginians who had attended Yale during Dwight's presidency "despised and hated our
manners, morals, industry, and religion." They were irreligious and
contemptuous of New England piety; the young Virginia blades considered Yankee industriousness fitting for "slaves and wretches only.
Your children," Dwight informed Taylor, "would probably dislike the
government of the college and the Faculty, and consider them as rigid,
superstitious, and mean-spirited. They would regard their New England companions as plodding drudges, destitute of talents as well as
of property. They would esteem New England life as slavery, unreason-
able and useless."

Taylor tried to reply in kind. Young men, he asserted, were not
capable of the malice and hatred Dwight had attributed to Virginians;

The Antebellum Era

on the contrary it was "unbending age, enslaved by habit, avarice, or ambition and blinded by nursing party or fanatic zeal" that was the "natural dwelling place" of contempt and condescension, and he agreed with Dwight "that it would be extremely injudicious in me to send my son in search of instruction to one who believes him to be a wretch destitute of morals, industry, and religion."[1]

Taylor's anger and polemicism gave way to his curiosity about the intellectual sources of Dwight's stereotype, and he took seriously the task of responding knowledgeably to Yankee invective. "Whether your letter was dictated by prejudice or civility," he told Dwight, "it merits an acknowledgement for the purpose of repaying the one by endeavoring to remove the other." However icy the tone, Taylor meant what he said. The charge of irreligiosity was the easiest to refute. Considering the legal establishment of Congregationalism in Connecticut with its "ambitious or repacious hierarchy," Taylor contrasted the way "our religious sects" in Virginia "mingle and worship in harmony and the state abounds with Christian ministers whose religion is not banished by intermeddling with civil government." Taylor was as much intrigued as irritated by Dwight's implication that "we are induced by wealth and idleness to hate your industry and poverty." The dichotomy, he insisted, was "morally incorrect," for it violated moral philosophy to attribute wealth to idleness and poverty to industry in the face of abundant evidence that just the reverse was true. Perhaps, Taylor suspected, this strange "breaking the ligaments between cause and effect" was a circuitous attack on slavery in Virginia. Taylor therefore responded with what would become, later in the antebellum period, staples of proslavery thought: first, the claim that industrial slavery in the North and in England was far more exploitive than chattal slavery in Virginia, and moreover, that the unprofitable and benign nature of southern slavery could be demonstrated "mathematically" with "figures, which tell the truth." However, Taylor harkened back to late eighteenth-century Virginian ambivalence about slavery, calling it "an evil forced upon us against our will," which "we regret" but "are unable to remedy." The defense of slavery, in any event, concerned him less than Dwight's assumed connection between social environment and moral character. "If your people are both industrious and poor," he warned Dwight, an ominous transformation might be taking place—New Englanders exhibiting the same "anomalous moral character" already visible in the wretchedness of English industrial squalor. Another explanation occurred to Taylor; wealth, he suggested

Proslavery Conservatism

to Dwight, was not a social constant but rather the product of human behavior. The "Boston nabob" who was able to spend in one evening's extravagance as much as a Virginia farmer earned in a year showed that the material "cause" for Virginia's alleged hauteur did not exist, and "it follows that the effect does neither exist." What did exist—as Dwight's vituperation made abundantly clear to Taylor—was institutionalized contamination of civic discourse in America. "Consider, Sir, the consequences of academical institutions which teach local prejudices, state enmities, and individual hatred." This trinity of evil, educational goals, pursued in a college as august and influential as Yale, could easily jeopardize "the union and national happiness," which were innocent, vulnerable preconditions of civil order.[2]

Taylor and Dwight were typical of the intellectuals in the new republic in their determination to preserve from degradation the sources and the design of republicanism inherited from the founders of the nation. Dwight spoke for New England Federalists who, in James Banner's words, valued "harmony, unity, order, and solidarity"[3] and conceived of their world as a "social body . . . composed of various members, mutually connected and dependent."[4] Taylor, in contrast, was a Jeffersonian agrarian convinced that northern Federalists were producing the "chains which the ambitions and avarices of particular men in all countries are continually forging for the weak and defenseless." Liberty, for Taylor, was the voluntary pooling by individuals of society's limited store of virtue, energy, and knowledge in order to ward off assaults by the powerful and acquisitive upon the public good. Conceiving of the world in Manichaean terms, assigning the task of libertarian vigilance to farmers and planters, and understanding the whole enterprise of self-government as risky, fragile, and requiring tireless perseverance, like farming itself, Taylor was a defensive, instinctive conservative.[5] He knew agrarian, democratic virtue or commercial, elitist vice when he saw it. Slavery might be regrettable but it was also integral to the social order from which his kind of democracy arose, and its critics were no friends to agrarian liberty. "Negro slavery is a misfortune to agriculture, incapable of removal, and only within the reach of palliation," he wrote in his famous *Arator . . . Essays* on the revitalization of southern agriculture.[6]

Taylor connected his lamentation about slavery to his diagnosis of the decline of Virginia agriculture in the early nineteenth century. His *Inquiry into the Principles and Policy of the Government of the United States* was a brilliant exposition on the breakdown of classical whig republicanism in the fluid, individualistic milieu of the new republic; his *Arator* essays identified the severe limitations on change that were inherent in an agrarian social order, especially one wedded to virtuous individualism. A society resigned to postponing social change, until the interests and enlightenment of individuals dictated that change occur, was a profoundly conservative one. Nature and experience taught patience in the quest for social reform and moral improvement, Taylor insisted, and he pointed to the slave insurrection on the Caribbean island of Santo Domingo of 1791 as conclusive proof of the folly and criminality of emancipation. Hard-won wisdom and public morality dictated the response of the nation: "The fact is that negro slavery is an evil that the United States must look in the face," he declared; "to whine over it is cowardly; to aggravate it, criminal; to forbear to alleviate it because it cannot be wholly cured, foolish." This trilogy of inhibitions against meddling reformers, harsh masters, and careless husbandmen represented a formidable defense of slavery. The first two strictures were clear enough. Taylor dismissed Jefferson's anguished doubts about the morality of slavery as the product of "mental fermentations and moral bubbles"; the machinations of Quaker and Methodist abolitionists and the pernicious influence of free blacks on slaves were a criminal threat to public safety. "Forbear[ing] to alleviate" was the active and intelligent element in Taylor's prescription, and its meaning went to the heart of his social and racial conservatism.[7]

The most convincing explanation of the agrarian sources of Virginia proslavery is Duncan MacLeod's discovery of "twin foundations" of nature and moralitiy in all of Taylor's thought. "A nation is both a natural and a moral being," Taylor wrote. "If it is deprived of its physical powers," bestowed by nature, "it is like a man possessed of reason, bound; if [deprived] of its intellectual," or moral, faculties, "it is like a maniac, unbound." Safety and survival required the preservation and mutual vitality of both natural and moral bases of human life. Taylor found the way to achieve that goal in the writings of the classical English economist, David Ricardo, on the labor theory of value. It held that all wealth arose from labor invested in production. For Taylor, land was a natural endowment and agriculture a naturally moral activity. He went further; the labor that was the key to extracting wealth from the land was a natural capacity and bestowed a moral right to the wealth the labor produced. Political freedom gave the individual control over his pursuit of wealth (what Jefferson called

Proslavery Conservatism

"happiness"), and labor made that freedom an existential reality in the experience of the laborer. "The occupations of men," he declared, "are the men themselves." Putting slaves to work in the labor-intensive activity necessary to revive Virginia agriculture—"hedging, ditching, deep ploughing, manuring, and fertilizing," MacLeod summarized— was an exercise of farmers' liberty to pursue all their natural rights and utilize all of their moral capacities to the uttermost, to seize the day and make life whole.[8]

Senator Nathaniel Macon of North Carolina also articulated a defense of slavery in republican, libertarian terms. A loyal Jeffersonian Republican and reluctant supporter of James Madison during the War of 1812, Macon felt strong emotional and intellectual ties to the Old Republican purists among Jefferson's followers, who were suspicious of every governmental expenditure and exercise of authority. The essence of Macon's republicanism was the belief that governmental frugality and simplicity were themselves a bond holding people and rulers together. "In proportion as men live easily and comfortably," Macon severely declared, "in proportion as they are free from burdens of taxations, they will be attached to the government in which they live."[9] The intelligence and self-reliance of the people were the social energy that fed republican government, and the innate genius of the people proscribed legislators and officials from imposing their sense of the public good on the people. "I confide in the people," he declared, "firmly believing that they are able to take care of themselves without the aid or protection of any set of men paid by them to defend them from their worst enemies—themselves. . . . I think better of the people than most of the men I have met with," he said calmly of himself and referring to his constituents; "I have tried them in every way and never found them faithless."[10]

No less important than Macon's faith in "the people" was his skepticism about the blessings of modernization. He lived all of his adult life in a spare, two-room house in Warren County and viewed debt, rapid accumulation of wealth, the clamor for internal improvements, and feverish pursuit of speculative gain as a social pathology that contributed nothing intrinsically valuable to human existence. Economic development only spawned dissatisfaction with the physical facilities for trade and transportation that only government, operating on a vast scale of activity, could satisfy. Development, moreover, created an artificial hierarchy of the newly enriched and the hard-working, slowly improving, mass of the populace. In place of social

The Antebellum Era

hierarchy in an enlightened republic, Macon contended, was the natural ebb and flow of reason and passion: "Only leave the people alone to their good sense," Macon explained, "and they will set things right themselves. This government is founded on the principle that the people have enough sense to govern themselves; if passion should sometimes show itself, it will burn out, and reason will resume her throne and the thing will come right."[11] By creating the dangerous mirage of political solutions for every imagined social ill, internal improvements were a step toward governmental tampering in social relations: "If Congress can make canals, they can with more propriety emancipate. Be not deceived, . . . let not the love of improvement or a thirst for glory blind that common sense with which the Lord has blessed you."[12]

The end result of this innocent view of individual intention and faith in the popular will, Macon fervently wished and expected, was a state of social equipoise in which humane, white mastery elicited, and merged with, deeply felt black loyalty. "It is a fact," he told the Senate during the Missouri compromise debates, that northerners who go to the South and there acquire slaves

expect more labor from them than people brought up among them. . . . The old ones are better taken care of than any poor in the world and treated with decent respect by all their white acquaintances. I sincerely wish that [northern colleagues] would go home with me, or some other southern member, and witness the meeting between the slaves and the owner, and see the glad faces and shaking of hands. . . . The owner can make more free in conversation with his slave, and be more easy in his company, than the rich man . . . with the white hireling who drives his carriage. He has no expectation that the slave will, for that free and easy conversation, expect to call him fellow citizen or act improperly.[13]

Macon felt no inconsistency in this demeaning portrayal of "white hirelings" who did not know their place and his professed love of the people. Life in a republic of free individuals, he knew, meant always being on one's guard; slavery created for Macon a haven where a master could afford to allow his gentler impulses wider scope. "I have heard of the situation of my negroes," he wrote to a minister in North Carolina not long after entering the Congress, "and I do not recollect many circumstances in my life that gave me more uneasiness. Because their situation in life put it out of their power to act in their sickness as they might wish, and because myself, the only person

Proslavery Conservatism

who they might have a right to expect assistance from, . . . was far from them, . . . I hope they took care of one another."[14] A few years later Macon expressed the same anguish when he called slavery "a curse . . . there was no way of getting rid of. . . . "[15]

The happy vision of glad, black faces meeting the returning master was precarious, and Macon spoke from deep conviction when he pleaded with the Senate to respect the sensitivities of slaveowners: "Why depart from the good old way which has kept us in quiet, peace, and harmony—everyone living under his own vine and fig tree, and none to make him afraid? Why leave the road of experience, which has satisfied us all and made us all happy, to take this new way . . . which leads to universal emancipation, of which we have no experience?"[16] An admiring contemporary biographer recognized Macon's emotional investment: "There can be nothing more contemptible than a man who dedicates all the energies of his mind to indulgences of any kind. . . . If they are not held in subjection . . . they will usurp upon all other subjects and convert the mind into a scene of tumult and confusion. It is from such discipline as this that such men as Mr. Macon always possess a certain calmness of temper, superior to the ordinary classes of mankind."[17]

Macon's "calmness of temper" and his dour view of human progress found confirmation in Edmund Burke's "Speech in Support of . . . Conciliation with the American Colonies" where in he warned that slaveowners in Virginia and the Carolinas were "proud and jealous of their freedom" and therefore unlikely to acquiesce even in the face of British military superiority.[18] "To this I will not attempt to add a word," Macon declared: "No man can add to Mr. Burke." Except Mr. Burke himself. What Macon omitted from Burke's point about liberty-loving slaveowners was significant: "Freedom is to them not only an enjoyment, but a kind of rank and privilege. . . . In such a people, the haughtiness of domination combines with the spirit of freedom, fortifies it, and renders it invincible."[19]

Macon's younger colleague, John Randolph of Roanoke, shared with him many values and beliefs, and none more so than the probable linkage between internal improvements and slavery. "If Congress have the power" to build roads in the West, he trumpeted in 1824, it may with the same constitutional propriety *emancipate every slave in the United States.*"[20] Unlike the hopeful Macon, Randolph was fully open to the awful possibility that social ruin and moral catastrophe were to be the fate of the South and the republic as he had known it.

The Antebellum Era

Randolph's volcanic political style and personality and his acute intelligence produced a strain of proslavery republicanism that moved beyond Macon's fear of power or Taylor's sense of the finite possibilities of human happiness.

Robert Dawidoff defines this position so insightfully that he ought to be quoted at length. "The facts" about Randolph's involvement in slavery, Dawidoff explains, are at once simple and confusing:

> Randolph was the chief slaveholder in his county, and he freed his slaves in the will finally recognized by the courts; Randolph was an architect of the defense of the slavery interest within the Union, and he never ceased to stigmatize slavery as a curse upon his country; Randolph believed the African nations inferior to the white European, and he loved and cared for particular black slaves whom he kept closer to himself than he allowed almost anybody else to be.... Randolph understood from his own experience how volatile the question of slavery was. He knew that the reluctance to broach it indicated that it was a touchy subject, not a settled one. He knew that the conscience of the South was unlikely to prevail over the circumstances of its power. He was aware of the masters' fear of retribution and their inability to envision a way out from under slavery at once safe and profitable. He recognized that the South did not really intend to free its slaves, not yet anyhow, and that made to feel defensive, the South might turn fierce. Understanding all this, and with motives clouded by the kaleidoscopic volatility of his own nature, Randolph said things that were almost never said. Knowing the slavowners' hearts and fears, he argued in a way that might be counted on to move them.[21]

In Dawidoff's view, Randolph pitted his emotions against his reason, not knowing which would prevail; he knew the destructive power of slavery, and he knew of no other interest besides slavery that could knit southern whites together in purposeful action in behalf of their own survival. Here too was a troubled equipoise. Although Randolph's realistic conservatism was the mirror opposite of the benign mingling of duty and gratitude which Macon saw as the cement of the social order, it also resembled Macon's Burkean appreciation of the habitual pride and combativeness among slaveowners as a source of their political energy. Because they were republicans who believed that virtue resided in the people, Macon and Randolph knew that political power could only be exercised in limited actions taken in behalf of the people. Because they were successful antebellum politi-

Proslavery Conservatism

cians fired with ambition, eloquence, and purpose, their own exercise of legislative power tapped only a small portion of their own energy. Disciplining, containing, channelling the unspent social passion of a democratic political culture was the supreme test of nerve and will in the Old South, and the code of behavior surrounding public conduct was called *honor.* "The central problem of political life for antebellum Southerners," Kenneth S. Greenberg concludes in a major new appraisal of proslavery politics, "was how to avoid becoming an enslaver or a slave. It was an insoluble problem for men who sought both republicanism and honor. Whereas republicanism demanded a renunciation of all forms of unrestrained power, honor demanded its accumulation."[22]

Proslavery conservatism—like all credible normative discourse—owed its vitality to its knitting together of competing moral assumptions, social visions, and political prescriptions. Recent studies of the Virginia debates over slavery from 1829 to 1832 examine the defense of slavery by men ambivalent about its blessings and therefore determined to discredit once and for all the presumptuous views of abolitionists, southern reformers, or blacks themselves. Alison G. Freehling finds proslavery conservatives in Virginia pinioned between two controversies: the movement for democratization of the state's 1775 constitution, which culminated in the Convention in 1829 and 1830, and Thomas Jefferson Randolph's proposal for gradual emancipation passionately debated by the legislature in 1832. Virginia resolved the constitutional question with an elaborate compromise between east and west by basing apportionment on the white population only (a western demand) and by adopting property and tax-paying qualifications for voting (an eastern stipulation). What enabled this package to win ratification was the approval of the new Constitution by sixty-four percent of voters in the Valley of Virginia, most of them from counties into which substantial slaveholding had spread. Only the trans-Appalachian remained unreconciled to continued eastern dominance.

The debate over slavery during 1831–1832, initiated by Thomas Jefferson's grandson, occurred in the charged atmosphere of the aftermath of Nat Turner's uprising. Though the insurrection in Southampton County emboldened the critics of slavery to advocate gradual emancipation and colonization and opponents of reform to point to the horrors of black violence as evidence of the impossibility of any relaxation of white hegemony, both view points crystallized before

The Antebellum Era

1831. Nor did the rejection of emancipation by the legislature mark a decisive turning point in Virginia history. Freehling shows that the conflict continued into the 1840s and 1850s. The classic proslavery document of the period was Thomas R. Dew's *Review of the Debate in the Virginia Legislature of 1831–1832*, a withering denunciation of reform proposals but also a prediction that Virginia would and should ultimately become a free labor state. Jesse Burton Harrison likewise argued that Virginia was fundamentally unlike South Carolina and the Gulf Coast states in climate and soil in its suitabilitiy for slave labor. Opposed to mandatory emancipation or other abrupt change, Harrison nonetheless predicted that an industrious white middle class, rather than slave labor, would ultimately transform the state's economy.[23]

Freehling's reconstruction of political discourse reveals that Virginia neither embraced slavery nor eschewed the visionary antislavery of its Jeffersonian youth in 1832 but rather discovered that it was a "house-divided," drifting "Hamlet-like" toward 1861.[24] Within that outer shell of perceptions and stances operated a body of intellectual and moral assumptions explicated by Dickson D. Bruce. The very occurrence of a debate over constitutional reform in 1829 and over slavery two years later drove Virginia gentlemen back to the resources of learning and value formation they cherished the most. "Given the relationship Virginia conservatives perceived between rousing the passions and the requirements of political deliberation," Bruce explains, "rhetoric would... be a discipline of some importance to them." Their favorite guide on rhetoric was the Scottish moral philosopher and teacher of rhetoric, Hugh Blair, whose *Letters on Rhetoric and Belles Lettres* (1783), dealt extensively with "the problem of passion in oratory and deliberation." Through the study and practice of rhetoric, the Virginia aristocrats sought to combine controlled, passionate arousal of their audience with precise articulation so that unruly public issues remained within a controlling framework of responsible, spirited discussion. "Passionate discourse and sincerity were inextricably tied" in Blair's rhetoric, Bruce explains, and "whatever its dangers... passion... was inseparable from honesty and candor."[25]

John Randolph considered Blair's rhetoric a quick fix. "Blair ought to be banished from 'our schools," he declared; "Horace's 'Art of Poetry,' Quintilian, Cicero, Longinus, among the ancients; Boileau and Martinus Scriblerus among the moderns—these should be our textbooks."[26] Randolph's rhetorical models and educational goals drew

Proslavery Conservatism

strands of serenity, courage, discrimination, and toughness from classical and early modern sources. Horace's *Ars Poetica* argued for the appropriateness of form to forensic purpose; Quintilian called for manliness, linguistic training, and skilled instruction in oratory; Cicero summoned the republican virtues of gravity and legality in a doomed defense of a passing order; Longinus, a first-century A. D. Greek writer of *On the Sublime*, superficially resembled Blair in his celebration of an evocative spirit but demanded rigorous adherence to the best Greek philosophical models; Nicholas Boileau, the seventeenth-century poetic critic, championed neo-classical standards of balance, restraint, and astringency; both Alexander Pope and his friend, Johh Arbuthnot, used the pseudonym, Martinus Scriblerus, and with Jonathan Swift, organized Tory satirists in the Court of Queen Anne into the Scriblerus Club in 1713.

Lacking knowledge of that heritage, Randolph lamented, Virginians performed pantomime acts of courage under the guise of candidly speaking the unspeakable. Gholson's antiemancipation speech reminded legislators that where "our political fathers" conducted indelicate debates in secret, "we debate it" in public, "and all this is done as if the slaves around us had neither eyes nor ears—or having ears, they heard not, and having eyes, they saw not." The Nat Turner uprising, in Gholson's view, had triggered a failure of nerve among those planters now advocating emancipation; he considered the proposal to be "monsterous and unconstitutional." The paramount danger was not that slaves would imitate Turner. In Lockean terms, Gholson recognized that the compact, on which government rested, was a delicately structured antidote to terror and irrational fears within the *body politic*. To arouse false apprehensions was to jeopardize the very climate of security on which political stability depended. "The people of our country again sleep quietly on their pillows and would, in all probability, have enjoyed uninterrupted repose, had it not been for this false legislative cry of 'Wolf! Wolf!' [by] gentlemen in the heat of their own intemperance and by the aid of their own disturbed and distempered fancies."[27] When William Henry Brodnax replied to Gholson, opposing emancipation but vigorously defending the prudence of debating its dangers, he likewise fused candor, danger, and statesmanship: "I do not regard it as a characteristic of true courage and manly firmness ... to shut our eyes and rush blindfold against danger without having examined it. So far as fear is involved, I hope we shall never be afraid to examine our real situation." Brodnax

The Antebellum Era

proposed the colonization outside of Virginia, first of free blacks and then of slaves whose masters agreed to their slaves' transportation to Africa in return for fair market compensation. The *Richmond Enquirer* praised Brodnax for his candor and courage in seizing the "true ground ... the middle ground" between two "ultra parties."[28]

Blair's rhetoric laid the groundwork for Burke's esthetics as a way of focusing political emotions. Not only did Burke associate slaveowning with daring, headstrong defense of liberty, he also divided the world of human action into categories of the "sublime" and the mundane, which stirred deep appreciation in southern aristocrats. "What made Burke's views so compelling," Bruce explains, "was the way he connected the reliance on principles" of limited government and property rights "with the kind of human concern that stressed the necessity of moral sentiment in any human organization.... Burke equated the sublime with passions of pain and, ultimately, with feeling the need for self-preservation."[29]

Between the external face of proslavery as antidote to disorder and its internal soul of sublime recklessness and passionate candor was a reliance on republicanism as refined and tested for Virginians in the crucible of the Alien and Sedition Acts, and remembered for a generation as "the principles of '98." Kathryn Ruth Malone argues that Virginians considered that "fidelity to ... the concept of limited government was the determinant of" their "survival." Gholson's anti-emancipation speech in 1832 was the very embodiment of such fidelity. The sanctity of private property under the Virginia Constitution of 1776, Gholson declared, bore directly on "the protection of *individual rights against governmental usurpation.* This sacred principle does not derive its sanction from constitutional charters—it has its foundations deep laid in the principles of justice—it is the very ligament which binds society together."[30]

Virginia's doctrines of '98 were also Janus-faced. They affirmed limited government, courageous principled defiance of unconstitutional centralization, and the dignity of individuals within a republican order, but also celebrated the political skill, knowledge, and discretion of Virginia's aristocratic leadership and a tradition of self-denying fealty to the common weal. Those social and intellectual costs meant that the doctrines were not necessarily exportable to other parts of the South nor applicable to constitutional crises outside of Virginia. When South Carolina's governor, James Hamilton, sought to enlist Virginia's support in the struggle against the tariff of abomina-

Proslavery Conservatism

tions in 1828, he explicitly acknowledged both admiration and reservation:

> Will Virginia, chivalrous, high-spirited as she is, passively and quietly stand by and see us immolated for no other crime than a devotion to her faith, not by a worship of mere lip-service but by a dedication of our life blood to her principles? If she will, then is she fit for a slave's portion? Let her put out all the lights that have blazed upon her altars. Let her strike from the escutcheon of her glory the names of her Washington, her Jefferson, her Madison, her Henry, her Mason, and her Grayson, and prepare to lay down herself in base and contented servitude.[31]

John C. Calhoun rose in the Senate on February 15, 1833 to denounce the Revenue Collection bill, better known as the Force bill—a measure providing for off-shore collection of customs duties under the 1828 tariff—which outflanked South Carolina's declared intention to nullify the measure and prevent its enforcement in the Palmetto State. That speech was a significant juncture in Calhoun's career as an American, and southern, conservative. Almost all of his political education to this date taught him that political and social order rested on a compact, not the hypothetical transaction prior to the institution of government that he later ridiculed in *A Disquisition on Government* but rather a rational, mutually acceptable, and almost instinctual agreement among contending, potentially antagonistic, elements of society.

The crisis of 1833, however, agitated deeper levels in Calhoun's political imagination than traditional issues of human nature and consent. The nullification controversy awakened in him a fresh revulsion against corrupt and chaotic forces operating just below the surface of public life and discernible less by conscious scrutiny than by a visceral appreciation of human self-destructiveness. While superficially Calvinist, this pessimistic romanticism and fixation with the coarser human appetites resembled, and probably echoed, Machiavelli's dark predictions of how *fortuna* would finally overwhelm *virtu* if visionary agitation and mindless tampering with delicate social arrangements were permitted to plunge society into a contagion of violence and unbridled passionate advocacy.

The warfare raging in Calhoun's mind—and in his political environment—between these respective Lockean/Calvinist and Machiavellian/romantic visions had only begun when he made his

The Antebellum Era

speech attacking the Force bill; his opening words, nonetheless, revealed his deeply divided political mind: "Mr. President, I know not which is more objectionable, the *provisions* of this bill or the *temper* in which its adoption has been urged." On one hand, "the rapid progress of despotism in our country" and "the deep decay of that brotherly feeling which once existed between these states" raised Calhoun's combativeness and alarm, clarifying his duty of "not... permitting" slanders on his native state to "pass unnoticed." On the other hand, he reminded his contemporaries how "indebted we are for our beautiful federal system" now jeopardized by the "deep constitutional question" that "lies at the bottom of the controversy."[32] System and imperilled constitutionalism or corruption and slander? Which side of the American political imagination should he excite and arouse? Which set of ideas would effect the right kind of human response?

The lure of constitutionalism and system was a strong one. In 1828 Calhoun had worked behind the scenes to guide South Carolina's opposition to the new tariff by writing an *Exposition* providing the Carolina radicals with a sophisticated theoretical doctrine. In place of the popular "co-department" theory of the Union, which saw state and federal governments dividing sovereignty between them, Calhoun held that sovereignty was indivisible and that the states governed one another through the agency of the federal government in areas of national concern without sacrificing any of their sovereignty in the process. Nullification of a federal statute by a state was therefore an exercise of this kind of transcendent state sovereignty. "This ascendency... of the Constitution over the law-making majority... can only be preserved through the action of states as organized bodies, ... judging the extent of their separate powers and interposing their authority to arrest the enactments of the general government," he explained to show how nullification was implicitly sanctioned by the Constitution's concept of federalism.[33]

The assumptions at work in this analysis were thoroughly Lockean and Calvinist. "What is that constitution of our nature which, while it impels man to associate with others of his kind, renders it impossible for society to exist without government?" he would later ask rhetorically in his *Disquisition on Government*. "It would seem to be," he answered, "essentially connected with the great law of self-preservation which pervades all that feels, from man down to the lowest... insect. In none is it stronger than in man. His social feelings may indeed, in a state of safety and abundance combined with high

Proslavery Conservatism

intellectual and moral culture, acquire great expansion and force, but not so great as to overpower this all-pervading and essential law of animated existence." Because individuals will respond differently to these animal impulses, "the tendency to a universal state of conflict between individual and individual" embued with "passions of suspicion, jealousy, anger, and revenge" compelled mankind to accept a "controlling power" called "government." The concurrent majority simply carried that controlling, self-denying function of the state one step further. Recognizing the seriousness of that step, however, Calhoun was ready as early as the Force bill speech with a compelling historical precedent: the common respect for a rule of law hammered out between patricians and plebeians in the Roman Republic. "The result" of the Roman constitution "was that men possessing those qualities which would naturally command confidence—moderation, wisdom, justice, and patriotism—were elevated to office." This kind of respect for strength and confidence in civic-mindedness was exactly the way in which a compact should work.[34]

One purpose of such theoretical elegance was to forestall South Carolina extremists bent on using the tariff issue as a vehicle to disrupt the Union before the question of legislation on slavery ever arose. He sensed better than anyone else the intensity of the polarization of the nation between abolitionists and slaveowners—polarization that jeopardized his own chances of succeeding Jackson in the White House. But it was not just thwarted ambition or prophetic understanding of the slavery controversy that drove Calhoun to traffic in the language of sectional intransigence. Calhoun embodied a view of the good society that had crystallized suddenly in South Carolina between 1800 and 1810—a decade of coalescence between low-country and up-country farmers, the spread of slavery and cotton cultivation throughout the whole state, and the ability of political newcomers and social upstarts like the Calhouns to win respect from the older, low-country aristocracy. Nurturing unity within South Carolina became essential to preserving the prosperity and security of both regions within the state, and Calhoun's fondness for a national compact of brotherly forbearance between gentlemen north and south meshed nicely with his realization that his political career, family interests, and newfound fame all rested on the same kind of compact within South Carolina.[35]

The fight over the Force bill made it all the more imperative to Calhoun that compact government give full play to the energies held

The Antebellum Era

in fruitful tension by reciprocal obligations of protection and liberty—especially within the South. When Prince Edward County, Virginia, invited Calhoun to attend its Fourth of July celebrations in 1834, he declined due to the press of official business but appended a fervent lecture on the nature of representative government:

> the present alarming condition of the country is not to be attributed to our own institutions, or to the want of capacity on the part of the people for self government but to the principle of consolidation which has concentrated all the powers of the system in the General Government, contrary to the original intent and genius of our institutions.... Let us not be deceived; consolidation irresistibly leads to faction, corruption, anarchy, and finally, if not arrested, to military despotism.

Prince Edward County's representatives in Congress, John Randolph and Thomas T. Bouldin, Calhoun emphasized, had fully recognized these dangers and had stood by South Carolina during the Force bill debates. Bouldin had died shortly thereafter, "resisting with all the ardor of a warm and enlightened patriot the usurpations of the Executive" while Randolph's reelection to Congress, despite his feeble health, "inspired terror in the ranks of power and corruption." Representatives such as these, Calhoun reminded the people of Prince Edward County, kept alive the doctrines of '98 on which South Carolina's and the South's liberties now depended.[36]

Calhoun was prepared in 1833 to denounce the Force bill as a violation of the compact among the states. When proadministration Senator William Rives of Virginia used the same co-department argument, that some South Carolina nullifiers had earlier employed, to *defend* the Force bill, Calhoun found himself in a quandary. "I understood the Senator from Virginia [Mr. Rives] to say that sovereignty was divided and that a portion remained with the states severally and that the residue was vested in the Union." Rives's purpose in so arguing was to show that the power to collect duties was part of that "residue." "If such be his meaning, ... our opinions do not disagree, ... but if the Senator ... means to assert that the twenty-four states form but one community with a single sovereign power as to the objects of the Union, it will be but a revival of the old question of whether the Union is a union between states as distinct communities or a mere aggregation of the American people."[37] Calhoun was charitable in giving Rives this benefit of the doubt. Citing Madison's *Federalist, No. 45,*

Proslavery Conservatism

Rives had reminded the Senate of the spirit as well as the letter of the Constitution on the subject of state sovereignty:

> So far as a sacrifice of a portion of state sovereignty shall be necessary to the objects of the Union ... the voice of every good citizen must be, let the sacrifice be made. Sir [Rives was responding directly to Calhoun], the sacrifice was freely made, to the extent required by the great objects of the Union, but that portion of sovereignty not necessary to be vested in the Union for those high purposes still remains unimpaired in the respective states.[38]

Those words from a Virginian—that tortured reading of Madison's intent as Calhoun understood it—and glib assumption that sovereignty could be divided into portions surrendered and portions retained suggested to Calhoun that South Carolina would have to chart its own course to safety, that the honored doctrines of '98 would no longer suffice.

If not the principles of '98, what? One available form of protection was the armor of individual honor in an intensely personalized political culture. Educated by high Federalists at Yale and Tapping Reeve's Law School, Calhoun saw the nation as a collectivity of communities needing the same bracing fraternal affection and bonds to other communities as low-country and up-country South Carolina. During the first fifteen years of his political career as war-hawk nationalist, he strived to maintain, what he later would call in the Force bill speech, "our beautiful federal system" of brotherly forbearance in the American union. As a newcomer to the South Carolina elite, Calhoun was keenly aware of its code of individual honor and the sanctity of individual conscience that men like Wragg and Laurens had abstracted from the country ideology of the eighteenth century; in common with his early national contemporaries in South Carolina he incorporated these values into a personal code of political honor and self-presentation. That code, in Robert M. Weir's words, praised symbolic actions of "recklessness" and "heedlessness of self" as ways individuals could guarantee their devotion to the commonweal.[39]

Echoing the language of the late eighteenth century in South Carolina, Calhoun inserted into his speech a lengthy section on the purity of his own motives and the high personal cost of his position on nullification:

> Here I must pause for a moment to repel a charge which ... even the President has reiterated, ... that I have been actuated by feelings of

The Antebellum Era

disappointed ambition. . . . I deeply regret the necessity of noticing myself, . . . and . . . nothing can induce me to advert to my own course than
the conviction that it is due to the cause at which the blow is aimed
through me. It is only in this view that I take notice of it.[40]

All of the etiquette of personal self-denial found its way into Calhoun's vindication of his own conduct—the higher cause of liberty
that nullification served, the defensive action of rebutting slander, the
frequency and prominence of the slanderers, distaste for egocentric
display clothing a brooding concern with personal reputation, and
the modest nomenclature for his own actions—"the part I have
taken." To make that "part" fit the scenario of individual purity, Calhoun constructed a highly selective legislative history of the 1828 tariff premised on the unprovable notion that the Senate had been so
evenly divided on the bill that Calhoun's Vice Presidential vote might
have decided the issue. Fearing that defeat of the bill would cost Jackson's election, "the friends of General Jackson . . . earnestly en-
treated" Calhoun to abstain from voting. "My reply to this entreaty
was that *no consideration personal to myself* could induce me to take such
a course" (italics added). In contrast nearly everyone else in Congress
had capitulated to the greedy pursuit of a share of the booty that a
higher tariff would generate, what Calhoun coolly described as "an
immense revenue with means of absorption upon any legitimate or
constitutional . . . appropriation." The contrast between public greed
and private duty expanded in Calhoun's hands: "I was amazed at the
folly and infatuation of the period. So completely absorbed was Congress in the game of ambition and avarice . . . that none but a few
anticipated the present crisis," the damage to the Constitution and
the Union manifested by nullification. "The road of ambition lay
open before me," Calhoun recalled of his situation five years earlier;
"I had but follow the corrupt tendency of the times—but I chose to
tread the rugged path of duty."[41]

As his reference to "avarice and ambition" suggested, Calhoun
found even richer material for a post-Lockean, pessimistically romantic vision of politics in the insatiable appetites of greedy politicians
and interest groups and in the boundless opportunism of democratic
politics of the Jacksonian era. Romanticism became the dominant
cultural outlook of American artists and thinkers from the 1820s to
the 1880s, and it pervaded oratory, popular culture, and religion as
well. A reaction against eighteenth-century rationalism, romanticism

Proslavery Conservatism

located human creativity in the heart and elevated emotion and sub-
jectivity over reason and objectivity. Most romantics thrilled to the
discovery of vibrant human personalities and saw limitless possibilities for goodness and achievement. But for the most thoughtful
romantics—notably Herman Melville, Edgar Allan Poe, and Henry
David Thoreau—the autonomy and power of human emotions was a
deeply disturbing vision of bottomless anxiety and apprehension in
the universe.

After nullification, Calhoun increasingly succumbed to romantic
despair. His concurrent majority resembled an eighteenth-century
constitutional formulation with its clinical assessment of majority and
minority powers, but what impelled him to improvise the doctrine
was his realization that a new moral force, abolitionism, had captured
the imaginations and will of northern reformers and had the potential for electrifying the nation's politics. Calhoun was determined to
breathe into southern intransigence an equally potent blend of urgency and conviction. The material at hand for a passionate southern
persuasion was the abundant evidence of material greed and interest-
group politics in the North. Manufacturers and financiers bewitched
Congress with beguiling cries for subsidies, tariffs, and legal protection. Politicians, who competed for the lucrative privilege of bestow-
ing these benefits, bought their way into office with patronage and
demogoguery.

The concurrent majority, Calhoun confidently predicted, would
change all this. A section of the nation would be able to block the
reckless expenditure of government funds to satisfy the demands of
commercial and industrial interests, and by drastically reducing taxes,
the sectional veto would diminish the power that patronage gave to
administration officeholders. But Calhoun's own logic pointed to a
far more despairing conclusion. Corrupt northern politicians, he believed in his heart, were not simply opportunists playing for the main
chance and needing discipline from the section of the country they
had offended and wounded. They were demagogues with a limitless
capacity to delude the electorate, and they had discovered in the coin
of abolitionism a way of purchasing public favor for decades to
come.[42]

Because he believed that he had sacrificed personal ambition to
the survival of liberty in his native state, because his civic gestures
were meant to enhance the well-being of the community rather than
glorify the individual, and because he believed he had diagnosed the

The Antebellum Era

licentiousness of democratic politics, Calhoun had to take pains to demonstrate that liberty could not be equated with personal freedom. Regarding liberty as a blessing for the community required Calhoun to deny the quintessential Lockean myth of a hypothetical contract between people and state, lest such a contract entitle all to liberty as a natural right or imply a natural equality between virtuous and debased members of society. "These great and dangerous errors have their origin in the prevalent opinion that all men are born free and equal . . . ; nothing can be more unfounded and false." Liberty existed only as a consequence of the existence of government; the same gracious act of the creator that sanctioned government made human beings subject "not only to parental authority but to the laws and institutions of the country where [they are] born and under whose protection they draw their first breath."[43]

The term "protection" echoed the Lockean formulation, even as it denied the libertarian implications of the contract. In the same eclectic fashion, Calhoun embraced and internalized an exotic Lockean concept—what Gillis J. Harp calls "the theory of political disharmony," the capacity and potential of government itself to spawn disorder and conflict. "For Calhoun," Harp explains, "government existed 'to preserve and perfect society'; but considering the intrinsic nature of government it was inevitably also the creator of 'disorder' through 'the abuse of powers'." As Calhoun later explained in *A Disquisition on Government*, laws "must be administered by men in whom . . . individual [feelings] are stronger than . . . social feelings. And hence the powers vested in them to prevent injustice and oppression on the part of others will, if left unguarded, be by them converted into instruments to oppress the rest of the community."[44] Government was hence a consequence of, and antidote to, sinfulness, and as a human enterprise it partook of that sinfulness. To "counteract . . . this tendency of government," Calhoun drew a rigid distinction between law and constitution. Government and law were axiomatic, "like breathing," while a constitution "is a contrivance of man," and men have the perplexing task of trying to bring their flawed constitutions into conformity with "the wisdom of the Infinite." The greater the threat to the liberty of the community the greater the deviation from the will of the creator and the bolder and more artistic the constitutional remedies men would have to devise to correct their own mistakes. Neither by creating virtuous hierarchies, nor by limiting power, nor by making government "too feeble to protect and preserve

Proslavery Conservatism

society," would the mischievous tendencies of politicians be curbed; greedy officeholders would always find ways of turning those devices to their own purposes. Rather men could preserve their liberty by recognizing that "self-preservation is the supreme law ... with communities as with individuals." On this assumption of communal self-preservation, Calhoun then based his whole elaborate system of the concurrent majority in which a section of the nation could claim a veto over national legislation and thereby reconcile its vital interests with membership in the Union.[45]

Having demolished to his satisfaction Lockean notions of natural rights arising from the protection/ obedience contract, Calhoun reinvented a protection/ obedience compact between entities called sections. Writing "at a moment when the South's fear of the North and its love of the Union" held "each other in perfect balance," Louis Hartz hypothesized, Calhoun seemed oblivious to requirements of consistency, but also highly inventive in his own effort to legitimize southern defiance of constitutional federalism.[46] Calhoun can therefore be seen as hopelessly inconsistent—a brilliant abstract thinker embittered by frustrated ambition—who lost himself in his own convoluted efforts to defend as traditional and orthodox constitutional innovations that were novel and haphazard. Gillis Harp's explanation—building on Hartz and Freehling—is less dramatic. Calhoun, he suggests, "intermingl[ed]" Lockean contractual explanations of political obligation with Machiavellian notions of purity, corruption, and the need for leadership grounded in heroic dedication to the preservation of virtue. Calhoun seems to have appreciated what Harp calls "the inter-relatedness of different political languages" as he moved from Locke on social bonding to the country ideology on public integrity, then to Bolingbrokean fixation over corruption, next to an exotic Lockean denial of natural rights and enshrinement of communal protection against government, and finally to a Machiavellian despair over capricious fortune and insufficient virtue.[47]

The clearest expression of Calhoun's Machiavellian resignation was a phrase he loved to repeat—"a mysterious providence." "A mysterious Providence ... brought together two races from different portions of the globe and placed them together in nearly equal numbers in the southern portion of this Union," he told the Senate in 1838; "experience has shown that the existing relation between them"— Calhoun's euphemism for slavery—"secured the peace and happiness of both.... To destroy it [slavery] was to involve a whole region in slaughter, carnage, and desolation." Just as unmerited adversity struck prosperous and enlightened societies without warning, so the abolitionist frenzy with all its pernicious implications "produced one happy effect.... It has compelled us of the South to look into the nature and character of this great institution ... [and] to see it in its true light as the most safe and stable basis for free institutions in the world."[48] During a debate on public land policy in 1841 Calhoun spoke of the "occupation" of North America by English settlers and the expulsion of "the aborigines" as a source "of the prosperity and greatness of our country." These circumstances, he suggested, arose "through the mysterious dispensation of Providence." Fortuitous chance had pitted English settlers motivated by religious zeal, adventure, enterprise, or a "devotion to liberty" against "aborigines ... too weak to prevent our people from spreading out over the vast extent of the continent." This exceptional ease of possession had preserved the colonists' slender store of civility; otherwise they would "have lost all the arts of civilized life and become fierce herdsmen and barbarians, like our ancestors ... in their frequent inundations over southern Asia and Europe." From unmerited historic good fortune of this kind, Calhoun concluded, "we owe our enterprise, energy, love of liberty, and capacity for self-government."[49]

In the *Disquisition on Government* Calhoun linked political maturity to the unscrutable will of "an all-wise Providence" who granted "liberty... as the noblest and highest reward for the development of our faculties, moral and intellectual;

> A reward more appropriate than liberty could not be conferred on the deserving nor a punishment inflicted on the undeserving more just than to be subject to lawless and despotic rule. This dispensation seems to be the result of some fixed law; and every effort to disturb it or defeat it, by attempting to elevate a people in the scale of liberty above the point to which they are entitled to rise, must ever prove abortive.[50]

The providential theme in Calhoun's later thought was not particularly religious; he said nothing of eschatology or the nature of the divine will or the redemptive purpose of divine intervention. But "mysterious Providence" *was* a perfect synonym for Machiavelli's concept of *fortuna*, what J. G. A. Pocock calls "the circumstantial insecurity of political life," the "pure, uncontrolled, and unlegitimated contingency" that compromises every human effort to control destiny or to

Proslavery Conservatism

make prudence an absolute security against misfortune. "No *virtu*," Pocock paraphrases Machiavelli, "can so completely dominate *fortuna* as to ensure that the same strategy remains always appropriate. . . . No *virtu* . . . gives men the power to change their own natures or consequently to act 'in time' "—that is quickly enough to outwit all that is contingent and unexplainable in the course of history.[51] Calhoun believed that leadership operated on just such a knife-edge of uncertainty and sheer nerve: "The contest" over tariff enforcement and nullification

> will in fact be a contest between power and liberty, . . . a contest in which the weaker section with its peculiar labor, production, and institutions has a stake in all that can be dear to freemen. Should we be able to maintain in their full vigour our reserved rights, liberty and prosperity will be our portion; but if we yield . . . then will our fate be more wretched than that of the aborigines whom we have expelled.[52]

Presbyterian civic orthodoxy in the South contained the same uneasy ambivalence about compact and corruption that energized Calhoun's Force bill speech. "Who knows," mused Robert Lewis Dabney in 1840, "but that this uproar of the abolitionist, which has almost broken the ties of our Union and thrown the poor slave back from his hope of approaching emancipation at least half a century, may have been designed by Providence as a check upon our imprudent liberality?" Even this bizarre scenario of social decay and divine regeneration operated within a context of reciprocal duties and obligations. "I cannot conceive of any duty arising to love my neighbor as myself," Dabney explained, "which compels me to inflict ruinous injury on that neighbor, and such would immediate freedom be to our slaves."[53]

Twenty years later Dabney still equated the claims of the compact with reconciliation of hostile, divergent demands arising from the slavery controversy. "It is a matter of life and death to Virginia to prevent being thrust into . . . the miserable dilemma of helpless submission to her northern enemies or of unwilling submission to a dirty, slave-trading, filibustering, proslavery cotton league, of which she is to be the poor, harrassed, tattered *selvage*, to be held between the body and danger." A freely chosen place of dignity and safety outside the vortex of conflict was what the compact should have guaranteed Virginia, and the defense of that bulwark was the "Christian . . . duty in staying the tide of passion and violence. . . . I had been more hopeful before this, believing that surely the people could not be so forsaken

The Antebellum Era

of God and their own senses"—underscoring the Calvinist, Lockean framework of his thought—"to go to cutting each other's throats."[54]

Caught inescapably between these moral polarities—of respect for property rights and concern for the well-being of blacks who were unprepared for freedom, of the destructiveness of northern and southern extremists whose conduct sadly vindicated the need for a controlling government and a loving, sovereign God—Dabney posited his own criticism of slavery. It was a system that ought to die because it was "liable to the most erroneous abuses." Yet responsibility for those abuses lay only with the slaveowners who committed them and with the slavetrading "forefathers of the Yankee abolitionists who entailed the curse upon us." As slavery was "an obstacle to the *Prince of peace*," he argued, "so it is our duty to overcome" it. But considering the apparent impossibility of abolition, overcoming slavery became a matter of "modify[ing] the system and remov[ing] the abuses . . . while we retain the good parts of it."[55]

The positive side of Dabney's civility remained a conservative Lockean view of obligation: the Declaration of Independence did not apply to "African barbarians"; abolitionism had its intellectual roots in the "Socinian [antitrinitarian] and rationalistic" apostasy of Unitarians who deceitfully regarded Boston as the "American Athens." Even if slavery could be shown to violate the golden rule, that rule did not necessarily require treating others as we would want to be treated, Dabney objected in a tortuous rationalization, but as *"we should, in that case, be morally entitled"* to be treated. Viewing moral and social obligation as a trade-off of duties and liberties very narrowly circumscribed, Dabney insisted, was all a southern Christian could do about slavery:

> The propriety of slavery, like that of the restraints and punishments of civil government, rests on the fact that man is depraved and fallen. Such is his character, that the rights of the whole, and the greatest welfare of the whole, may, in many cases, demand the subjection of one part of society to another, even as man's sinfulness demands the subjection of all to civil government. Slavery is, indeed, but one form of the institution, *government*. . . . And this is the Scriptural account of the origin of slavery, as justly incurred by the sin and depravity of man.[56]

Albert Taylor Bledsoe mixed contractual assurance with republican pessimism more freely. Personal liberty, he argued with reference to slavery in 1860, is simply something taken by society from one person

Proslavery Conservatism

and given to another. "Liberty is ... created by the bonds of civil society. ... The bonds or laws by which this liberty is created are imposed not on the natural right, but on the natural tyranny, of man," Bledsoe contended. Liberty was a fortuitous attainment within the community rather than an intrinsic right. Only "that public order alone which cherishes the true liberty of the individual is strong in the approbation of God and in the moral sentiments of mankind," he declared, moving toward the awful possibility of societal degeneracy; "all else is weakness, death and decay."[57]

Benjamin Morgan Palmer's *National Responsibility before God: A Discourse, Delivered on the Day of Fasting, Humiliation, and Prayer, Appointed by the President of the Confederate States of America, June 13, 1861* rescued as much moral virtue as a sinful past and a dangerous present would allow. The war was indeed a judgment for American, as well as southern, sins of "idolatry," irreverence, "flagrant abuse of the elective franchise," "grievous want of reverence for the authority and majesty of the law," and "a grovelling to merely material interests." There were, however, limits—imposed by historical fortune—on the practice of penitence, and what Palmer saw situated beyond those limits was the intractability of human affairs and an inscrutability closely resembling what Calhoun called "mysterious Providence":

I had designed ... *to speak of the obligations we owe to our slave population.* But the subject is excluded by its own largeness from discussion now. It will bear postponement. When this unnatural war shall be concluded, and we shall be free from the impertinent interference with our domestic affairs by which we have been so long annoyed, there will be opportunity to say all that the moralist and Christian should utter, and what it will be fitting the legislator and the master should hear. We can afford to bide the time.[58]

The perplexity of conservative southern Protestants over consent and corruption—whether to fasten attention on order or on disorder—was only a part of the religious culture of the Old South. This ill-defined yet persistent conundrum was important because it arose from the tensions between revered traditions, drawn from Old World and colonial experience, and fresh possibilities thrust before southerners by changes taking place in the wider world. One of those changes was the intrusion into the South of the national and international market economy, which placed slaveowners under unprece-

The Antebellum Era

dented pressure to maximize profits and expand the capital base of their operations; another was the spread throughout the middle and upper ranks of society of a pervasive concern with social order. Not surprisingly, a new kind of proslavery thought in the 1850s found expression—one that comported well with expanding economic risk and opportunity and with rising demands for social discipline.

The most explicitly religious variety of the new proslavery ideology was millenialist. The pages of the *Southern Presbyterian Review*, Jack P. Maddex has discovered, "regularly referred to the coming millennial age" in which the current generation of Christians could participate by quickening the pace of social progress and intensifying personal piety and morality as prologue to the final eschatalogical drama. Rather than ignoring the seeming embarrassment of slavery, these millennialists brought it to the center of their prophetic work.

To see the Kingdom required a pure faith that the issue of emancipation was in God's hands and that the Father might or might not will that it occur and that criticism of slavery usurped God's sovereign disposal of the matter. It also required solemn affirmation of the conventional, proslavery wisdom that slavery was no worse than northern wage slavery and a prescient view that modernization would produce more regimentation of labor and extremes of leisure, wealth, and servile labor.

These views harbored two exciting social prophesies that the world was moving into an era of industrial as well as agricultural exploitation of labor in which the South was uniquely experienced and that Christian paternalism was the secret to maintaining social harmony in a culture of privilege and oppression.[59]

Proslavery millenialists proclaimed without a trace of irony that slavery's infinite capacity for improvement and moral enhancement made it an ideal activity within which to observe the onset of the millennium. Were slavery "carried out in a *scriptural sense*," the Virginia Presbyterian minister Samuel J. Cassells declared, "I can scarcely imagine a better state of society than what might thus exist."[60] Charles Colcock Jones, the preeminent advocate of evangelization of slaves and use of Christian doctrine to attack the evils of slavery from within, explained that the "*changes* in the system, which justice and mercy may require, may be happily effected by the tranquil yet powerful and conservative influence of the Gospel." Moved by his dislike of slavery, his distrust of human efforts to alter it, and his commitment to the building of the Kingdom of God, Jones testified that "the Gos-

Proslavery Conservatism

pel will certainly improve [slavery], as it will every other defective form of government in the world." If masters would become fully imbued with loving attentiveness to their slaves' needs, human qualities, and capacity to give and receive love, there could be no limit to how much the spirit might transform master-slave relationships.[61] When that day arrived, the Mississippi minister, James A. Lyon predicted, "not that one man will not serve the other, but [rather] all minds and hearts being completely under the control of Christianity, there can be no antagonism of will, since what will be the unselfish right of the one ... will be the pleasing duty of the other."[62]

James Henley Thornwell, the most important figure among the proslavery millennialists, and the intellectual leader of Presbyterianism in the Old South produced the fullest examination of these possibilities. His treatise, *The Rights and Duties of Masters: A Sermon Preached at the Dedication of a Church, Erected in Charleston, S.C., for the Benefit and Instruction of the Coloured Population* on May 26, 1850 celebrated an auspicious occasion. Not until page 41 of this sermon did Thornwell exhaust the standard litany of Christian proslavery: the evils existing in the North and in England, "the insane fury of philanthropy" that condemned slavery on humanitarian grounds while threatening to incite "insurrection in our midst," the "excesses of unchecked democracy" elsewhere in the world, scriptural sanction for slavery , as well as the more novel contentions that slavery was compatible with Christianity to the extent that it did not discourage "piety," "communion with God," or "the onward progress of man" and that slavery enslaved only the labor, and not the body, of the slave. He devoted extensive attention to the notion that true slavery was bondage to sin and made the astonishing concession that slavery was "part of the curse which sin introduced into the world," though presumably not a sin in and of itself.

After disposing of all of these problems, Thornwell finally came to the mysterious process by which slavery, in the hands of Christian masters, would purge itself of evil. At first the formulation was familiarly Lockean: "Let masters and servants, each in their respective spheres, be impregnated with the principle of duty, ... masters ... never transcending the legitimate bounds of their authority—and servants ... never falling short of the legitimate claims on their obedience." But instead of next contemplating regretfully the evidence that slaves were not equipped for such demands, and admitting that it was unrealistic to expect masters to perform such acts of moral grandeur,

The Antebellum Era

Thornwell proceeded to describe how Providence implanted within slavery the seeds of benevolence. Slavery, he argued,

> is one of the conditions in which God is conducting the moral proba-
> tion of man . . . one of the schools in which immortal spirits are trained
> for their final destiny. . . . The Christian beholds [the slave], not as a
> tool, not a chattel, not a brute or a thing—but an immortal spirit, as-
> signed to a particular position in this world of wretchedness and sin, in
> which he is required to work out the destiny which attaches to him, in
> common with his fellows, as a man.[63]

Proslavery millennialism saw master-slave relationships as intimate and continuous conduits of Christian spirituality into actual
behavior and consciousness. Optimistic, persuaded of the systemic
nature of change in a middle-class culture, yet driven by the specter of
what slavery might become without amelioration, these churchmen
equated the moral regulation of slavery with the march of progress.
Acting on these principles, Christians could "eat the heart of slavery
even as slavery continues."[64]

Calvin Henderson Wiley—a lay Presbyterian preacher raised in
Eli Caruthers's Alamance Presbyterian Church, who became in 1853
the first Superintendent of Common Schools in North Carolina—
brought Christian proslavery to its apogee in his book-length manuscript on "The Duties of Christian Masters" written between 1855 and
1859. "The existence of African slavery in the United States, a free
and Christian land, offers an exceedingly wide and interesting field
for the labors of the followers of Christ," he declared at the outset of
his exceedingly long discussion. Slavery provided Christian masters
with an accessible and infinitely varied laboratory in which to practice and study morality and discipleship. And slavery could become—
in the hands of diligent and pious masters—the means of
communicating to slaves themselves their fallen moral nature, their
due subordination to those God had placed over them, and the vital
distinction between physical and spiritual freedom. Conceiving of
slavery as an educational enterprise, Wiley imbibed fully the utopian
proslavery notion that modernization put all human relationships on
a new and hopeful footing:

> No rational being can be held, but by force, in non-reasonable bond-
> age, and as the Negro is a reasonable being, and from his position and
> association ever making some progress in knowledge and becoming

Proslavery Conservatism

more observant and reflective, it is essential to the well being of society that he should receive right ideas as to its origin and character. Of course he is not capable of comprehending abstruse and abstract principles and systems or fine metaphysical distinctions, but it must be remembered that the greatest, most important, and most practical truths are the simplest and most easy to learn.

Of the principles on which society was founded and on which men and women could build their lives, none were as important as the truth "that happiness here can only be secured by a conscientious discharge of duty and a well grounded hope of a blessed immortality beyond the grave."[65] The powerful role of "well grounded hope" in immortality, and ever-present mindfulness of "duty" to perform, constituted the mature form of evangelical commitment in the Old South. The apprehensive defense of slavery hastened the attainment of that maturity.

Excursus III

Culminations:
The Moral Economy of the Old South

The problem of authority had troubled three generations of conservatives and evangelicals in the South. The nature of freedom and the dimensions of human creativity bulked larger in the cultural consciousness of northern and western American society, but the discussion of authority bestowed a fitting gravity on religion and politics in the early South. Eighteenth-century Augustan thought located authority in hypothetical social spheres like benevolent bureaucracies or symbiotic fusions of church and state. Revolutionary whigs did them one better by making the people as an abstract entity the repository of authority. Republican constitutionalists believed that popular authority could be expressed by concrete actions in behalf of the public good taken by people entrusted with power by the community. Antebellum romantics thrilled to the possibility of transforming society in light of authoritative moral visions, or they brooded over the human passions in their own and in others' breasts that made those visions chimerical. The end-product of these definitions and redefinitions of authority was a commonly shared understanding of how people—in the light of their history and ethics—ought to behave and could be expected to behave. Historians sometimes call this understanding "the moral economy" of a group of people. An episode in Georgia, on the eve of the Civil War, revealed clearly how religion, social ethics, and folkways coalesced.

"Sir, you entered my family on a friendly arrangement, . . . " began a letter from the Reverend Charles Colcock Jones to a former friend and houseguest whose name Jones's modern editor suppressed. During a lengthy visit in the Jones plantation house, "Maybank," in Liberty County, Georgia, during the summer of 1860, Jones alleged, the guest had seduced and impregnated a young slave chambermaid.

> The proof of your criminality is of so clear a character as to remove all doubt. *There is the free, unconstrained confession of the Negro woman herself in full detail; there is the correspondence between the time of your connection with*

Excursus III. Culminations

her and the birth of the child—a mulatto, now some time born; and there is a resemblance to you beyond mistake.

The heart of Jones's letter, however, was not this allegation, nor his challenge to the culprit to report his offense to the Session of his own Presbyterian Church for disciplinary action; it was a description and explanation of the moral organization of antebellum southern life that ought to have prevented this particular outrage from ever occurring in the first place. "You ... became particularly known to me ... when a guest of my neighbors," Jones explained;

> you were introduced to me as an educated man, the son of a venerable and highly esteemed minister of South Carolina, whose full name you bear; as a married man, having but recently married your second wife, who was then absent at the North for her health; as a prominent member of the Presbyterian church in Columbus, Georgia, the superintendent of the Sunday school, the president of the Young Men's Christian Association, and the principal of a female high school in that city, and recommended on your school circular by names of the first respectability. You had also taught a school within the bounds of our own congregation in Liberty County, and had associated with the active members of the church resident in the village, and taken part in their religious meetings, and I believe aided them in their efforts to give religious instruction to the Negroes. You came to my acquaintance under these favorable circumstances, and were received for what you were considered and professed yourself to be—a gentleman, a married man, and a Christian. You had my confidence as unreservedly as any stranger possibly could have, and enjoyed the kind hospitality of my family from the day you entered to the day you left it. You rendered yourself agreeable, and conducted yourself with every mark of respect and propriety; were always present morning and evening at family worship, and also in our weekly neighborhood prayer meeting. You were the guest of a gentleman, a professing Christian and minister of the gospel, and witnessed from week to week his efforts to instruct religiously the servants of his family and household.[1]

The key words in that passage were "stranger" and "family." The family and the household stood at the center of expanding rings of concentric circles through which strangers had to pass from the unknown outside world as they sought access to the intimate places of society. The miscreant's own parentage and family identified him as a trusted member of another community of virtue and his marriage

The Antebellum Era

marked him as someone who would not be suspected of illicit sexual designs. By becoming a church member, a Sunday School Superintendent, a Y.M.C.A. President, and the principal of an elite school for young girls, he had secured entry into more and more intimate social situations. These credentials, in turn, helped qualify him—as a visitor to Liberty County—to attend prayer meetings and teach religion to slaves in the Presbyterian Church in Jones's own neighborhood. (A long-time historian of the church and nationally recognized advocate of Christianization of blacks, as well as a wealthy planter, Jones was no longer a parish minister.)

This tableau of sin and retribution illustrates two critical features in the moral economy of the Old South. First, white southerners divided their social world into two groups, strangers and homefolk. The latter were family, friends, and neighbors; the former were outsiders who might be homefolk somewhere else but bore close watching until their trust-worthiness and moral credentials could be checked. Strangers, therefore, carried with them indelible badges of virtue or vice that could be seen by the careful observer. Name and family connections headed the list of questions to be asked a stranger. Body language, dress, voice intonation, facial expression, demeanor, and horsemanship were further "ascriptive" indicators of upbringing, motivation, and social training. How one dealt with social inferiors and superiors and with members of the opposite sex further revealed a person's character. No one ventured very far into the life of a neighborhood, a local church, or into the inner sanctum of the home and family without undergoing close scrutiny. "I have never been more deceived in a man in all my life," Jones exclaimed; "what disgrace of ruin and character you have brought upon yourself.... Of the hundreds of men,... who have been guests in my house,... you... are the only man who has ever dared to offer *to me personally and to my family and to my neighbors* so vile and so infamous an insult.... Had you been detected, I should have driven you instantly out of the house and off the premises with all the accompanying disgrace which you merited." The ferocity and anguish of this language accurately measured Jones's incredulity at witnessing the breakdown of a system of moral regulation that, in his view, was all that set the South apart from the rest of the sinful world.[2]

Second, when "ascriptive" tests of virtue failed to deter or prevent sinful aggression, a dual system of law enforcement dealt with crimes committed in the Old South. Sheriffs, judges, and juries consti-

Excursus III. Culminations

tuted formal machinery of justice; vigilantes and popular exuberance were the informal means by which the community dealt with wrong-doing. Public officials knew better than to interfere when white ruffians, sometimes with planter leadership, decided that some miscreant had escaped punishment for some offense against the community.[3] Charles Colcock Jones was no vigilante, but there were hints in his reaction to the seduction of his chambermaid that he would have to invoke popular outrage if he was to secure satisfaction against the school principal from Columbus, Georgia. Within hours after receiving Jones's letter, the accused gentleman did show it to two discreet, friendly members of the Session of the Columbus Presbyterian Church. He probably thereby evaded Jones's demand that he lay the matter before the entire Session. After some deliberation the two replied to Jones pleading their unwillingness to take formal disciplinary action against the accused or exposing him to public censure.

> In looking at the evidence so far as appears by your letter, it is: first, the birth of a mulatto child at a time corresponding to the time Mr. [Lee] was in your family; second, the declarations of the mother of the child; and, third, the resemblance of the child to the accused. The first part of the evidence—time—is satisfactory as far as it goes. The second—the mother's declaration—is what usually has to be mainly relied upon in similar cases when the mother is a free white woman; but courts and juries have not always convicted the accused when the mother's declaration upon oath has been positive. The third—to wit, resemblance—is of very doubtful character at best. You can doubtless readily call to mind the very striking resemblance that is often found to exist between persons where there can be no kindred, and then again the absence of resemblance between brothers and sisters, parents and children, where the fidelity of the parents would not be questioned by anyone acquainted with them.

Community attitudes about scorned women could protect as well as jeopardize an accused person. Jones's wistful desire that he had caught his houseguest in the act of fornication so that he could have personally driven him from Maybank, with clothing askew and the sound of Old Testament moral denunciation echoing through the stillness of the night, further evoked the notion of informal justice. Having missed that opportunity, Jones did the best he could. He investigated and discovered an earlier case in which this culprit had allegedly fathered a bastard child by a slave girl "in the village where he

The Antebellum Era

taught school," had "denied the charge before the trustees of the school," and had succeeded in having the slave girl whipped for her insolence.[4]

The dispute between Jones and the two members of the Columbus Church Session who came to the defense of the alleged seducer was, on one level, over which system of justice ought to operate in this case. Because the law offered him no relief, Jones could only hope that other Christians would consign the miscreant to disgrace; the members of the Session preferred legal institutions to community sentiment because courts and lawyers instinctively protected the reputations of males from feminine vengeance and slander. At a deeper level, however, the argument dealt with *which* informal code of justice ought to prevail: sanctions against sexual licence, which Jones believed had been breached, or those against racial and sexual presumption, which the chambermaid had violated in making reckless allegations against a respectable white male. In an unintended but delicious irony of nomenclature, the *Columbus* laymen confronted the *Liberty* County minister with the veiled demand to know just how far he was willing to go in jeopardizing white male solidarity in the exposure of alleged sexual misconduct—whether he was willing to rend the social order every time a black woman accused a white man of fornication.

The exercise of authority, by society over individuals and by individuals over family members, slaves, and even houseguests was therefore fraught with ambiguity and uncertainty. In "The Duties of Christian Masters," Calvin Wiley devoted a long chapter to the subject of "Human Authority" in an effort to subsume all of these difficulties beneath a covering theological law. "It is the will of God that there should be authority of man over man," Wiley contended. When God ordered Adam to "be fruitful and multiply and replenish the earth and subdue it and have dominion over... every living thing," He placed authority in the hands of human fathers. Following the fall from grace— "a wreck in moral nature and the harmony and beauty of all its material and immaterial surroundings"—God allowed human beings to occupy "an intermediate state between Heaven and Hell where a rebellious race could be held in temporary bondage." Cursed with knowledge of "the blessedness" they had lost and "the horrors" of the fall, humans there lived in a "probationary state" and enjoyed only limited capacity to escape enslavement to the Devil. One of the few resources available to fallen humanity was "the establish-

Excursus III.   Culminations

ment of human authority" through the agencies of government and the family.[5]

In an imperfect world, however, those embodiments of authority had to contend with "the new instincts of the race" in which "those unlike in sex, in age, color, and strength" would "war on and devour or oppress each other." God therefore gave humans a further compensating gift; "it was subordination ... peaceful and legal subjection ... to prevent a perpetual war for ... mastery." Wiley then ransacked the Old Testament for evidence that God expected human creatures to subject themselves to political rulers, and children, servants, and sojourners to the head of their household. Thus the Ten Commandments had special meaning for slaveowners by compressing into a short list the spiritual discipline masters should impose upon their slaves. Prohibitions on theft, murder, adultery, and falsehood represented the active side of moral subjection while those on idolatry, covetousness, disrespect of parents, and violations of the Sabbath taught the correct spirit of reverence toward the deity and the hierarchical system God had ordained.[6] By seizing the "missionary opportunity" to inculcate obedience and piety in their slaves, the master and his wife could escape the self-absorption and callousness of well-to-do northerners. Wiley seized on the distinction between the codified and informal law to liberate the master from guilt and fear. "The true course," he wrote,

> is to regard slavery as an existing system which cannot now be abolished with justice to either master or servants; and conducting it in strict accordance with Divine precepts, and with an honest and conscientious view to the interests of both races, and with the understanding that this is the path of moral duty only under existing circumstances, to be ready and willing to leave the future to the Providence of God, in the development of time, whatever this may be.[7]

As an educator, Wiley expressed the southern evangelical desire first enunciated by Samuel McCorkle: that together the religion of the heart and the discipline of the mind prepared people to respond to offerings of Providence. "Christians ought to be warm and zealous friends of learning and philosophy," the *Evangelical and Literary Magazine* declared in Virginia in 1822; "ministers of the gospel ought especially to be among the foremost in intellectual attainments.... A mere smattering of knowledge ought not to satisfy them. Their adversaries

The Antebellum Era

are learned, acute, and industrious. . . . Unless literature and philosophy [can] be made subservient to the cause of vital Christianity, they will be powerful auxiliaries of infidelity."[8]

Convinced of the existence of an overarching, infinite, and benevolent web of Christian purpose, action, and intention, southern evangelicals perceived it their duty to thrust spiritual energy into the cosmos and toward that web, trusting that God would permit their acts of charity and expressions of piety to adhere to the gossamer veil. "The religion of the South is a do-it-yourself religion, something I as a Catholic find painful and touching and grimly comic," Flannery O'Connor would later observe; "it's full of unconscious pride that lands them in all sorts of ridiculous predicaments. They have nothing to correct their practical heresies and so they work them out dramatically."[9] Charles Colcock Jones invoked just such a limitless sense of the efficacy of Christian volition when he predicted that, for the pious, diligent slaveowner, "light will insensibly break into his mind. Conscience will be quickened and before he is aware perhaps, his servants will be greatly elevated in his regards and he will feel himself bound and willing to do more and more for them."[10] Black evangelicals during slavery also believed, as John Jasper put it, that "Ev'body got to rise to meet King Jesus, in th' morning," but they saw the great human homecoming in starkly egalitarian terms: "th' high and th' low, th' rich and th' po', th' bond and th' free, as well as me."[11]

Epilogue:

Political Legacies of Early Southern Evangelicalism

By the close of the antebellum period, evangelicalism had spilled across the social landscape of the South for more than a century. From Whitefield to McCorkle to Thornwell, evangelical Christianity had passed through a life cycle from youth to maturity to old age. A religious as well as a political age ended in 1861. In the next century the creation of autonomous, black evangelical denominations as well as the rise of fundamentalism and pentecostalism would alter in significant ways the religious impulses examined in this book. Alter but not obliterate. Viewed from the perspective of conservative political discourse, three distinct legacies of early southern evangelicalism—traditional, combative, and prophetic—continued and continue to shape southern history.

For *traditional* southern evangelicals, the Christian message of redemption comes to people living in a world shaped by past experience and indebted to received tradition. They pride themselves on accepting history and thought and theology as necessary disciplines for a nation and its citizens. A good example of the influence of this tradition was the academic career of Woodrow Wilson, which took him to Connecticut and New Jersey but had deep roots in southern Presbyterianism. His father, Joseph Ruggles Wilson, an Ohio native of Scots-Irish ancestry who spent virtually his entire ministry in the southern Presbyterian Church, had a profound influence on his famous son. He wholeheartedly embraced Thornwell's covenant theology under which God expected the faithful to govern the world according to a Biblical moral law, even using that law to expunge evil from slavery. "Slavery is embedded in the very heart of the moral law itself," the elder Wilson told his Augusta, Georgia, parishioners in an obligatory proslavery sermon in 1861, "a law which constitutes... the very *constitution* of that royal kingdom whose regulations begin and

Epilogue

end in the infinite holiness of Jehovah." Woodrow's lifetime fascination with written constitutions began with his father's teaching about the divinely instilled sources of order in human affairs.

He also absorbed his father's Calvinist orientation toward ambition and striving—searing self-examination and painful resignation to the workings of Providence. The elder Wilson had great ambitions as a minister and seminary professor, but church politics and denominational poverty blighted his career. In mid-life, he wrote that "the ambitious man trusts to the people to lift him into eminence of position" but knows that "people and princes . . . cannot confer that smile which lights up the living-room of the soul" or clarify God's purpose for a person's life. Thus paternal injunctions to Woodrow to "dismiss *ambition* and replace it with hard industry," to "go out from your own personality" into public service, "not to regard ego as the center of the universe," to remember that "genius" for such service consisted of "the ability to work with painstaking self-denial," and seek this fulfillment through a regimen of devotional introspection and humility, were the bond between Wilson and the person he called "my incomparable father." In an informal religious service led by one of his father's theological students near Wilson's seventeenth birthday, he had an intense conversion experience; as a student at Davidson College he underwent a typical crisis of faith; and during a protracted revival at Princeton he placed on his door a sign which read "I am a Christian, but studying for exams." [1]

Whether his progressivism after 1910 was liberal or conservative, the central theme in Wilson's teaching and scholarship was bringing British conservative thought to bear on the revitalization of American civic life. At the time of his graduation from Princeton in 1879, Wilson and a close friend drew up "a solemn covenant" to strive with "all our powers and passions for the work of establishing the principles we held in common" through "persuasion" and leadership. By the mid-1890s, when he had returned to teach political science at Princeton, social unrest in the country had convinced Wilson that Burke's conservatism provided the best material for a persuasive analysis of freedom and responsibility. Wilson admired Burke's ability to formulate a system of political principles, his bold exhortations to others to rethink the fundamental grounds of their political beliefs, and his emotional volatility and vulnerability. Burke's concept of party as a fellowship of highminded men sharing common principles seemed to Wilson to salvage the best of human attributes—friendship, personal

Political Legacies

honor, generosity—from the tawdry environment of politics, and to put them to service in behalf of the state. Burke's celebration of the political process answered Wilson's yearning for wholeness in public life: "All government, indeed human benefit and enjoyment, every virtue and prudent act," he quoted approvingly from Burke, "is founded upon compromise and barter. . . . We choose . . . to be happy citizens [rather] than subtle disputants." [2]

A decade later, as President of Princeton, he repeatedly urged graduating seniors to emulate the Burkean ideal. "Our function in life is not that of critics merely, to perceive this is good and that evil. . . . We must be active lovers of the good, propagandists of the excellent." And he emphasized how closely this ideal conformed to the moral covenant he had learned in his father's church. "Whether. . . you are aware of it or not," he told the class of 1904, "the air you have breathed here is Christian, saturated with influence and the traditions of men who have followed the divine master and sought to learn of Him. . . . We breed a type of men . . . morally noticeable, . . . less servile, more individual, full of an energy which is of the heart as well as the mind." [3]

Wilson's emphasis on persuasion, on the burdens of duty, and on the need to instill high intellectual standards into conservative thought contrasted sharply with the political values of Presbyterians in North Carolina in the 1920s, who demanded a law prohibiting the teaching of evolution. They were concerned less with Biblical literalism than with the threat that modernism in the schools and in the study of science would erode respect for the work of the deity. And they needed to preserve the seamless unity of faith and knowledge so essential to order and the subordination of individuals to the morally upright will of the community. "We wish it clearly understood," the editors of the *Presbyterian Standard* declared, "that we are not discussing the truth or falsity of evolution. . . . The question before us is whether the Christian people of this state are going to support any institution that countenances an open attack upon our cherished beliefs." [4] Against this moral and intellectual prescription stood William Louis Poteat, biology professor and President of Wake Forest College, who declared that in forty years of teaching, "I have discredited neither the Genesis account of the origin of man nor the gospel account of the origin of Jesus Christ. . . . I frankly believe that God created all things and animals, man included, by the method of evolution." [5] Poteat's former students in the legislature provided the crucial votes to

Epilogue

defeat the bill outlawing the teaching of evolution. He regarded the intellectual traditions of the western world, including Darwinian science, as necessary means of pursuing truth.

A later twentieth-century example of southern Baptist intellectual independence is Jimmy Carter, the other southern evangelical to occupy the White House. Carter shared Poteat's candor and straightforwardness, and, like Wilson, he drew deeply, though more indirectly and selectively, on European tradition in search of intellectual and moral discipline for himself and his contemporaries. A chief influence on Carter was the work of Reinhold Niebuhr, whose major treatise, *The Nature and Destiny of Man* and subsequent books on politics and theology, reintroduced a generation of American religious and political readers to the European philosophical context within which Protestant and early Christian theology took shape. Beginning when he was a member of the Georgia Senate, Carter turned repeatedly to *Moral Man and Immoral Society*, *The Irony of American History*, an anthology entitled *Reinhold Niebuhr on Politics*, and a discerning biography of Niebuhr by June Bingham. Carter grasped the "two centers of Niebuhr's own thinking, love and justice on one hand; pride, power, and interest on the other." [6]

When Carter's interest in Niebuhr became political news, religiously literate observers wondered how a candidate who celebrated the "goodness" of the American people could be a serious thinker about what Niebuhr had called "the sad duty of politics ... to establish justice in a sinful world." The affinity between the two men lay beneath surface appearances. Niebuhr was a synthesizer of elements from Protestant tradition and the intellectual history of western civilization. He readily linked the radicalism of democratic evangelicals in the eighteenth century and abolitionist evangelicals of the nineteenth century to the demands of justice in the Old Testament, in European natural law, and in various kinds of libertarian thought. This mixture of ideas exactly meshed with Carter's experience as an opponent of segregation in the deep South in the 1950s and 1960s. Those battles taught Carter that evil could be perpetrated by neighbors and that justice could be vindicated by small, imperfect acts of obedience to the law and to principles of equality. Niebuhr's ironic view of history in which flawed human beings achieve imperfect justice and mercy therefore struck a responsive chord in Carter. "Niebuhr does say that there is inherent selfishness, or failure, callousness, pride—they exist," Carter told an interviewer early in his presidency, but "there comes a

Political Legacies

time of crisis when the superb qualities of human beings in a collective fashion are evoked in a religious concept or in a governmental structure that transcends the mundane commitments of people."

Carter told his Sunday School class in Washington that the Bible is "a debate between God and man, God and woman, over the laws of God, a constant interchange between God and human beings in which we struggle to justify ourselves." That comment showed how far Carter had come from the Biblical literalism of his Georgia roots and suggested that a critical feature of his Georgia experience was a painful reexamination of social attitudes in the light of Scripture. It also echoed Niebuhr's injection that "we are made to be in dialogue not only with ourselves but also with our fellows, and ultimately with God. The Bible . . . is not the record of a monologue on the part of God or man, but of a spirited exchange between them."[7]

In fashioning leadership from regional tradition and the western heritage, Wilson, Poteat, and Carter bore what C. Vann Woodward has called "the burden of southern history."[8] They leavened southern political life and discourse in the same way Witherspoon had hoped Princeton graduates would enrich American politics with values of moral philosophy. Their paradoxical mixture of pride and humility violated the combative southern notion that evil comes like an intruder in the dark, that moral and political leadership must strike a posture of defiance against alien presumption. In contrast with traditional evangelicalism, which had a pervasive impact on some segments of the region's elite but less popular influence, two remaining public faces of southern evangelicalism struck exposed nerves in the political consciousness of the South. One is *combative* evangelicalism, the acerbic and aggressive assault on modern political liberalism conducted in the name of voters whom Senator Jesse Helms praised for sending "a message throughout the world that North Carolina is a conservative God-fearing state."[9]

The political appeals of Helms and of Jerry Falwell for a righteous crusade to purify America have deep roots in southern religious and public life. Helm's caustic television editorials in the 1960s excoriated civil rights leaders for their failure to condemn "crime and immorality" by blacks while having the temerity to demand the dismantling of segregation. Helms re-emphasized the nineteenth century belief that in a bi-racial society, informal justice imposed by moralistic whites on disturbers of community norms of whatever race was an unavoidable social discipline and that this reality should be recog-

Epilogue

nized and respected by everyone, especially black people. In 1963, a white Post Office employee from Baltimore, was murdered while engaged in a quixotic civil rights march across Alabama; by Helms's account, he carried a sign questioning the divinity of Jesus along with others advocating racial integration. Responding to public outrage over the killing, Helms declared that while "we regret . . . the death of Mr. Moore, . . . the record should be clear. Mr. Moore was a deliberate, calculating trouble-maker . . . who went looking for trouble and found it in a heavier dose than he expected." [10] Falwell's warning that "for the last twenty or thirty years we have suffered shame and . . . international embarrassment because we have been violating God's principles" invoked Old Testament images of a sinful people rebelling against God's sovereign authority. [11]

History, for these evangelicals, is not an education so much as it is a polemical weapon to be used in the fight against what Helms has called "the inseparable entities of atheism and socialism—or liberalism—which tends in the same direction." The right use of history for Helms is the construction from examples in the past of stark alternatives between good and evil. [12] Harking back to the "germ theory" of western political development popularized in the late nineteenth century, Helms has declared that "our indebtedness for the freedom Americans enjoy" goes not to "the Syrians, the Egyptians, or the Romans" but to the Germanic tribes who invented local self-government. From that development, as well as from early Greek and Roman precedents and New Testament sources, he drove quickly to a typical Helmsian polarity: "Liberty . . . is not guaranteed by edicts or proclamations or slogans from the mob, but by order and discipline and fundamental self-control." [13]

Lack of discipline in modern society, for Helms, is the greatest single affront to the heritage of the past. A prime example was public school desegregation, which he traced to the radicalism of the French Revolution, an "ideology" contemptuous of "law and custom." Consequently, the virulent political tendency of "equality, as a mowing down of every person to a mass man, has been a pitiable, corrosive force in modern society." That harsh set of alternatives is, for Helms, the only way history can instruct. He told with relish the story of the Pilgrims attempting communal ownership of property and then discovering, under the leadership of William Bradford, that only private property and individual enterprise provided the necessary incentives for the colony to survive. The lesson of the Pilgrims discredited what

Political Legacies

Helms called modern liberalism's abandonment of "personal initiative and responsibility."

In Helms's implacable view of history, the American past was a long, usually losing struggle between license and self-restraint, between "the patrons of the indolent and unproductive" and those who "adhered to ideals of limited and frugal government." From the date of the adoption of the sixteenth amendment, permitting the income tax, "the people of the United States began to lose their liberty. From then on, Congress knew where and how to get the money to push its citizens around."[14] The people should push back. "Above all," Helms has written, "Americans must rise up and reclaim their nation from the slothful, divisive, prodigal, and treacherous individuals who have bartered away our freedom for a mess of pottage."[15] Sloth, divisiveness, prodigality, and treachery defined the spectrum of human sins the combative evangelicals wish to discredit. This accusatory religious rhetoric—like the small town, Protestant, southern culture from which it arises—defines sin only in personal terms and attributes most temptation to external cultural contamination.

In addition to traditional and combative southern evangelicalism, a third body of belief—one not often thought of as conservative but one deeply concerned with defining norms in light of Scripture, tradition, and experience—remains to be acknowledged. The black churches in the South have traditionally combined a Calvinist appreciation of human depravity with an older, *prophetic* Christian view that the suffering of the people of God under persecution and tyranny is a focus of true spirituality. Martin Luther King, Jr., who began his Baptist ministry in the mid-1950s in Alabama about the same time Jerry Falwell did in Virginia, declared early in the civil rights movement that

> when we lay our lives bare before the scrutiny of God, we admit that though we know truth, yet we lie; we do know how to be just, yet we are unjust; we know that we should love, yet we hate; we stand at the juncture of the high road, yet we deliberately choose the low road. "All we like sheep have gone astray."[16]

King's high road/low road dualism drew on sources far removed from Calvinism. Like other strands of evangelicalism, this one combined, in fruitful tension, the givens of a sinful world and a redeeming Creator with imperatives to participate in the drama of salvation.

Epilogue

"If one is truly devoted to the religion of Jesus," King declared, "he will seek to rid the world of social evils. The gospel is social as well as personal. I still believe that standing up for the truth of God is the greatest thing in the world. The end of life is to do the will of God, come what may."[17]

Notes

PROLOGUE

1. Leonard I. Sweet, "The Evangelical Tradition in America," in Leonard I. Sweet, ed., *The Evangelical Tradition in America* (Macon, Ga.: Mercer University Press, 1984), chap. 1; Robert M. Calhoon, review of Fred J. Hood, *Reformed America*, Anne C. Loveland, *Southern Evangelicals and the Social Order*, and Donald G. Mathews, *Religion in the Old South*, *William and Mary Quarterly*, 3rd ser., 39 (1982): 386–90 and "Southern Evangelicalism," *Evangelical Studies Bulletin*, 2 (1985): 7–9.

2. Scott H. Hendrix, *Luther and the Papacy: Stages in a Reformation Conflict* (Philadelphia: Fortress Press, 1981), pp. 49, 52.

3. John Doberstein, trans. and ed., *Luther's Works* (Philadelphia: Fortress Press, 1959), vol. 51, p. 70.

4. I Tim. 3:15

5. Jaroslav Pelikan, *The Christian Tradition: A History of the Development of Doctrine*, vol. 4, *Reformation of Church and Dogma (1300–1700)* (Chicago: University of Chicago Press, 1984), p. 211.

6. Rupert E. Davies, *The Problem of Authority in the Continental Reformers: A Study of Luther, Zwingli, and Calvin* (1946; reprint, Westport, Conn.: Greenwood Press, 1978), pp. 154, 145.

7. Donald R. Kelley, *The Beginning of Ideology: Consciousness and Society in the French Reformation* (Cambridge, Eng.: Cambridge University Press, 1981).

8. Quentin Skinner, *The Foundations of Modern Political Thought*, Vol. 2, *The Age of Reformation* (Cambridge, England: Cambridge University Press, 1978), pp. 16, 193

9. Ibid., pp. 15, 16.

10. Ibid., p. 192.
11. Ibid., p. 199.
12. Ibid., p. 202, Skinner's paraphrase.
13. Ibid., pp. 206–17.
14. Ibid., chap. 4 and 5.
15. Ibid., p. 320.
16. John Dunn, *Political Obligation in its Historical Context: Essays in Political Theory* (Cambridge, Eng.: Cambridge University Press, 1980), pp. 58–59.
17. Richard Ashcraft, *Revolutionary Politics & Locke's Two Treatises on Government* (Princeton: Princeton University Press, 1986), p. 265.
18. Ibid., p. 195.
19. Leonard Woods Labaree, *Conservatism in Early American History* (New York: New York University Press, 1948), p. viii.
20. Clinton Rossiter, *Conservatism in America* (New York: Knopf, 1955); Allen Guttmann, *The Conservative Tradition in America* (New York: Oxford University Press, 1967), pp. 148–80; George H. Nash, *The Conservative Intellectual Movement in America Since 1945* (New York: Basic Books, 1976), pp. 72–83, 163–71; William R. Harbour, *The Foundations of Conservative Thought: An Anglo-American Tradition in Perspective* (Notre Dame: Notre Dame University Press, 1982); Michael D. Clark, *Coherent Variety: The Idea of Diversity in British and American Conservative Thought* (Westport, Conn.: Greenwood Press, 1983), pp. 212–15; George F. Will, *Statecraft as Soulcraft* (New York: Simon and Schuster, 1983); and Robert M. Calhoon, "Watergate and American Conservatism," *South Atlantic Quarterly*, 83 (1984): 127–37.

CHAPTER 1.

1. John B. Boles, "Evangelical Protestantism in the Old South: From Religious Dissent to Cultural Dominance," in Charles R. Wilson, ed., *Religion in the South* (Jackson: University of Mississippi Press, 1985), pp. 16–26.
2. "Extract of a Letter from the Rev. Mr. *Davies* at *Hanover* in *Virginia* to the Rev. Mr. F[awcett], Feb. 7, 1757," in *Letters from the Rev. Samuel Davies &c. Shewing the State of Religion in Virginia, particularly among the Negroes* (London, 1757), pp. 27–30.
3. Ernest Trice Thompson, *Presbyterians in the South* (Richmond: John Knox Press, 1963), vol.1, 52–53. See also Richard Beale Davis, *Intellectual Life in the Colonial South, 1585–1763* (Knoxville: University of Tennessee Press, 1978), vol. 2, pp. 684–94, 758–74.

Notes to Pages 17–22

4. "Old Documents," *Virginia Evangelical and Literary Magazine*, 4 (1821): 543.

5. Susan O'Brien, "A Transatlantic Community of Saints: The Great Awakening and the First Evangelical Network, 1735–1755," *American Historical Review*, 91 (1986): 811–32. The Philip Doddridge Papers, Dr. Williams's Library, London, contain several transcriptions of Davies's letter to Mr. Fawcett, cited above in note 2, which apparently circulated among English evangelicals before its publication.

6. Philip Doddridge, *The Rise and Progress of Religion in the Soul: Illustrated in a Course of Serious and Practical Address, Suited to Persons of Every Character and Situation* (1744; reprint, London, 1835), pp. 2, 176.

7. "Old Documents," p. 552

8. Samuel Davies, *The Duty of Christians to Propagate Their Religion Among the Heathens, Earnestly Recommended to the Masters of Negro Slaves in Virginia; a Sermon Preached in Hanover, January 8, 1757* (London, 1758), pp. 38–39.

9. "Old Documents," p. 544.

10. Richard Beale Davis, "The Colonial Virginia Satirist," *Transactions of the American Philosophical Society*, 67 (1967): 47.

11. Elizabeth Colson to the Countess of Huntington, Jan. 10, 1773, Countess of Huntington Papers, A/3/4/4, Westminster College, Cambridge, England.

12. "A Narrative of the Lord's Wonderful Dealings with John Marrant, a Black, (Now Gone to Preach the Gospel in Nova Scotia) Born in New York, in North America ... in Richard Van Der Beets, ed., *Held Captive by Indians: Selected Narratives, 1642–1836* (Knoxville,: University of Tennessee Press, 1973), pp. 181–83.

13. William Howland Kenney, III, "Alexander Garden and George Whitefield: The Significance of Revivalism in South Carolina, 1738–1741," *South Carolina Historical Magazine*. 71 (1970): 1–16.

14. Ibid., p. 4; George Whitefield, *Three Letters from the Reverend G. Whitefield: Viz. Letter I. To a Friend in London Concerning Archbishop Tillotson. Letter II. To the Same on the Same Subject. Letter III. To the Inhabitants of Maryland, Virginia, North and South Carolina, concerning their Negroes* (Philadelphia, 1751), pp. 2–5.

15. *George Whitefield's Journals (1737–1741) ... A Facsimile Reproduction ... with an Introduction* by William V. Davis (Gainesville Fla.: Scholars' Facsimiles & Reprints, 1969), pp. 382, 386–87.

16. S. Charles Bolton, *Southern Anglicanism: The Church of England in Colonial South Carolina* (Westport, Conn.: Greenwood Press, 1982), pp. 50–52.

Notes to Pages 22–29

17. Whitefield to Alexander Garden, Mar. 18, 1739/40, in *Six Letters to the Reverend Mr. George Whitefield . . . by Alexander Garden* (Boston, 1740), p. 6.

18. *Whitefield's Journals*, pp. 398–99; *Six Letters . . . by Alexander Garden*, p. 7; *Three Letters from . . . G. Whitefield*, pp. 13–14.

19. Ibid., p. 15.

20. James D. Essig, *The Bonds of Wickedness: American Evangelicals Against Slavery, 1770–1808* (Philadelphia: Temple University Press, 1982), p. 10.

21. *Six Letters . . . by Alexander Garden*, p. 50.

22. Ibid., pp. 51–52.

23. Ibid., pp. 53–54.

24. Hugh Bryan to his sister, Feb. 5, 1740/41, Mrs. Hugh Bryan to her sister, October 1739, *Living Christianity Deliniated in the Diary and Letters of Mr. Hugh Bryan of South Carolina* (London, 1760), pp. 6–20.

25. "A Letter from Mr. Hugh Bryan to a Friend, Nov. 20, 1740, *South Carolina Gazette,* Jan. 1–8, 1741; Harvey H. Jackson, "Hugh Bryan and the Evangelical Movement in Colonial South Carolina," *William and Mary Quarterly,* 3d ser., 48 (1986): 594–614.

26. James H. Easterby and Ruth S. Green, eds., *The Journal of the Commons House of Assembly, 1741–1742* (Columbia,: Historical Commission of South Carolina, 1953), pp. 405–407, 461–62.

27. Eliza Pinckney to Mary Bartlett, n.d. [March 1742], in Elise Pinckney and Marvin R. Zahnizer, eds., *The Letterbook of Eliza Lucas Pinckney, 1739–1762* (Chapel Hill: University of North Carolina Press, 1972), pp. 29–30.

28. Eliza Pinckney to George Lucas, n.d. [June 1742], in Pinckney and Zahnizer, eds., *Letterbook of Eliza Pinckney*, pp. 44–45; see also pp. 51–54.

29. "A Letter from Hugh Bryan," *South Carolina Gazette,* Jan. 1–8, 1741.

30. Lam. 2:14; Jer. 23:1.

31. Ez. 24:2–10

32. "A Letter from Hugh Bryan," *South Carolina Gazette,* Jan. 1–8, 1741; Dan. 5:25–28

33. "A Letter from Hugh Bryan," *South Carolina Gazette,* Jan. 1–8, 1741.

34. Kenney, "Alexander Garden and George Whitefield," p. 14; Anne Dutton to Philip Doddridge, Jan. 30, 1743/44, Doddridge Papers.

Notes to Pages 30–36

35. John S. Moore, ed., "John Williams' Journal," *The Virginia Baptist Register*, no. 17 (1978): 798. For the identification of Rev. Dick, see Joan Rezner Gunderson, "The Anglican Ministry in Virginia, 1723–1776: A Study of Social Class," Ph.D. diss., Notre Dame University, 1972, appendix, p. 268

36. Rhys Isaac, *The Transformation of Virginia, 1740–1790* (Chapel Hill: University of North Carolina Press, 1982), pp. 59–60.

37. Moore, ed., "John Williams' Journal," p. 798; see also Sandra Rennie, "Virginia's Baptist Persecution, 1765–1778," *Journal of Religious History*, 12 (1982): 430–41.

38. Mill Creek Baptist Church Minutes, 1757–1928, Virginia Baptist Historical Society, Richmond, Va., pp. [1–3]; see also J. Stephen Kroll-Smith, "Transmitting a Revival Culture: The Organizational Dynamic of the Baptist Movement in Colonial Virginia, 1760–1777," *Journal of Southern History*, 50 (1984): 551–68.

39. Samuel Frink to Rev. Daniel Burton, Secretary, society for the Propagation of the Gospel, Jan. 4, 1769, S. P. G. Archives, London, England, C/AM, 8/45.

40. *Memoirs of Rev. George Whitefield by John Gillies* (Middletown, Conn., 1837), p. 465.

41. Richard J. Hooker, ed., *The Carolina Backcountry on the Eve of the Revolution: The Journal and Other Writings of Charles Woodmason, Anglican Itinerant* (Chapel Hill: University of North Carolina Press, 1953), pp. 102–103.

42. Anon., "Biography of Rev. Dr. Richard Furman," Richard Furman Papers, Furman University Library, Greenville, S.C.

43. G. A. Rawlyk, *Ravished by the Spirit: Religious Revivals, Baptists, and Henry Alline* (Kingston and Montreal: McGill-Queen's University Press, 1984), pp. 5, 11, 24, 75–77.

44. Josiah Smith, *The Character, Preaching, &c. of the Reverend Mr. George Whitefield . . .* (Charlestown, 1765), p. 9.

CHAPTER 2.

1. Robert M. Weir, ed., *The Letters of Freeman, Etc.: Essays on the Nonimportation Movement in South Carolina Collected by William Henry Drayton* (Columbia: University of South Carolina Press, 1977), pp. 32, 82, 88.

2. Ibid., pp. 16, 140.

3. Ibid., p. xxvii.

Notes to Pages 37–46

4. See Isaac Kramnick, *Bolingbroke and His Circle: The Politics of Nostalgia in the Age of Walpole* (Cambridge, Mass.: Harvard University Press, 1968); Robert M. Weir, "A Review Essay," *South Carolina Historical Magazine*, 70 (1969):267–73; Jack P. Greene, ed., *The Nature of Colony Constitutions: Two Pamphlets on the Wilkes Fund Controversy in South Carolina by Sir Egerton Leigh and Arthur Lee* (Columbia: University of South Carolina Press, 1970), pp. 42–55.

5. William Eddis, *Letters from America*, Aubrey C. Land, ed. (Cambridge, Mass.: Harvard University Press, 1969), where this quote and the rest of the epigraph for this chapter can be found on pp. 71–72.

6. Weir, ed., *Letters of Freeman*, pp. xiv–xxxvi.

7. "American Loyalists," *Southern Quarterly Review*, 4 (1843): 115.

8. George C. Rogers, "The Conscience of a Huguenot," *Transactions of the Huguenot Society of South Carolina*, 67 (1962): 4–5.

9. Ibid., p. 6.

10. "American Loyalists," p. 145.

11. Ibid., pp. 117–118. Italics added.

12. *South Carolina and American General Gazette*, Oct. 7, 1768.

13. Weir, ed., *Letters of Freeman*, pp. 26–29.

14. "American Loyalists," p. 120.

15. Ibid., p. 119.

16. Ibid., p. 124.

17. Ibid., p. 142; John Locke, *Two Treatises of Government*, Peter Laslett, ed. (Cambridge: Cambridge University Press, 1966), pp. 350–51.

18. Samuel Clarke, *Sermons* (London, 1744), vol. 7, p. 12.

19. Ibid., vol. 3, pp. 1–59, 145–66; vol. 6, pp. 1–27, 319–60.

20. "American Loyalists," pp. 143–44.

21. W. W. Abbot, *The Royal Governors of Georgia, 1754–1775* (Chapel Hill: University of North Carolina Press, 1959), chap. 4–7; and Patrick J. Furlong, "Civilian-Military Conflict and the Restoration of the Royal Province of Georgia, 1778–1782," *Journal of Southern History*, 38 (1972): 415–42.

22. Wright to Hillsborough, Aug. 15, 1769, Colonial Office Papers, Series 5, Vol. 660, ff. 95–98, Public Record Office, London.

23. Robert M. Calhoon, ed., "William Smith, Jr.'s Alternative to the American Revolution," *William and Mary Quarterly*, 22 (1965: 105–118.

24. Jack P. Greene, "Travails of an Infant Colony: The Search for Viability, Coherence, and Identity in Colonial Georgia," and Edward J. Cashin, "Sowing the Wind: Governor Wright and the Georgia Back-

country on the Eve of the Revolution," in Harvey H. Jackson and Phinizy Spalding, eds., *Forty Years of Diversity: Essays on Colonial Georgia* (Athens: University of Georgia Press, 1984), pp. 297–99, 233–46.

25. Bull to Dartmouth, Mar. 28, 1775, CO 5/396, ff. 245–47.

26. Bull to Hillsborough, Dec. 6, 1769, Mar. 2, 1770, CO 5/393:9–11; 396: 245–47.

27. Bull to Hillsborough, Dec. 6, 1769, CO 5/393: 9–11.

28. Robert M. Weir, "Rebelliousness: Personality Development and the American Revolution in the Southern Colonies," in Robert M. Weir, ed. *"The Last of American Freemen": Studies in the Political Culture of the Colonial and Revolutionary South* (Macon, Ga.: Mercer University Press, 1986), pp. 105–31.

29. Bull to Hillsborough, Oct. 18, 1768, CO 5/391, ff. 135–36.

30. Ibid.

31. Bull to Hillsborough, Dec. 12, 1769, CO 5/393: 21–24. Cf. Samuel Johnson's observation that "whether to see life as it is, will give us much consolation, I know not; *but the consolation which is drawn from truth, if any there be, is solid and durable,"* Walter Jackson Bate, *The Achievement of Samuel Johnson* (New York: Oxford University Press, 1955), p. 143, Johnson's italics.

32. Ibid., pp. 134–35.

33. Ibid.

34. Bull to Dartmouth, Aug. 3, 1774, CO 5/396, ff. 97–99.

35. Bull to Dartmouth, Mar. 10, 1774, CO 5/396, ff. 21–23.

36. Leigh to Gower, Jan. 15, 1775, in Jack P. Greene, ed., "The Political Authorship of Sir Egerton Leigh," *South Carolina Historical Magazine*, 75 (1974): 145–49

37. Connolly to Clinton, Nov. 25, 1780, Clinton Papers, William L. Clements Library, Ann Arbor, Michigan.

38. Goodrich to Clinton, Nov. 2, 1780, ibid.

39. *Royal Georgia Gazette*, July 27, 1780.

40. *South-Carolina and American General Gazette*, Aug. 2, 1780

41. *Royal Georgia Gazette*, Aug. 3, 1780.

42. Ibid., Sept. 28, 1780. See also additional citations in Janice Potter and Robert M. Calhoon, "The Character and Coherence of the Loyalist Press," in Bernard Bailyn and John B. Hench, eds., *The Press & the American Revolution* (Worcester, Mass.: American Antiquarian Society, 1980), pp. 266–72.

43. Joseph B. Lockey, ed., *East Florida, 1783–1785* (Berkeley: University of California Press, 1949), p. 97.

44. *The Case of the Inhabitants of East-Florida, with an Appendix Con-*

taining Papers by Which All the Facts in the Case Are Supported (St. Augustine, 1784), p. 17.

45. Lockey, ed., *East Florida*, pp. 301–302.

46. Ibid., pp. 96–99.

47. Ibid., pp. 154–56; Cf. Jack P. Greene, *Peripheries and Center: Constitutional Development in the Extended Polities of the British Empire and the United States, 1607–1788* (Athens: University of Georgia Press, 1986), p. 12.

EXCURSUS I

1. [Arthur Dobbs], "A Scheme to Enlarge the Colonies and Increase Commerce and Trade," Dobbs Papers, Public Record Office of Northern Ireland, Belfast, pp. 19–25.

2. Michael Anesko, "So Discreet a Zeal: Slavery and the Anglican Church in Virginia, 1680–1730," *Virginia Magazine of History and Biography*, 93 (1985): 247–78.

3. This concession to the Vestry had significant ramifications; in 1765 Tryon had broken a fifty year impasse between the Crown and the Lower House of the legislature when he persuaded it to pass an establishment bill that neither affirmed nor denied the power of the governor to appoint Anglican clergymen in the colony, and, in the face of dissenter opposition to further inductions of Anglican clergymen, Tryon apparently believed it important to perpetuate nominal ambiguity about who controlled clerical patronage; see Jack P. Greene, *The Quest for Power: The Lower Houses of Assembly in the Southern Royal Colonies, 1689–1776* (Chapel Hill: University of North Carolina Press, 1963), pp. 352–53; and Paul Conkin, "The Church Establishment in North Carolina, 1765–1776," *North Carolina Historical Review*, 32 (1955): 11–16.

4. Drage to Tryon, May 29, 1770, in William S. Powell, ed., *The Correspondence of William Tryon*, vol. 2, *1768–1818* (Raleigh: Division of Archives and History, 1981), pp. 460–67.

5. Tryon to Drage, July 9, 1770, in Powell, ed., *Correspondence of William Tryon*, pp. 476–77. Tryon allegedly blamed the Regulator uprising on "a faction of *Quakers* and *Baptists*," William K. Boyd, ed., *Some Eighteenth Century Tracts Concerning North Carolina* (Raleigh: Edwards and Broughton Company, 1927), p. 280.

6. Seymour to [Burton], Aug. 24, 1772, S. P. G. Archives, C/AM, 8/84.

Notes to Pages 62–70

7. Tryon to Drage, July 9, 1770, in Powell, ed., *Correspondence of Tryon, 1768–1818*, p. 477. For an analysis of Tryon as an official devoted to "a social organization based upon discipline, order, and organization," see Gary Freeze, "Like a House Built Upon Sand: The Anglican Church and Establishment in North Carolina, 1765–1776," *Historical Magazine of the Protestant Episcopal Church*, 48 (1979): 405–13.

8. Powell, ed., *Correspondence of Tryon, 1768–1818*, p. 409, n. 1.

9. Ibid., p. 893.

10. Jon Butler, "Enlarging the Body of Christ: Slavery, Evangelism, and the Christianization of the White south, 1690–1790," in Sweet, ed., *The Evangelical Tradition in America*, p. 111.

11. Ottolenghe to [Rev. John Waring], Nov. 19, 1753, in John C. Van Horne ed., *Religious Philanthropy and Colonial Slavery: The American Correspondence of the Associates of Dr. Bray, 1717–1777* (Urbana : University of Illinois Press, 1985), p. 112.

12. Ottolenghe to [Waring], Nov. 18, 1754 in Van Horne, ed., *Religious Philanthropy*, p. 116.

13. Ottolenghe to Waring, July 12, 1758, in Van Horne, ed., *Religious Philanthropy*, p. 129.

CHAPTER 3.

1. A common denominator among the politically successful recent British emigrants—Hamilton, Wilson, Witherspoon, and Iredell but not Lee—was that British society and culture equipped them with a richer cultural understanding of political moderation as a prudent orientation to a dangerous and unpredictable world than their colonial contemporaries. See Philip Greven, *The Protestant Temperament: Patterns of Child-Rearing, Religious Experience, and The Self in Early America* (New York: Knopf, 1977), pp. 206–20, 341–47; cf. Robert M. Calhoon, "John Adams and the Psychology of Power" and " 'Inescapable Circularity' : History and the Human Condition in Revolutionary Virginia," *Reviews in American History*, 4 (1976): 520–21 and 11 (1983): 41.

2. Don Higginbotham, "The Making of a Revolutionary," in Higginbotham, ed., *The Papers of James Iredell* (Raleigh: Division of Archives and History, 1976), vol. 1, pp. xxxvii–lviii.

3. Ibid., p. 187.

4. Ibid., pp. 443, 436.

5. Ibid., p. 443.

Notes to Pages 70–76

6. Ibid., pp. 441–42, 436.

7. Ibid.

8. Ibid., p. 378. For the influence of the country ideology on Iredell, see p. 241, note 2.

9. Ibid., p. 379

10. Ibid., p. 443

11. Ibid., pp. 264–67.

12. Ibid., p. 267; Jack P. Greene, " 'Not to be Governed or Taxed but by . . . Our Own Representatives': Four Essays in Opposition to the Stamp Act by Landon Carter," *Virginia Magazine of History and Biography*, 76 (1968): 291–92.

13. Jack P. Greene, ed., *The Diary of Colonel Landon Carter of Sabine Hall* (Richmond: Virginia Historical Society, 1965), p. 1015.

14. Ibid., p. 1112.

15. Gordon S. Wood, *The Creation of The American Republic, 1776–1787* (Chapel Hill : University of North Carolina Press), pp. 132–43; Paul K. Conkin, *Self-Evident Truths: Being a Discourse on the Origins & Development of the First Principles of American Government—Popular Sovereignty, Natural Rights, and Balance & Separation of Powers* (Bloomington: Indiana University Press, 1974), pp. 48–73.

16. Francis Newton Thorpe, ed., *The Federal and State Constitutions, Colonial Charters, and Other Organic Laws of the States, Territories, and Colonies Now or Heretofore Forming the United States of America* (Washington, D.C. : Government Printing Office, 1909), vol. 7, p. 3813.

17. Ibid.

18. Ibid., vol. 3, p. 1686

19. Ibid., vol. 5, p. 2787

20. Ibid., vol. 2, p. 778.

21. Jerome J. Nadelhaft, *The Disorders of War: The Revolution in South Carolina* (Orono, Me.: University of Maine at Orono Press, 1981), pp. 31, 33; Ronald Hoffman, *A Spirit of Dissension: Economics, Politics, and the Revolution in Maryland* (Baltimore: Johns Hopkins University Press, 1973), pp. 180–81.

22. Thorpe, ed., *Federal and State Constitutions*, vol. 5, pp. 2789–90; Robert L. Ganyard, *The Emergence of North Carolina's Revolutionary State Government* (Raleigh: Division of Archives and History, 1978), pp. 68–89.

23. For a discussion of recent scholarship, see Robert M. Calhoon, review of Jeffrey J. Crow and Larry E. Tise, eds., *The Southern Experience in the American Revolution* and Don Higginbotham, ed., *Recon-*

Notes to Pages 76–81

siderations of the Revolutionary War: Selected Essays, Journal of Interdiscipli-
nary History, 10 (1979): 367–70.

24. Hoffman, *Spirit of Dissension,* pp. 183–95, 223–41; and Harold
B. Hancock, *The Loyalists of Revolutionary Delaware* (Newark: University
of Delaware Press, 1977), pp. 37, 82, and 96.

25. Hoffman, *Spirit of Dissension,* pp. 227–30; Hancock, *Loyalists of
Delaware,* pp. 80–86; Keith Mason, "Localism, Evangelicalism, and Loy-
alism: Popular Opposition to Elite Authority on the Eastern Shore of
Maryland during the American Revolution" paper read at the Conference on the Colonial Experience of the Eighteenth Century Chesa-
peake, George Peabody Library, Baltimore, Maryland, Sept. 14, 1984.

26. Hancock, *Loyalists of Delaware,* p. 3.

27. Jeffrey J. Crow, "Liberty Men and Loyalists: Disorder and Disaffection in the North Carolina Backcountry," in Ronald Hoffman,
Thad W. Tate, and Peter J. Albert, eds., *An Uncivil War: The Southern
Backcountry During the American Revolution* (Charlottesville: University
of Virginia Press, 1985), pp. 147–48.

28. John S. Watterson, "The Ordeal of Governor Burke," *North
Carolina Historical Review,* 48 (1971): 95–102.

29. Lindley S. Butler, ed., *The Narrative of Col. David Fanning* (Davidson, N.C.: Briarpatch Press, 1981), pp. 6–10; Harry Eckstein, "On
the Etiology of Internal Wars," *History and Theory,* 4 (1964): 133–63.

30. Robert M. Weir, " 'The Violent Spirit,' the Reestablishment of
Order, and the Continuity of Leadership in Post-Revolutionary South
Carolina," *The Last of American Freemen",* pp. 139–40.

31. Ibid., p. 147

32. Samuel E. McCorkle, "The Curse and Crime of Plundering: A
Sermon," McCorkle Papers, Duke University Library, Durham, North
Carolina.

33. Melvin Yazawa, *From Colonies to Commonwealth: Familial Ideology
and The Beginnings of the American Republic* (Baltimore: Johns Hopkins
University Press, 1985), p. 143.

34. Donald R. Come, "The Influence of Princeton on Higher
Education in the South before 1825," *William and Mary Quarterly,* 2
(1945): 372–96

35. Jack Scott, ed., *An Annotated Edition of Lectures on Moral Philosophy by John Witherspoon* (Newark : University of Delaware Press, 1982),
p. 49.

36. Mark A. Noll, "The Irony of the Enlightenment for Presbyterians in the Early Republic," *Journal of the Early Republic,* 5 (1985): 164.

37. Ibid.

38. Douglas Sloan, *The Scottish Enlightenment and the American College Ideal* (New York: Teachers College Press, 1971), pp. 113–14; Noll, "Irony of the Enlightenment," p. 154.

39. Scott, ed., *Lectures on Moral Philosophy*, p. 1.

40. Timothy M. Barnes and Robert M. Calhoon, "Moral Allegiance: John Witherspoon and Loyalist Recantation," *American Presbyterians: The Journal of Presbyterian History*, 63 (1985): 273–77, 279–80.

41. Scott, ed., *Lectures on Moral Philosophy*, pp. 109–112. Three surviving notebooks on Witherspoon's lectures, kept by Madison's classmates, survive, and according to Ralph Ketcham "there are major differences between the student notebooks" and the version of the lectures published in 1815 after his death, Ketcham, *James Madison: A Biography* (New York: Macmillan, 1971), pp. 41–42, notably Witherspoon's later appreciation of the Anglican rationalist, Samuel Clarke. The passages I have cited from Witherspoon's *Lectures* are identical with the John Ewing Calhoun notebook, Firestone Library, Princeton University.

42. Scott, ed., *Lectures on Moral Philosophy*, pp. 143–47, 150–65 *passim*, 186–87.

43. Sloan, *Scottish Enlightenment* p. 125.

44. Noll, "Irony of the Enlightenment," p. 158; Sloan, *Scottish Enlightenment* p. 135.

45. Anon., "Fathers of the Presbyterian Church in Virginia," ca. 1800, Brock Collection, Henry E. Huntington Library, San Marino, California, no. 645, pp. 24–25.

46. Douglass Adair, "James Madison," in Trevor Colbourn, ed., *Fame and the Founding Fathers: Essays by Douglass Adair* (New York: W. W. Norton, 1974), p. 128.

47. William T. Hutchinson, William M. E. Rachal, Robert A. Rutland, eds., *The Papers of James Madison* (Chicago: University of Chicago Press, 1962), vol. 10, pp. 263–70.

48. Ibid., pp. 476–80; Scott, ed., *Lectures on Moral Philosophy*, p. 49.

49. Arthur O. Lovejoy, *Reflections on Human Nature* (Baltimore: Johns Hopkins University Press, 1961), pp. 58–65; Hutchinson, Rachal Rutland, eds., *Papers of Madison* vol. 10, p. 418.

50. Ibid., pp. 365–66.

51. Colbourn, ed., *Fame and the Founding Fathers*, pp. 20–26.

Notes to Pages 88–93

52. Thomas E. Buckley, S. J., *Church and State in Revolutionary Virginia, 1776–1787* (Charlottesville: University of Virginia Press, 1977), pp. 71–102.

53. Hutchinson, Rachal, Rutland, eds., *Papers of Madison*, vol. 8, p. 299.

54. Ibid., pp. 299–300; Buckley, *Church and State in Revolutionary Virginia*, pp. 131–33. See two dissenter petitions, Oct. 25, 1776; Amherst County Presbyterian, Baptist, and Methodist petition, Nov. 1, 1779; Albemarle County petition, Oct. 28, 1785, Religious Petitions, 1774–1802, Presented to the General Assembly of Virginia, Virginia State Library, Richmond.

55. Hutchinson, Rachal, Rutland, eds., *Papers of Madison*, vol. 8, pp. 300–302; Buckley *Church and State*, p. 190. See Amherst County Presbytery petition, June 5, 1775; Albemarle, Amherst, and Rockingham dissenters petition, Oct. 22, 1776; Surry County petition, Oct. 26, 1785, Religious Petitions, 1774–1802.

56. Hutchinson, Rachal, Rutland, eds., *Papers of Madison*, vol. 8, p. 300. See Prince Edward County Baptist petition, June 20, 1776; miscellaneous petitions, June 3, 1782, Religious Petitions, 1774–1802.

57. Hutchinson, Rachal, Rutland, eds., *Papers of Madison*, vol. 8, p. 304. See Albemarle petition, Nov. 1, 1776; Prince Edward petition, Oct. 16, 1776; miscellaneous petition, Nov. 11, 1784; Presbytery of Hanover petition, Nov. 12, 1784, Religious Petitions, 1774–1802.

58. William Hooper, quoted in first epigraph for chapter 3.

CHAPTER 4.

1. James H. O'Donnell, ed., "A Loyalist View of the Drayton-Tennent-Hart Mission to the Upcountry," *South Carolina Historical Magazine*, 67 (1966): 15–28; Oliver Hart to James Hart, Mar. 24, 1778 Oliver Hart Papers, South Caroliniana Library, University of South Carolina: Newton B. Jones, ed., "Writings of the Reverend William Tennent, 1740–1777," *South Carolina Historical Magazine*, 61 (1960): 143–45, 189–93; William Tennent, *An Address Occasioned by the Late Invasion of the Liberties of the American Colonies by the British Parliament* (Philadelphia, 1774), pp. 17–18.

2. William L. Saunders, Walter Clark, and Stephen B. Weeks, eds., *Colonial and State Records of North Carolina* (Raleigh, 1886–1914), vol. 9, pp. 1160–61.

Notes to Pages 93–101

3. Eli W. Caruthers, *A Sketch of the Life and Character of the Reverend David Caldwell* (Greensboro, 1842), pp. 273–284.

4. *Colonial and State Records of North Carolina*, vol. 7, pp. 813–14; vol. 9, pp. 98–99.

5. Perry Miller, "From the Covenant to the Revival." in Perry Miller, *Nature's Nation* (Cambridge, Mass.: Harvard University Press, 1967), pp. 99–107; Melvin B. Endy, Jr., "Just War, Holy War, and Millennialism in Revolutionary America," *William and Mary Quarterly*, 42 (1985): 24.

6. [Richard Furman], "To the inhabitants of South Carolina who resided between Broad & Saluda Rivers at the time they were embodying in . . . opposition to the . . . American Congress," Furman Papers, recently published in James A. Rogers, *Richard Furman: Life and Legacy* (Macon, Ga.: Mercer University Press, 1985), App. A, pp. 267–73.

7. Ibid., pp. 267–68, 272.

8. Jeffrey J. Crow and Paul D. Escott, "The Social Order and Violent Disorder: An Analysis of North Carolina in the Revolution and the Civil War," *Journal of Southern History*, 52 (1986): 389.

9. Rogers, *Furman*, p. 270.

10. Elmer T. Clark, J. Manning Potts, and Jacob S. Payton, eds., *The Journal and Letters of Francis Asbury* (Nashville: Abingdon Press, 1958), vol. 1, pp. 215–16.

11. John B. Boles, *The Great Revival, 1787–1805: The Origins of the Southern Evangelical Mind* (Lexington: University of Kentucky Press, 1972), pp. 4–5.

12. Donald G. Mathews, *Religion in the Old South* (Chicago: University of Chicago Press, 1977), p 31.

13. Clark, et al., *Journal and Letters of Asbury*, vol. 1: 216.

14. Ibid., p. 211.

15. Rhys Isaac, *The Transformation of Virginia, 1740–1790* (Chapel Hill; University of North Carolina Press, 1982), p. 263.

16. Clark, et al., *Journal and Letters of Asbury*, vol. 1, p. 208. Another useful account is the Thomas Mann Journal, 1805–1806, Duke University Library, Durham, North Carolina.

17. Isaac, *Transformation of Virginia*, pp. 301–302.

18. Greven, *The Protestant Temperament*, pp. 87–109.

19. Stith Mead Letterbook, 1792–1795, Virginia Historical Society, Richmond, pp. 21–29; M. H. Moore, *Sketches of the Pioneers of Methodism in North Carolina and Virginia* (Nashville: Southern Methodist Publishing House, 1884), pp. 219–228.

Notes to Pages 102–108

20. "Random Sketches of Rev. James O'Kelly" by "Icon No. 6," bound volume of clippings from the *Christian Sun* (Suffolk, Va.) in the Church History Room, Elon College Library, Elon College, North Carolina.

21. James O'Kelly, *Hymns and Spiritual Songs* (Raleigh, 1816), p. 15. O'Kelly called himself "the author, or rather the compiler" of this hymnal, "a small part of these hymns are ... of my composing," pp. [i-ii]. The hymn quoted does not appear in David Mintz, *Spiritual Song Book* (Halifax, N.C., 1805) and may well be O'Kelly's composition. Almost certainly, he would have spoken of his own conversion in these terms.

22. Peter Berger, *The Sacred Canopy: Elements of a Sociological Theory of Religion* (New York: Doubleday, 1967), p. 51.

23. Aaron Spivey, "A Succinct Account &c.," Cashie Baptist Church Record Book, 1791–1832, Baptist Collection, Wake Forest University Library, pp. 87–104.

24. The Will of Aaron Spivey, Bertie County Wills, North Carolina Archives.

25. Spivey, "A Succinct Account &c.," pp. 87–96.

26. Piercy to the Countess of Huntingdon, Feb. 22, 1773, Huntingdon Papers, A/4/1/1.

27. Sketch of Dr. Edward D. Smith, n.d., South Caroliniana Library; [?] to Margaret Peyton, Aug. 23, 182[?], Peyton Family Papers, Virginia Historical Society; "Extract from an Eulogy delivered by G. C. Memminger," n.d., South Caroliniana Library.

28. Ms. sermon, Brock Collection, no. 120.

29. Richard Furman to [?], Dec. 3, 1789, Furman Papers. Lk. 9:23; paraphrase of Rom. 8:9, see p. 139.

30. Lewis O. Saum, *The Popular Mood of Pre-Civil War America* (Westport, Conn.: Greenwood Press, 1980), p. 94.

31. Harriet Hedren to [?], Jan. 1857, Brock Collection, no. 118. Mk. 15:34; Is. 66:12.

32. Stith Mead to David Meade, April 26 or 27, 1812, Charles W. Andrews Papers, Duke University Library.

33. Undated fragment, Furman Papers.

34. B. Cullen to [?], May 26, 1799, Village Itinerancy Association Papers, Vol. 41 (v), Dr. Williams's Library, London. Rom. 3:17.

35. Ms. sermon, Robert Johnston Miller Papers, North Carolina Archives.

36. Ms. sermon by Robert Buchan, Brock Collection, no. 120.

Notes to Pages 109–115

37. Berger, *Sacred Canopy*, p. 48. For a comparison of physical and emotional deterioration to clay in the hands of the potter, see William Black (in Baltimore, Maryland) to the the Wesleyan Missionary Society, April 5, 1820, Methodist Missionary Society Archives, London.

38. Fishing Creek [S.C.] Presbyterian Church Records, Historical Foundation of the Presbyterian and Reformed Churches, Montreat, North Carolina.

39. W. D. Blanks, "Corrective Church Discipline in the Presbyterian Churches of the Nineteenth Century South," *Journal of Presbyterian History*, 44 (1966) :89–105; Fred J. Hood, "The Restoration of Community: The Great Awakening in Four Baptist Churches in Central Kentucky," *The Quarterly Review*, 39 (1978): 73–83.

40. Henry S. Stroupe, " 'Cite Them Both to Attend the Next Church Conference': Social Control by North Carolina Baptist Churches, 1772–1908," *North Carolina Historical Review*, 52 (1975): 170.

41. Mathews, *Religion in the Old South*, p. 42.

42. Robert M. Calhoon, ed., *Religion and the American Revolution in North Carolina* (Raleigh: Division of Archives and History, 1976), pp. 56–58; see above chapter 1, note 38.

43. Stroupe, " 'Cite Them Both,' " p. 157.

44. Translated "jumping" by Professor Ritter (see below note 45), suggesting that this offense referred to Separate Baptist excess during worship services; in the context of "gluttony, drinking, and dancing," *springen* seems more likely to refer to physical abandon.

45. Guy A. Ritter, ed. and trans., Official Record book of Brick Union Lutheran Church Howrytown (Greenville), Botetourt County, Virginia (typescript), Roanoke College Library, Salem, Virginia.

46. Joseph Biggs, *A Concise History of the Kehukee Baptist Association* (Tarborough, N.C., 1834), p. 139.

47. Henry Pattillo, *The Plain Planter's Family Assistant; Containing an Address to Husbands and Wives, Children and Servants; With some Helps for Instruction by Catechisms; and Examples of Devotion for Families* (Wilmington, 1787), pp. 50–51.

48. *Minutes of the Chowan Baptist Association, 1806* (Edenton, 1806), pp. 6–7: Daniel Calhoun, *The Intelligence of a People* (Princeton: Princeton University Press, 1973), p. 207.

49. *Minutes of the Chowan Baptist Association, 1807* (Halifax, N.C. 1807), pp. 5–8.

50. Ibid. and *Minutes of the Chowan Baptist Association, 1810* (Edenton, 1810), pp. 6–8.

51. See the striking similarities between Ethridge and Maurice Merleau-Ponty, *Phenomenology of Perception*, Colin Smith, trans. (London: Routledge and Kegan Paul, 1962), p. 377; and Maurice Merleau-Ponty, *The Visible and the Invisible*, Alphonso Lingis, trans. (Evanston: Northwestern University Press, 1968), p. 148.

52. *Minutes of the Chowan Baptist Association, 1823* (Newbern, 1823), pp. 6–11.

53. I John 1:4–5.

54. Calhoun, *Intelligence of a People*, p. 312; Samuel Eusebius McCorkle, journal, Historical Foundation of the Presbyterian and Reformed Churches, ff. 31A–34A, 40A–46B; for a convenient transcription of the Old Testament portion of the journal, see John Lucien Setzler, "Journal of an 18th Century Preacher," B.D. thesis, Lutheran Southern Theological Seminary, Columbia, South Carolina. Cf. sermon on Job 14: 14–15, Eli Caruthers Papers, Duke University Library.

55. Job 7:5, 19; Tit. 2:12; 3:18; II Tim. 4:8.

56. Reference to Polycarp and Justin Martyr, martyred in 155 and 165 A.D. respectively, reflected McCorkle's familiarity with his namesake, see Robert M. Grant, *Eusebius as Church Historian* (Oxford: Clarendon Press, 1980), pp. 115–16.

57. II Cor. 5:2; I Cor. 13:12.

58. *Minutes of the Chowan Baptist Association, 1825* (n.p., 1825), pp. 6–20.

59. *Minutes of the Chowan Baptist Association, 1806* (Edenton, 1806), pp. 6–7. Heb. 2:14. Cf. Moses Black to the Wesleyan Missionary Society, Dec. 24, 1802, Methodist Missionary Society Archives.

60. *Minutes of the Chowan Baptist Association, 1809* (Edenton, 1809), pp. 6–10.

61. Ibid., p. 6.

EXCURSUS II

1. Blackwell P. Robinson, *William R. Davie* (Chapel Hill; University of North Carolina Press, 1957), p. 261.

2. R. D. W. Connor, comp., Louis R. Wilson and Hugh T. Lefler, eds., *A Documentary History of the University of North Carolina, 1776–1779* (Chapel Hill,: University of North Carolina Press, 1953) vol. 1, pp. 375–79.

3. Robinson, *William R. Davie*, pp. 248, 406–410; Robert M.

Notes to Pages 123–129

Calhoon, "William Richardson Davie," David C. Roller and Robert Twyman, eds., *The Encyclopedia of Southern History* (Baton Rouge: Louisiana State University Press, 1979), p. 330; McCorkle to Ernest Haywood, Dec. 20, 1799, Haywood Papers, Southern Historical Collection, University of North Carolina Library, Chapel Hill, N.C.

4. Thomas T. Taylor, "Samuel E. McCorkle and the Christian Republic, 1792–1802," *American Presbyterians: The Journal of Presbyterian History*, 63 (1985): 375–85.

5. Roger Ascham, *The Schoolmaster* (1570, republished by Lawrence V. Ryan, ed., Charlottesville: University of Virginia Press, 1967), pp. 24–25.

6. Henry Allason Notebook, unpaginated, Birmingham University Library, Birmingham, England; see Moses Black to the Methodist Missionary Society, Oct. 18, 1802, Methodist Missionary society Archives. For a discussion of other evangelical educators on republicanism, see Melvin Yazawa, *From Colonies to Commonwealth: Familial Ideology and the Beginnings of the American Republic* (Baltimore: Johns Hopkins University Press, 1985), pp. 151–94.

7. Richard K. McMaster, "Liberty or Prosperity? The Methodists Petition for Emancipation in Virginia, 1785," *Methodist History*, 10 (1971): 48–49; 151 out of 505 slaveowners in Lunenburg County signed this petition, see Richard R. Beeman, *The Evolution of the Southern Backcountry: A Case Study of Lunenburg County, Virginia, 1746–1832* (Philadelphia: University of Pennsylvania Press, 1984), p. 165.

8. Fredrika Teute Schmidt and Barbara Ripel Wilhelm, "Early Proslavery Petitions in Virginia," *William and Mary Quarterly*, 30 (1973): 138–40, 145–46. Italics added.

9. Drew Gilpin Faust, "Evangelicalism and the Meaning of the Proslavery argument: The Reverend Thornton Stringfellow of Virginia," *Virginia Magazine of History and Biography*, 85 (1977): 3–17.

10. James O'Kelly, *Essay on Negro Slavery* (Philadelphia, 1789), pp. 33–34; Judges 16:30; Mark A. Noll, Nathan O. Hatch, George M. Marsden, *The Search for a Christian Republic* (Westchester, Ill.: Crossways Books, 1983), pp. 16–17, 108–10.

11. Robert L. Brunhouse, ed., "David Ramsay, 1749–1815: Selections from his Writings," *Transactions of the American Philosophical Society*, new ser., 55, pt. 4 (1965): 195.

12. Ibid., pp. 66, 64.

13. Ibid., p. 123.

14. Ibid., pp. 34–35.

15. Ibid., pp. 34–85, italics added.

16. Ibid., p. 84 n. 2.

17. The Writings of Conrad Speece, vol. 1, Brock Collection, no. 81, pp. 3–20. Cf. anon. sermon on Ps. 147:12–14, ibid.

18. Writings of Conrad Speece, Brock Collection, no. 81, p. 54.

19. Marvin Meyers, *The Jacksonian Persuasion: Politics and Belief* (1957; reprint, New York: Vintage Books, 1960), pp. 45–54.

CHAPTER 5.

1. Mary J. Bratton, ed., "Fields's Observations: The Slave Narrative of a Nineteenth Century Virginian," *Virginia Magazine of History and Biography*, 88 (1980): 75–79.

2. Karl J. Weintraub, "Autobiography and Historical Consciousness," *Critical Inquiry*, 1 (1975): 830.

3. "Fields's Observations," p. 82.

4. Ibid., pp. 85–93.

5. Alrutheus A. Taylor, *The Negro in the Reconstruction of Virginia* (Washington, D.C.: Association for the Study of Negro Life and History, 1926), pp. 254–59; Philip S. Foner and George E. Walker, eds., *Proceedings of the Black State Conventions, 1840–1865* (Philadelphia: Temple University Press, 1980), vol. 2, pp. 267–68. John 21:7.

6. James Rapier to John Rapier, April 27, 1857, James Rapier Papers, Moorland-Spingarn Research Center, Howard University, Washington, D.C. (copies in the possession of Professor Loren Schweninger).

7. Ibid.; Loren Schweninger, *James T. Rapier and Reconstruction* (Chicago: University of Chicago Press, 1978), pp. 21, 32; Rapier's father bequeathed a lot in Florence, Alabama "in which the present African Church stands" to the church, Lauderdale County, Alabama wills, Book B (Sept. 13, 1869), pp. 78–80 (notes in the possession of Loren Schweninger).

8. James Rapier to John Rapier, April 27, 1857, Rapier Papers.

9. Ibid.

10. Loren Schweninger, "James T. Rapier of Alabama and the Noble Cause of Reconstruction," Howard N. Rabinowitz, ed., *Southern Black Leaders of the Reconstruction Era* (Urbana: University of Illinois Press, 1982), pp. 79, 93–94.

11. Psalm 119: 19–20.

Notes to Page 141

12. William L. Andrews, ed., *Sisters in the Spirit: Thee Black Woman's Autobiographies of the Nineteenth Century* (Bloomington: Indiana University Press, 1986), pp. 98–99, 100; see also Jean M. Humez, " 'My Spirit Eye': Some Functions of Spiritual and Visionary Experience in the Lives of Five Black Women Preachers, 1810–1880" in Barbara J. Harris and JoAnn K. McNamara, eds., *Women and the Structure of Society* (Durham, N.C.: Duke University Press, 1984), pp. 133–43.

13. Albert J. Raboteau, *Slave Religion: The "Invisible Institution" in the Antebellum South* (New York: Oxford University Press, 1978), p. 301.

14. [?] to John Fort, ca. summer, 1821, Neill Brown Papers, Duke University Library. The full text of this letter reads:

Master John I want permation of you pleas to speak a few words to you—I hope you will not think me too bold Sir. I make my wants known to you because you are, I believe, the oldest and most experienced that I know of, in the first place. I want you to tell me the reson you allwaze preach to the white folks and keep your back to us is because we sit up on the hill we have no chance a mong them we must be forgoten because we cant get near enoughf without getting in the edge of the swamp behind you we have no other chance because your stand is the edge of the swamp, if I should ask you what must I do to be saved perhaps you would tel me pray let the bible be your gide this would be very well if we could read I do not think there is one in fifty that can read but I have been more fortunate than most of the black people I can read and write in my way as to be understood I possess a weak mind about the duties of religious people If God sent you to preach to sinners did he direct you to keep your face to the white folks constantly or is it because these give you money but it is handed to you by our master did he tell you to have your meeting houses just as long as to hold the white folks and let the black people stand in the sone and rain as the brook in the field are charged with inatention it is impossible for us to pay good attention with this chance in fact some of us scarc think we are preached to at all. Money appears to be the object weare carid to market and sold to the highest bider never once inquire whether you sold a heathon or christian if the question was put, did you not sel a christian, what would be the answer I cant tell you what he was gave me my price thats all was interested in Is this the way to heavin if it is there will be a good miny go there if not there chance will be bad for there can be many witnesses against them If I understand the white peole they are praying for more religion in the world of may our case not be forgoten in the prairs of the sincear I now leave it to you and your aids to consider on I hope you will read it to their church if you think it proper it is likely I never will hear from you on this subject as I live far from you I dont wish you to take any of these things to your self if nothing is due do your god justis in this case and you will doo me the same

Your Sirvent Sir

15. Anne Randolph Meade Page to [?], n.d., Charles Wesley Andrews Papers, Duke University Library. Although this incident was a topic of family conversation in the 1820s, it must have occurred sometime around 1805. Mary Francis Page was married in 1810, Richard C. W. Page, *Genealogy of the Page Family in Virginia* (New York: Publisher's Printing Co., 1893), p. 141. On this theme, see Jean E. Friedman, *The Enclosed Garden: Women and Community in the Evangelical South, 1830–1900* (Chapel Hill: University of North Carolina Press, 1985), pp. 35–37.

16. Anne Randolph Meade Page to [?], n.d., C. W. Andrews Papers.

17. William G. McLoughlin, "Evangelical Childrearing in the Age of Jackson: Francis Wayland's Views on When and How to Subdue the Willfulness of Children," *Journal of Social History*, 9 (1975): 35–43; Anne Randolph Meade Page to Mary Fitzhugh Custis, n.d., [ca. 1833], C. W. Andrews Papers.

18. Bertram Wyatt-Brown, *Southern Honor: Ethics and Behavior in the Old South* (New York: Oxford University Press, 1982), pp. 99–114.

19. Ms. sermon on John 5:42–43, preached in Richmond, Sept. 12, 1824, Brock Collection, no. 51. Titus 2:14.

20. Ms. sermon on Hebrews 9:28, preached in Richmond, July 9, 1820, Brock Collection, no. 120.

21. Ann B. Glove [?] to Margaret C. Peyton, Dec. 20, 1831, Peyton Family Papers, Virginia Historical Society. The following discussion is grounded in the findings of Jan Lewis, *The Pursuit of Happiness: Family and Values in Jefferson's Virginia* (New York: Cambridge University Press, 1983).

22. Ann B. Glove [?] to Margaret C. Peyton, July 10, [1832?], Peyton Family Papers, Virginia Historical Society.

23. Copybooks of William S. Pettigrew, 1827–1829, Pettigrew Family Papers, vol. 15; Louisa Lenoir, copybook, Lenoir Family Papers, vol. 136, Southern Historical Collection, University of North Carolina at Chapel Hill Library, Chapel Hill, N.C. For their internalization of these values, see Calhoun, *The Intelligence of a People*, (Prince-

Notes to Pages 148–152

ton; Princeton University Press, 1973), pp. 194–95, Eugene D. Genovese, *Roll, Jordan, Roll: The World the Slaveowners Made* (New York: Knopf, 1974), pp. 369, 374–78: Francis Griffin, *Less Time for Meddling: A History of Salem Academy and College, 1772–1866* (Winston Salem, N.C.: John Blair, 1979), pp. 163–64. On the shift in the Lenoir Family from eighteenth century rationalism to nineteenth century "Christian fortitude," see Richard A. Schrader, "William Lenoir, 1751–1839," Ph.D. diss., University of North Carolina at Chapel Hill, 1978, p. 207.

24. Philip Greven, *The Protestant Temperament,* pp. 159–70.

25. Louisa Lenoir copybook, pp. [1–2,] [14–16].

26. Ibid., pp. [2–3.]

27. Ibid., pp. [4–10, 23].

28. Ibid., pp. [11–14].

29. Ibid., pp. [17–20, 23–24].

30. Ibid., pp. [9, 17–19, 21–23].

31. Pettigrew copybook, July 8–Dec. 30, 1828.

32. Ibid., Feb. 27–Oct. 30, 1827.

33. Ibid.

34. Ibid., July 8–Dec. 30, 1828.

35. Ibid., Feb. 27–Oct. 30, 1827.

36. Ibid.

37. Ibid., Sept. 1827.

38. Ibid., Feb. 27–Oct. 30, 1827 and Sept. 8–Nov. 19, 1829.

39. Ibid., July 8–Dec. 20, 1828.

40. Ibid., Sept. 8–Nov. 19, 1829.

41. Ibid., Feb. 27–Oct. 30, 1827; Pettigrew omitted "persons black and white" after the first entry.

42. Ibid., Sept. 1827.

43. Ibid., Feb. 27–Oct. 30, 1827.

44. Ibid.

45. Ibid.

46. Ibid., cf. note 34.

47. Ibid., Sept. 1827

48. Jesse Mercer to D. B. Mitchell, Oct. 9, 1816, Brock Collection, no. 119 (2).

49. [?] to Mary C. Penn, Mar. 16, 1834, Green Penn Papers, Duke University Library.

50. J. A. Brown to Duncan Black, May 1, 1840, Neill Brown Papers.

51. Donald G. Mathews, *Slavery and Methodism: A Chapter in American Morality* (Princeton: Princeton University Press, 1965), chap. 1; and

Orville Vernon Burton, *In My Father's House Are Many Mansions: Family and Community in Edgefield, South Carolina* (Chapel Hill: University of North Carolina Press, 1985), pp. 20, 24, 54, 57–61, 64, 69, 114, 122.

52. Ibid., chap. 2.

53. "James O'Kelly," *Encyclopedia of Religion in the South*, p. 553.

54. Donald G. Mathews, "North Carolina Methodists in the Nineteenth Century: Church and Society," in O. Kelly Ingram, ed., *Methodism Alive in North Carolina* (Durham: Duke University School of Divinity, 1976), pp. 64–65.

55. Petition to the South Carolina General Assembly, ca. 1838, ND 2822, South Carolina Department of Archives and History, Columbia, South Carolina; the signers of the petition were members of the Cedar Springs Associate Reformed Presbyterian Church, Abbeville District, South Carolina.; Religious instruction of slaves was for Hemphill an integral part of his campaign to colonize blacks in Africa, "Address on Colonization," July 1840, Hemphill Family Papers, Duke University Library.

56. Samuel Benedict to Richard Holloway, June 21, 1839, Holloway Collection, College of Charleston, Charleston, S.C.

57. [?] to [Margaret C. Peyton?], Aug. 23, 1822, Peyton Family Papers.

58. George Haltiwanger to the President and members of the North Carolina Synod, April 2, 1833, Early Synod Documents, Archives of the Lutheran Synod of North Carolina, Salisbury, North Carolina.

59. Raymond Morris Bost, "The Reverend John Bachman and the Development of Southern Lutheranism," Ph.D. diss., Yale University, 1963, pp. 343–55; *Lutheran Observer*, July 21, 1843.

60. Ibid., Aug. 21, 1843.

61. Bost, "John Bachman," pp. 351–52.

62. Ibid., p. 354. For further evidence, see David R. Keck, "The Lutheran Church in the South as Mentioned in the Lutheran Observer from 1837 to 1847 (Index and Study)," B.D. thesis, Lutheran Theological Southern Seminary, 1964, pp. 29–31.

63. David F. Bittle, *Remarks on New Measures* (Staunton, Va., 1839) and R. Weiser, "Essay on Revivals," in J. T. Tabler, ed., *Sermons and Essays in Two parts: The First Containing Popular and Evangelic Sermons by the Late Rev. G. D. Flohr, . . . The Second Containing Sermons and Essays for the Most Part by Living Ministers* (Baltimore, 1840), pp. 271–304.

64. James Oakes, *The Ruling Race: A History of American Slaveholders* (New York: Knopf, 1982), pp. 103, 120, 121, 110.

65. E. Brooks Holifield, *The Gentlemen Theologians: American Theology in Southern Culture, 1795–1860* (Durham, N.C.: Duke University Press, 1978), pp. 39, 43.

66. Ibid., pp. 87–88, 151–52; see Mark A. Noll, "Common Sense Traditions and American Evangelical Thought," *American Quarterly*, 37 (1985): 226. An example is John H. Rice to Thomas Chalmers, July 25, 1817, Thomas Chalmers Papers, New College Library, University of Edinburgh, Scotland.

67. C. C. Goen, *Broken Churches, Broken Nation: Denominational Schisms and the Coming of the American Civil War* (Macon: Mercer University Press, 1985), p. 169.

68. John R. McKivigan, *The War against Proslavery Religion: Abolitionists and the Northern Churches, 1830–1865* (Ithaca: Cornell University Press, 1985), pp. 51, 103

69. Goen, *Broken Churches*, p. 75.

70. James Oscar Farmer, *The Metaphysical Confederacy; James Henley Thornwell and the Synthesis of Southern Values* (Macon Ga.: Mercer University Press, 1986), p. 223. For an early formulation, see Drury Lacy, "Sermon . . . on . . . the Death of . . . Henry Pattillo, . . . *North Carolina Presbyterian*, May 21, 1875.

CHAPTER 6.

1. Dwight to Taylor, Sept. 3, 1805, Taylor to Dwight, n.d., in David R. Barbee, ed., "A Sheaf of Old Letters," *Tyler's Quarterly Historical and Genealogical Review*, 32 (1950): 82–86; for the citation to this exchange and a valuable discussion of its context, see C. William Hill, Jr., *The Political Theory of John Taylor of Caroline* (Rutherford, N.J.: Fairleigh Dickinson University Press, 1977), pp. 223–233. Though I would not classify Dwight as a proslavery conservative, there is a great deal more ambiguity and irony in this exchange than I could have known before reading Larry E. Tise, *Proslavery: A History of the Defense of Slavery in America, 1701–1840* (Athens: University of Georgia Press, 1987), pp. 205–219. Dwight's charge that only one or two of the ten to twelve Virginians attending Yale during his recollection benefitted from the experience was essentially accurate. Between 1800 and 1805, Virginians William H. Buckner, Newton Calvert, Abel P. Upshur, and Arthur Upshur each left Yale after one year or sooner; William Maxwell of Norfolk entered Yale in 1798 and graduated in the class of 1802. He

was later President of Hampden-Sydney College. If Dwight remembered ten or eleven disruptive Virginians in 1805, it probably reflected his outrage over the conduct of Abel Upshur and his brother, Arthur. Abel led a brief student "rebellion" in after being disciplined for frequenting a tavern, cursing and insulting a tutor, and bringing liquor into the College. Upshur carried all of the Virginia attitudes that Dwight attributed to him into later life, writing a major refutation of Joseph Story, *Commentaries on the Constitution of the United States* in 1840, "Broadside Catalogues of Yale College," Yale University Archives. See also Claude H. Hall, *Abel Parker Upshur: Conservative Virginian, 1790–1844* (Madison: State Historical Society of Wisconsin, 1964), pp. 8–11.

2. Taylor to Dwight, "Sheaf of Old Letters," pp. 84–86.

3. James M. Banner, Jr., *To the Hartford Convention: The Federalists and the Origins of Party Politics in Massachusetts, 1789–1815* (New York: Knopf, 1970), p. 53.

4. Ibid.

5. Robert E. Shalhope, *John Taylor of Caroline: Pastoral Republican* (Columbia: University of South Carolina Press, 1980), pp. 70–107.

6. Ibid., p. 142.

7. Ibid., pp. 143, 145; Lance Banning, *The Jeffersonian Persuasion* (Ithaca, N.Y.: Cornell University Press, 1978), pp. 194–98.

8. Duncan MacLeod, "The Political Economy of John Taylor of Caroline," *Journal of American Studies*, 14 (1980): 389–90, 397.

9. Noble E. Cunningham, "The Politics of Nathaniel Macon," M. A. thesis, Duke University, 1949, p. 70.

10. Ibid., p. 37.

11. Ibid., p. 39.

12. Harry L. Watson, "Squire Oldway and his Friends: Opposition to Internal Improvements in Antebellum North Carolina," *North Carolina Historical Review*, 54 (1977): 118.

13. *Annals of Congress . . . Sixteenth Congress, First Session* (Washington, D.C., 1855), col. 226.

14. Cunningham, "Politics of Macon," p. 114.

15. Ibid., p. 115.

16. *Annals of Congress, Sixteenth Congress, First Session*, col. 225.

17. Edward R. Cotton, *The Life of Nathaniel Macon* (Baltimore, 1840), p. 59.

18. *Annals of Congress, Sixteenth Congress, First Session*. col. 228.

Notes to Pages 169–176

19. Elliott R. Barkan, ed., *Edmund Burke on the American Revolution: Selected Speeches and Letters* (New York: Harper and Row, 1966), pp. 84–85.

20. Robert Dawidoff, *The Education of John Randolph* (New York: W. W. Norton, 1979), p. 59.

21. Ibid., pp. 46–47, 57.

22. Kenneth S. Greenberg, *Masters and Statesmen: The Political Culture of American Slavery* (Baltimore: Johns Hopkins University Press, 1985), p. 146. Cf. David Donald, "The Proslavery Argument Reconsidered," *Journal of Southern History*, 37 (1971): 17.

23. Alison Goodyear Freehling, *Drift Toward Dissolution: The Virginia Slavery Debate of 1831–1832* (Baton Rouge: Louisiana State University Press, 1982), chaps. 3–5, pp. 208–10.

24. Ibid., pp. xiii, 263.

25. Dickson D. Bruce, Jr., *The Rhetoric of Conservatism: The Virginia Convention of 1829–30 and the Conservative Tradition in the South* (San Marino, Calif.: Huntington Library, 1982), p. 123.

26. Randolph to F. W. Gilmer, Mar. 15, 1817, in John Gilmer Speed, *The Gilmers in America* (New York, 1897), p. 63.

27. Freehling, *Drift Toward Dissolution*, pp. 137–40; Richmond *Enquirer*, Jan. 21, 24 1832.

28. Freehling, *Drift Toward Dissolution*, pp. 140–43.

29. Bruce, *Rhetoric of Conservatism*, p. 167.

30. Kathryn Ruth Malone, "The Virginia Doctrines, The Commonwealth and the Republic: The Role of Fundamental Principles in Virginia Politics, 1798–1833," Ph.D. diss., University of Pennsylvania, 1981, pp. 379–80.

31. "James Hamilton's Speech at Walterborough, October 21, 1828," William W. Freehling, ed., *The Nullification Era: A Documentary Record* (New York: Harper and Row, 1967), p.59, quoted in Malone, "The Virginia Doctrines," p. 417. William Grayson was a Virginia Anti-Federalist.

32. Robert L. Meriwether, W. Edwin Hemphill, and Clyde N. Wilson, eds., *The Papers of John C. Calhoun* (Columbia: University of South Carolina Press, 1959–), vol. 12, p. 46. Italics added. Cf. Richard N. Current, *John C. Calhoun* (New York: Washington Square Press, 1963), pp. 19–23.

33. William W. Freehling, *Prelude to Civil War: The Nullification Controversy in South Carolina, 1816–1836* (New York: Harper and Row, 1965), pp. 161–62; Meriwether et al., *Papers of Calhoun*, vol. 12, p. 88.

34. John C. Calhoun, *A Disquisition on Government and Selections from the Discourse*, C. Gordon Post, ed. (Indianapolis: Bobbs Merrill, 1953), pp. 4–5 Meriwether, Hemphill, and Wilson, eds., *Papers of Calhoun*, vol. 12, p. 90.

35. George C. Rogers, Jr., "South Carolina Federalists and the Origins of the Nullification Movement," *South Carolina Historical Magazine*, 71 (1970): 19–22: see also Pauline Maier, "The Road Not Taken: Nullification, John C. Calhoun, and the Revolutionary Tradition in South Carolina," *South Carolina Historical Magazine*, 82 (1981): 1–19.

36. Meriwether, Hemphill, and Wilson, eds., *Papers of Calhoun*, vol. 12: p. 60.

37. Ibid., pp. 72–73.

38. *Register of Debates*, 22nd Congress, 2nd Session (Washington, 1833), col. 499.

39. Meriwether, Hemphill, and Wilson, eds., *Papers of Calhoun*, vol. 12: p. 46; Weir, *"The Last of American Freemen,"* pp. 227, 230.

40. Meriwether, Hemphill, and Wilson, eds., *Papers of Calhoun*, vol. 12: p. 60.

41. Ibid., p. 61.

42. William W. Freehling, "Spoilsmen and Interests in the Thought and Career of John C. Calhoun," *Journal of American History*, 52 (1965): 25–32.

43. Calhoun, *Disquisition on Government*, pp. 44–45.

44. Gillis J. Harp. "Taylor, Calhoun, and the Decline of a Theory of Political Disharmony," *Journal of the History of Ideas*, 46 (1985): 114; Calhoun, *Disquisition on Government*, p. 7.

45. Ibid., pp. 8–9.

46. Louis Hartz, *The Liberal Tradition in America* (New York: Harcourt Brace and World, 1955), p. 166.

47. Harp, "Taylor, Calhoun, and Disharmony," pp. 107, 120.

48. Meriwether, Hemphill, and Wilson, eds., *Papers of Calhoun*, vol. 12, p. 346; vol. 14, p. 84.

49. Ibid., vol. 15, p. 491–92.

50. Calhoun, *Disquisition on Government*, p. 43.

51. J. G. A. Pocock, *The Machiavellian Moment: Florentine Political Thought and the Republican Tradition* (Princeton: Princeton University Press, 1975), pp. 38–39, 156, 180, 211, 541.

52. Meriwether, Hemphill, and Wilson, eds., *Papers of Calhoun*, vol. 12: pp. 92–93.

53. Frank Bell Lewis, "Robert Lewis Dabney: Southern Presbyte-

rian Apologist," Ph.D. diss., Duke University, 1946, pp. 40–41. See Scott, ed., *Lectures on Moral Philosophy*, p. 125 for Dabney's debt to Witherspoon on this point. Cf. Samuel Dunwoody, *A Sermon on the Subject of Slavery* (Charleston, 1837), p. 19.

54. Lewis, "Dabney," p. 46.

55. Ibid., pp. 51, 54, 56.

56. Ibid., p. 58.

57. John Joyce Bennett, "Albert Taylor Bledsoe: Social and Religious Controversialist of the Old South," Ph.D. diss., Duke University, 1942, pp. 209–11, 212–14, 216.

58. Doralyn Joanne Hickey, "Benjamin Morgan Palmer: Churchman of the Old South," Ph.D. diss., Duke University, 1962, p. 194.

59. Jack P. Maddex, Jr., "Proslavery Millennialism: Social Eschatology in Antebellum Southern Calvinism," *American Quarterly*, 31 (1979): 48–49.

60. Ibid., p. 53.

61. Ibid.

62. Ibid., p. 52.

63. (Charleston, 1850), pp. 43–44.

64. Bertram Wyatt-Brown, "Modernizing Southern slavery: The Proslavery Argument Reinterpreted," in J. Morgan Kousser and James M. McPherson, eds., *Region, Race, and Reconstruction: Essays in Honor of C. Vann Woodward* (New York: Oxford University Press, 1982), p. 35; Drew Gilpin Faust, ed., *The Ideology of Slavery: Proslavery Thought in the Antebellum South, 1830–1860* (Baton Rouge: Louisiana State University Press, 1981), pp. 15–20, 239–71; and Clarence L. Mohr, *On the Threshold of Freedom: Masters and Slaves in Civil War Georgia* (Athens: University of Georgia Press, 1986), chap. 8.

65. Calvin H. Wiley, "The Duties of Christian Masters," Calvin Henderson Wiley Papers, Southern Historical Collection. For an excellent examination of the Wiley manuscript and other unpublished fragments on slavery in his papers, see John B. Weaver, "Calvin Henderson Wiley and the Problem of Slavery, 1850–1865," M. A. thesis, University of North Carolina at Chapel Hill, 1975. For the inverse of these hopes, see the fears that American slaves bound for colonization in Africa had imbibed "too much of those airs and traits of superiority... from the example of their masters," Jeremiah Hubbard (Deep River, North Carolina) to Joseph Gates, Mar. 22 and July 28, 1834, American Colonization society Records, Library of Congress, Washington D.C.

Notes to Pages 193–198

EXCURSUS III

1. Charles C. Jones to [William States Lee], Aug. 26, 1861, Robert Manson Myers, ed., *The Children of Pride: A True Story of Georgia and the Civil War* (New Haven: Yale University Press, 1972), pp. 741–42. On the identification of the recipient, see *Columbus Enquirer*, Sept. 21, 1859, p. 3, George Howe, *History of the Presbyterian Church in South Carolina* (Columbia, S.C., 1870–83, vol. 2: 213, and transcriptions of Jones's letters from this episode made by the Reverend David L. Buttolph—Jones's own pastor, nephew by marriage, and neighbor who introduced Lee to Jones—Buttolph to Jones, October 16, 1861, Jones Papers, Tulane University Library, New Orleans, Louisiana. The 1860 census listed Lee as 35 years of age and his wife, aged 30 years who was born in Connecticut. Lee owned no taxable real property of record in Columbus; he briefly held office as Alderman in 1862–1863 and thereafter disappeared entirely from local records—circumstances confirming Jones's judgment that he was socially marginal, 1860 Manuscript Census, Miscogee County, Georgia, p. 155 and "Index of *The History of Columbus* by Mr. John Martin," typescript, Georgia Department of Archives and History, Atlanta, Georgia.

2. Bertram Wyatt-Brown, "The Ideal Typology and Antebellum Southern History: A Testing of a New Hypothesis," *Societas*, 5 (1975): 1–29; Myers, ed., *Children of Pride*, pp. 741–42.

3. Bertram Wyatt-Brown, "Religion and the Formation of folk Culture: Poor Whites in the Old South," Lucius F. Ellsworth, ed., *The Americanization of the Gulf Coast, 1803–1850* (Pensacola: Historic Pensacola Preservation Board, 1972), pp. 20–43.

4. John Johnson and A. G. Redd to C. C. Jones, Sept. 24, 1861, in Myers, ed., *Children of Pride*, pp. 752–54; C. C. Jones to John Johnson and A. G. Redd, Oct. 16, 1861, *Children of Pride* pp. 773–76. In all likelihood, Redd and Johnson were the only members of the Columbus Church Session to see Jones's letter; Redd endorsed Lee's initial advertisement for the Columbus High School for Young Ladies and John Johnson was either his landlord or host, *Columbus Enquirer*, Sept. 25, 1858, p. 3.

5. Calvin H. Wiley Papers, Southern Historical Collection.

6. Ibid.

7. Ibid.

8. "On the Reciprocal Influence of Literature and Religion," and "On Affording Religious Instruction to Slaves," *Virginia Evangelical and Literary Magazine* 5 (1822): 13, 67–71.

9. O'Connor to John Hawkes, Sept. 13, 1959, Sally Fitzgerald, ed., *The Habit of Being* (New York: Farrar, Straus, and Giroux, 1979), p. 350.

10. Anne C. Loveland, *Southern Evangelicals and the Social Order, 1800–1860* (Baton Rouge: Louisiana State University Press, 1980), p. 225.

11. Donald G. Mathews, *Religion in the Old South*, (Chicago: University of Chicago Press, 1977), p. 219.

EPILOGUE

1. John M. Mulder, *Woodrow Wilson: The Years of Preparation* (Princeton: Princeton University Press, 1978), pp. 9, 28, 45, 46, 1.

2. Arthur S. Link et al., eds., *The Papers of Woodrow Wilson* (Princeton: Princeton University Press, 1966), vol. 8, pp. 333–37.

3. Ibid., 16: 126; 15: 368; Arthur S. Link, "Woodrow Wilson and his Presbyterian Inheritance," in Arthur S. Link, *The Higher Realism of Woodrow Wilson and Other Essays* (Nashville: Vanderbilt University Press, 1971), pp. 7–8.

4. Willard B. Gatewood, "Professors, Fundamentalists, and the Legislature," Lindley S. Butler and Alan D. Watson, eds., *The North Carolina Experience: An Interpretive and Documentary History* (Chapel Hill: University of North Carolina Press, 1984), p. 375.

5. Willard B. Gatewood, *Preachers, Pedagogues, and Politicians: The Evolution Controversy in North Carolina, 1920–1927* (Chapel Hill: University of North Carolina Press, 1966), p. 67.

6. William L. Miller, *Yankee from Georgia: The Emergence of Jimmy Carter* (New York: Times Books, 1978), p. 224.

7. Ibid., pp. 211–12, 192–93, 203.

8. C. Vann Woodward, *The Burden of Southern History* (New York: Vintage Books, 1960), pp. 174–84.

9. *Greensboro News and Record*, Nov. 7, 1984, p. A-2.

10. WRAL-TV Viewpoint, no. 267 (Dec. 19, 1961), no. 443 (Dec. 17, 1962), no. 571 (Mar. 21, 1963), no. 586 (April 11, 1963), no. 601 (May 2, 1963), no. 610 (May 15, 1963), no. 614 (May 22, 1963), no. 802 (Feb. 26, 1964) no. 944 (Sept. 25, 1964), North Carolina Collection, University of North Carolina at Chapel Hill Library: *New York Times*, April 24, 1963, p. 19; John David Smith, *An Old Creed for the New South: Proslavery Ideology and Historiography, 1865–1918* (Westport, Conn.: Greenwood Press, 1985), pp. 81–93.

Notes to Pages 204–206

11. Noll et al., *Search for Christian America*, p. 126.

12. Gabriel Fackre, *The Religious Right and Christian Faith* (Grand Rapids, Mich.: William B. Eerdmans, 1982), pp. 13, 33, 40, 43, 48, 50–52, 72.

13. Jesse Helms, *When Free Men Shall Stand* (Grand Rapids, Mich.: Zondervan, 1976), pp. 20–21.

14. Ibid., pp. 99–100, 23–24, 48–50.

15. Ibid., p. 12.

16. Martin Luther King, Jr., *Strength to Love* (New York: Harper and Row, 1963), p. 91; Is. 53:6.

17. Hanes Walton, Jr., *The Political Philosophy of Martin Luther King, Jr.* (Westport, Conn.: Greenwood Press, 1971), p. 48. See also Will D. Campbell, comp., *The Failure and the Hope: Essays of Southern Churchmen* (Grand Rapids, Mich.: Eerdmans, 1972).

Index
to Biblical References

Index

Index

Index

Index